WRITING FAITH

WRITING FAITH

Text, Sign, & History in the Miracles of Sainte Foy

Miracles of sainte foy

Kathleen Ashley & pamela sheingorn

THE UNIVERSITY OF CHICAGO PRESS CHICAGO AND LONDON

KATHLEEN ASHLEY is professor of English at the University of Southern Maine. She is the editor of *Victor Turner and the Construction of Cultural Criticism* (1990) and coeditor of *Autobiography and Postmodernism* (1994).

PAMELA SHEINGORN is professor of history at Baruch College of CUNY and professor of history and theatre at CUNY Graduate School. She is the author of *The Easter Sepulchre in England* (1987) and editor and translator of *The Book of Sainte Foy* (1995).

Together Ashley and Sheingorn edited *Interpreting Cultural Symbols: Saint Anne in Late Medieval Society* (1990).

The University of Chicago Press, Chicago 60637
The University of Chicago Press, Ltd., London
© 1999 by The University of Chicago
All rights reserved. Published 1999

08 07 06 05 04 03 02 01 00 99   1 2 3 4 5
ISBN: 0-226-02966-2 (cloth)
ISBN: 0-226-02967-0 (paper)

Library of Congress Cataloging-in-Publication Data

Ashley, Kathleen M., 1944–
     Writing faith : text, sign, and history in the miracles of Sainte Foy / Kathleen Ashley and Pamela Sheingorn.
          p.   cm.
     Includes bibliographical references and index.
     ISBN 0-226-02966-2 (cloth : alk. paper). — ISBN 0-226-02967-0 (pbk. : alk. paper)
     1. Foy, Saint, ca. 290–303. 2. Christian child saints—France—Conques—Biography. 3. Bernardus, scholasticus, fl. 1010–1020. Liber miraculorum Sanctae Fidis. 4. Miracles—History of doctrines—Middle Ages, 600–1500. 5. Conques (Aveyron, France)—Religious life and customs. I. Sheingorn, Pamela. II. Title.
BX4700.F37A74   1999
235'.2—dc21   98-52096

Illustration credits—frontispiece (Portable Altar of Sainte Foy, ca. 1100), pp. 1, 136 (detail): Courtesy of Commune de Conques and Conservation des Antiquités et Objets d'Art de l'Aveyron; pp. 22, 46, 65, 117 (decorated letters from fols. 15r, 22v, 94v, 44v, *Liber miraculorum sancte Fidis,* eleventh century, MS 22, Sélestat, Bibliothèque Humaniste): Courtesy of Bibliothèque Humaniste (F. 67600); p. 100 (female saint, probably Saint Foy, ca. late eleventh or early twelfth century): Courtesy of Musée du Louvre, Paris, Département des Objets (OA 6273)

For Cliff

CONTENTS

PREfACE

Medieval literature is generally understood to be full of narrative reshaping to rhetorical ends, but this insight has only recently been extended to hagiographic texts. Underlying the "pious reading" of much hagiography was the belief that because the texts were religious they could not be political constructions and, further, that the results of any creative rewriting had to be measured against a truer original version. However, a revisionist group of scholars of early medieval monastic history, among them Thomas Head, Sharon Farmer, Felice Lifshitz, and Barbara Rosenwein, now argue that medieval hagiography has a place among "rhetorical sources" and tends to articulate "themes of power and authority."[1] We share this perspective, and therefore we start from these "methodological premises": that "narratives describing the activities of saints . . . are fully historiographical, and that the activities of producing historical narrative, on the one hand, and of instituting and elaborating saints' cults on the other, are generated by one and the same impulse, an impulse which is fundamentally 'political.'"[2] For us, every version of a hagiographic text is a rhetorical construction that serves historical purposes.

The hagiographical text we analyze here is the *Liber miraculorum sancte Fidis,* a compilation of Sainte Foy's miracles begun early in the eleventh century by scholar Bernard of Angers and continued by monastic authors in the course of that century. In our citations of the *Liber* we follow the principle of supplying original language quotations only when our argument depends upon close analysis of some aspect of the Latin. The Latin name of the saint, Fides, translates into English as Faith; in modern French she is Foi and in old French, Foy. We have chosen to refer to the saint throughout the book as Foy, both to emphasize the medieval, southern French setting of her cult and to distinguish this specific construction of a saint from the general hagiographic and scholarly projects of writing faith.

We refer to passages in the *Liber miraculorum* from book 1 through book 4, chapter 11, by book and chapter number—4.11, for example—following the convention used by both Bouillet and Robertini in their editions of the miracles. Beginning with 4.12, Robertini interpolated the miracles in the fragmentary Conques manuscript into book 4, whereas the previous editor, Bouillet, had designated them separately as C.1 to C.5. As a result, in Robertini's edition the numbers of chapters 12 through 29 of book 4 do not match Bouillet's edition. In referring to these chapters we give the Bouillet number first, followed by the Robertini number in parentheses. Most of the translations from the *Liber miraculorum* included here are taken from Sheingorn, *Book of Sainte Foy,* which follows the Bouillet numbering. Both Bouillet and Robertini print the later miracle narratives in appendices and designate them with reference to the manuscripts in which they are preserved: V (Vatican), L (London), A (Chartres), and R (Rodez).

Our research and travel were enabled by grants from the City University of New York's PSC-CUNY Research Award Program and the University of Southern Maine's Faculty Senate Research Committee. We are grateful to Hubert Meyer, Conservateur of the Bibliothèque Humaniste of Sélestat, for access to the rich holdings of that library, and to Pierre Lançon, Archivist at Conques, for continuing bibliographic assistance. We would like to acknowledge our debt to the many scholars whose work has contributed so much to our thinking about hagiography. Of this large and generous group, we especially want to thank Tom Head, Sharon Farmer, Ann Clark, and the New York Hagiography Group. The support of Richard Emmerson for this project over many years has been important to us. We are grateful to Sheila Delany for suggesting the pun in our title, to Gail Gibson for crucial assistance at a key moment, and to Carol Weisbrod for reading the entire manuscript and offering incisive commentary. Acute critiques by the two readers for the University of Chicago Press helped us strengthen our arguments, and the enthusiasm of our editor, Randy Petilos, spurred us to produce our final draft ahead of schedule.

The challenges of co-authorship were alleviated by the willingness of Mark Sheingorn and Jack Reuter to share their spaces in New Hampshire, Maine, and New York at intervals with this trickster saint and her obsessed writing team.

This book is dedicated to the memory of C. Clifford Flanigan. At an early stage of our project, he read the miracle narratives with us and gave us the benefit of his wide-ranging erudition. He also responded with delight to the rhetorical maneuverings of Bernard of Angers, a delight we share and that we hope we have conveyed to our readers.

INTRODUCTION: READING HAGIOGRAPHY

Our title, *Writing Faith,* signals the dual focus in our study of the eleventh-century Latin narratives produced for the cult of Sainte Foy. All authors of hagiographic texts "write faith" in the sense that they construct and reconstruct saints' lives and miracles for believers, but post-medieval scholars of hagiography also participate in writing faith as they interpret texts and write their histories. Thus, the medieval authors of the *Liber miraculorum sancte Fidis* wrote faith (pun intended) as they created their portraits of Sainte Foy out of materials available in their cultural milieux and in response to specific, often local, needs and agendas. Since every rewriting was a historical event, keyed to the needs of a particular audience, no redaction was more authentic than another. Medieval authors and copyists valued every version of a saint's life or miracles; whether written or re-written, each text was believed to deserve serious literary attention. It is this understanding of the relation between production and reception of texts that we bring to the *Liber miraculorum sancte Fidis.*

Just as there were multiple medieval portraits of Sainte Foy, so modern scholarly interpretation of medieval texts about the saints produces multiple versions of the past (especially of its religious beliefs and practices). Each version of history—including the one we offer in this book—results from a particular set of assumptions and analytic tools. We study here primarily the medieval but also the post-medieval reworkings of the miracles of one saint, attending to the conditions of production and the lenses of reception. Our concern is both with the functions of these texts in the eleventh century and with the uses to which scholars have subsequently put them.

To embed these miracle stories in their eleventh-century milieux, and to reveal the constraints of hagiographic scholarship, we have devised an approach that we characterize as post-disciplinary; that is, we draw our analytic methods from a number of individual disciplines, including anthropology, history, literary theory, philology, rhetoric, religious studies, and feminist and gender studies. Only by escaping the artificial confines of disciplinary boundaries can we assemble from multiple analytic perspectives a representation of a complex past that will, nonetheless, ultimately elude our complete grasp.

In introducing our discussion of the Foy miracle stories we first examine the trajectory of scholarship to reveal how successive generations and groupings of interpreters have written the history of medieval sainthood, or hagiography. The current scholarly meaning of "hagiography" can be easily understood from its etymology; the term comes from the Greek *hagios* (holy) and *graphia* (writings) and refers "to the full range of writings about saints, and, by extension, to the study of such works."[1] In this introductory chapter we take seriously both parts of this definition, and we especially engage the interrelation between the two parts, that is, between the medieval writings about saints and the study of those writings. Using a specific cult, that of Sainte Foy, we examine the ways that interpretation of hagiography has shaped understandings of medieval culture.

As religious historian David Knowles indicates, the scholarly study of hagiography seems to demand a daunting range of expertise:

The hagiographer is plunged at once into the nightmare of early medieval diplomatic and forgery, into all the tangled chronological difficulties of the *fasti* of half the sees of Europe, into the labyrinthine ways of martyrologies, necrologies and calendars, into the linguistic, social and psychological varieties of Christian sentiment—Greek, Persian, Egyptian, Syrian, Slav and Oriental, into the magical mists and colours of the Celtic wonderland, and into the changes and translations that lapse of centuries and popular devotion can bring about in a matter that is of its nature peculiarly dependent upon personal knowledge and popular acclaim. . . . Add to all this the theological background and the judgment of credibility, possibility and moral and spiritual sanity inseparable from the subject-matter.[2]

But before we enter this complex field, we need to situate the term "hagiography" historically and to gain an awareness of its shifting connotations. During the early Middle Ages *hagiographi* referred to "the 'holy writings' of the Bible"[3] rather than to writings about the saints. From the late fourth century, the time of Jerome's efforts to find the best biblical text, scholarly study of the Bible has especially concerned itself with establishing the pure sacred text; Christianity has persistently clung to the notion that there is *one* biblical text rather than many variants. When nondevotional study of writings about the saints began in the seventeenth century, scholars took study of the Bible as their unexamined model. The two groups of clerics engaged in the endeavor, those of the Congrégation de Saint-Maur and of the Société des Bollandistes, searched for the earliest version of a saint's life and the most accurate rendition of a saint's miracles. Thus only in the seventeenth century did hagiography come to mean "writings about the saints."

From the seventeenth century on, understanding of hagiography has been crucially shaped, first and foremost, by the professional religious, who needed such texts both to construct their own history and to reform their practices. The efforts of these early clerical scholars participated, of course, in the much larger scholarly project of textual editing, which had the goal of producing accurate and usable editions of writings inherited from the past, especially the classical past, and was highly critical of medieval editorial practices. The implication was that if medieval editors had understood the principles of textual scholarship, they would have preserved such hagiographic texts in the exact form in which they were first written. Scholarly study of hagiography thus originated within the ecclesiastical context and, as a result, a basic assumption was built into the discipline—that the scholar's task is reconstruction of an Ur-text. The textual editions that we use today to study the cult of Sainte Foy, and which we describe next, were all shaped by this assumption.

A primary function of writings about the saints, from the beginning, was to provide materials for use in Christian worship. Each saint was especially honored on a specific day, which for the martyrs was the day of death by execution. A martyrology (a calendrically ordered list of martyrs) provides the earliest reference to Sainte Foy; a simple statement about the saint was apparently added to the influential *Martyrologium Hieronymianum* late in the sixth century: "October 6 in Gaul, in the city of Agen, the anniversary of Saint Faith martyr."[4] The purpose of such an entry was to ensure that a saint was commemorated liturgically on the relevant feast day.

No further information about Sainte Foy appears until the mid ninth century, when we find a summary *Passio* of Sainte Foy and Saint Caprais in the *Martyrology* composed by Florus of Lyons.[5] Like every *Passio,* this text recounts the narrative of the saints' suffering, ending in triumphant death. For some early Christian saints, a *Passio* based partly on trial transcripts was written shortly after death. It functioned as a record of the holy person, was read aloud in full or excerpted form as part of the official religious celebration on the saint's feast day, and might also serve as the basis of sermons preached on that day. The text Florus used presumably corresponds to the earliest surviving *Passio* of Sainte Foy, which is preserved in two tenth-century manuscripts.[6] Known as *Passio I* to indicate its chronological primacy, this text gives no indication of author, date, or place of composition.

Passio I sets the martyrdom of a saint named Foy in the Gallo-Roman city of Agen during the period of Roman persecution of Christians (third or early fourth century). It describes a confrontation between Foy, a young Christian girl of a noble family, and a Roman prefect whose mission was to identify Christians. When Foy refused to foreswear Christianity and worship the pagan goddess Diana, the prefect had her stretched out on an iron grill, which was placed over a fire. Another Christian named Caprais watched these events from a hiding place and saw a heavenly dove lower a bejeweled crown onto Foy's head. This sight inspired Caprais to surrender to martyrdom as well, and finally both were beheaded. Later a bishop of Agen named Dulcidius built two churches, one for each martyr, and transferred each body from the pit or cave (probably outside the city) where they had been hastily hidden to the appropriate church inside the city walls.

Luca Robertini has recently demonstrated that the part of the *Passio I* text dealing with Foy derives from writing about another saint, a Fides who, along with her sisters Spes and Karitas (Hope and Charity), was reportedly taken to Rome by their mother Sophia (Wisdom) in search of martyrdom. According to the *Passio* of these three sisters, Fides was beaten, had her breasts amputated, and was finally burned on a red-hot grill.[7] This *Passio* survives in several different versions in Carolingian manuscripts. The lack of any early Christian text of Foy's *Passio,* in combination with Robertini's evidence that the extant version contains significant borrowed elements from the *Passio* of Fides, Spes, and Karitas, suggest that the hagiography of Sainte Foy developed mainly in the Carolingian period. Its author or authors presumably wrote *Passio I* in answer to the needs of the specific historical situation that Thomas Head describes:

The contours of hagiography changed dramatically in the 9th century. Ecclesiastical authorities came to rely increasingly on written documentation for the authenticity of saints and their veneration. In the *Admonitio generalis* of 789, Charlemagne renewed a canon borrowed from an ancient collection that ordered that "the false names of martyrs and the uncertain memorials of saints should not be venerated." Five years later, the bishops whom the emperor gathered at Frankfurt were more explicit: "No new saint shall be honored or invoked, nor shrines to them erected on the roads. Only those saints are to be venerated in a church who have been chosen on the authority of their Passion or on the merit of their Life." The "Passions and Lives" in question were hagiographic texts. In response to the perceived need for written documentation for the cults of saints, Carolingian clerics produced many works celebrating the saints of the distant past. Hincmar of Reims wrote about Remi, Hilduin of Saint-Denis about Denis, and Alcuin of York about Vedast, to cite only some of the best-known examples. They were forced to piece together bits of written and oral tradition, along with topoi borrowed from ancient and respected works of hagiography.[8]

Thus, based on Head's account, we might reasonably conclude that in the Carolingian period an extant cult of Sainte Foy required a text and that an unknown writer composed *Passio I* in response to that need. The writer may have lived in Agen, a site that presumably had the greatest interest in Foy's cult because tradition held that the body of a saint named Foy was buried there. It is probably significant that *Passio I* celebrates Agen: "We count the city of Agen a worthy and joyous place, for it merited to be the birthplace of martyrs, the site of their glorious struggle and burial."[9] In constructing a detailed biography of one of its saints, Agen simultaneously constructed itself as a holy place.

But soon another site was vying with Agen and producing texts in support of its claims. A charter of 883 in the cartulary of the monastery at Conques,[10] located east of Agen in a remote gorge of the Rouergue, asserted that Conques was the resting place of the bodies of Sainte Foy and Saint Vincent. Whether relics thought to be Sainte Foy's physical remains were transferred from Agen to Conques to protect them from Normans raiding the Garonne Valley, or were stolen from Agen by agents from Conques, or never left Agen, we do not know. What is clear is that the monks of Conques had been attempting to acquire the relics of a saint as early as about 855,[11] that they claimed to have possession of Foy's relics, and that they were persuasive.[12]

Although saints' relics were believed to be especially effective channels for the power to intervene on earth that God granted to the saints as reward for their suffering, the possessors of relics were not always successful in activating them. The monks of Conques apparently made convincing claims that their new saint had begun to exercise her power; by sometime in the tenth century she was gaining a reputation as a miracle worker. For the monastery at Conques Foy's reported activities had important economic consequences, since people who came there from the surrounding countryside in search of miracles enriched the monastery with offerings of thanksgiving.

According to his version of events, news of Foy's miracles reached a student at the cathedral school of Chartres, one Bernard of Angers, early in the eleventh century. Virtually all that we know of Bernard comes from the internal evidence of his own writing, in which he says that he was trained at Chartres, where he first heard of the martyr Foy and her amazing miracles. Bernard claimed that he was skeptical at first, but grew curious about the miracle-working saint and made a vow to visit her shrine at Conques, for him a remote and unknown place. In about 1010, Bernard was hired to teach at the cathedral school in Angers, but he says he managed to make the trip to Conques three years later in the company of another teacher, Bernier.[13]

Bernard reports that in Conques he was asked to record the many miracle stories about Foy that circulated in the region, and he explains that he listened and took notes which he revised to produce full texts when he returned north. As he describes his working method, Bernard interviewed oral informants who had witnessed miracles, made notes on scraps of parchment for the purpose of remembering precise details, and then turned the notes into prose narratives (1.7). These rough drafts were later polished to conform to the literary tastes of a sophisticated clerical readership.[14] The product of Bernard's initial visit to Conques was the first section or book of what came to be called the *Liber miraculorum sancte Fidis* (Book of Sainte Foy's Miracles).[15] Bernard returned to Conques sometime before 1020 to collect more miracle stories, and he made a third visit in 1020.[16] The two compilations resulting from these later visits were subsequently combined into book 2 of the *Liber.*

The Prologue to book 3 of the *Liber miraculorum sancte Fidis,* written by an anonymous monk of Conques, refers to Bernard's recent death. The monk writer proposes to carry on the task of composing narratives about the miracles of Foy, and the monks of Conques did exactly that. Before 1050 these individual miracle stories had been gathered into two more books, known as 3 and 4 (BHL 2943); additional narratives that the monks wrote until about 1075 we refer to here as the "late miracle narratives" (BHL 2944–2963).

In spite of the fascinating differences among the various layers of the *Liber miraculorum,* all of its authors display a keen awareness of the need for literary presentation and a striking sensitivity to the textuality of their materials. Throughout, Bernard of Angers reveals his consciousness that he is producing a book, and the monks understand that they are adding to Bernard's volume even as they reshape it. All authors share a deep commitment to demonstrating the authenticity of the miraculous events, but also a commitment to shaping the presentation in whatever way necessary to reach a particular audience. The *Liber miraculorum sancte Fidis* is a sophisticated literary text.

As the monks of Conques fostered the cult of their patron saint, they generated other necessary and desirable texts. A text telling their dramatic story of the way Conques acquired Foy's relics, a kind of text called a *Translatio,* was composed sometime between 1020 and 1060 (BHL 2939), and the *Passio* was rewritten both in prose (*Passio II,* BHL 2929–2930) and verse (BHL 2938) forms around 1050. Shortly after 1060 the *Translatio* was put into verse as well (BHL 2941).

Both Bernard's notes and the first manuscript containing his finished texts have, sadly, disappeared. We can only assume that about 1050 the monks of Conques produced in their own manuscript workshop one or more manuscripts gathering together the four books of the *Liber miraculorum.*[17] This may be identical with the earliest surviving manuscript containing miracles of Sainte Foy, dated between about 1050 and 1075 (Conques, Bibliothèque de l'Abbaye, 1), which is in fragmentary condition and includes only parts of book 4. Its twenty-seven leaves are enough, however, to reveal that five of its miracle narratives are unique to the manuscript; that is, they appear in no other surviving text. This suggests to Luca Robertini, the most recent editor of the *Liber miraculorum sancte Fidis,* that an early version of book 4 was longer than any version found in subsequent manuscripts; he is of the opinion that books 1 and 2 were longer as well.[18] We may conclude that compilers felt no compulsion to copy the Conques manuscript in its entirety, although it was, according to Robertini, the archetype for books 1 through 4 in all surviving manuscripts, and is, therefore, what modern scholars would call the "authoritative text."

Three manuscript traditions derive from the Conques manuscript. One of these depends upon a lost manuscript that Robertini calls alpha. Made in the Conques scriptorium about 1070/1080, this *libellus*—book made up of texts devoted to a single saint—contained a selection of miracle stories (including some of the late narratives), the texts of Sainte Foy's *Passio* and *Translatio,* and liturgical materials for celebrating the feast of Sainte Foy. Robertini suggests that alpha "was conceived as an instrument of propaganda for the cult of Sainte Foy and was probably sent to other monasteries that desired to receive documentation of the saint."[19] From alpha the scriptorium at Conques made a manuscript (today in four parts: Orléans, Bibl. mun. 296; Leiden, Bibl. univ. Voss. lat. O.60; Paris, BNF, Nouv. acq. lat. 443; and Vatican, Reg. lat. 467) that included the only surviving copy of a Provençal version of Sainte Foy's *Passio* and *Translatio* known as the "Chanson de Sainte Foy."[20]

Also deriving from alpha is the selection of miracles in a passionary redacted in England, at St. Augustine's monastery in Canterbury, between 1100 and 1125 (London, BL Arundel 91). This manuscript illustrates the spread of Foy's cult to sites where she was not the primary saint, but where her feast was celebrated as one of many saint's days during the liturgical year. Sufficient for that purpose were the text of Foy's *Passio* and a small selection of miracles to be read during the Office on October 6.

Another major branch of the manuscript tradition deriving directly from the Conques manuscript leads to the priory of Sainte Foy in Sélestat (Alsace), which owned the most complete surviving copy of Sainte Foy's miracles. The Sélestat manuscript was the source of the spread of Foy's miracles into Germanic lands, which is documented by a number of copies and partial copies. This manuscript includes a rare miracle narrative about the founding of the Sélestat priory.

In spite of the spread of Foy's cult to new sites, which was evidently enabled by the collection of miracles begun by Bernard of Angers and continued by monks at Conques, virtually no new material was added to the body of texts we have already discussed. Foy's miracles remain those of a high medieval saint. It would nonetheless be erroneous to conclude that the texts of Foy's miracles were handed down exactly as their authors composed them. First, there is a sense in which every selection created a different Sainte Foy; for example, the London manuscript entirely omitted the kind of miracle called a joke or trick. Editing or abridgment also shifted emphasis. A fourteenth-century manuscript based on the Sélestat manuscript (Oxford, Bodl., Lyell 64) revised individual miracle narratives to eliminate all mention of Bernard of Angers and to erase his distinctive personality. In addition, materials about Foy were composed in the vernacular languages; this began with the "Chanson de Sainte Foy," but most such texts date from the fourteenth and fifteenth centuries. These include versions of Foy's *Passio* in the Middle English *Gilte Legende,* an Anglo-Norman poem of 1242 lines, "La vie sainte fey, virgine et martire," by Simon of Walsingham, and a life of Saint Faith in Osbern Bokenham's *Legendys of Hooly Wummen.*[21] By the fifteenth century, the medieval cult of Sainte Foy had thus generated a rich and varied repertoire of texts celebrating the saint and her powers. In the chapters to follow, we concentrate on the miracle narratives contained within the *Liber miraculorum sancte Fidis.*

We now reach the period in which scholarly study of hagiography, including the *Liber miraculorum sancte Fidis,* began. The upheavals of the sixteenth century, the Protestant Reformation and Catholic Counter-Reformation, had a profound impact upon the cults of the saints. Protestants tended to make a sharp distinction between biblical and post-biblical saints, withdrawing their veneration from the latter; Catholics revised their practices, omitting a number of saints from the reformed breviary of 1568.[22] Since Sainte Foy survived these changes her feast continued to be celebrated, which means that a core of texts about her continued to be available in liturgical and devotional books. Scholarly studies of these texts also appear; the Catholic scholar Surius published an edition of Sainte Foy's *Passio* in 1569.[23] His claim that his texts were taken from "very old manuscripts" ("pervetustis manuscriptis codicibus") reveals the common assumption of the time that the oldest manuscript to be found was most likely to contain the best, that is, the most accurate, version of a text. Such editions also participated in a general project of putting manuscript texts into print in order to make them available to other Catholic scholars. The first printed edition of Foy's miracles was included in such a project: Labbe's *Nova bibliotheca manuscriptorum librorum* (New Library of Manuscript Books). For the second volume of his *Nova bibliotheca* (Paris, 1657), Labbe transcribed twenty-two Foy miracle narratives, probably all that his now-lost manuscript source contained.

In 1770, the vast undertaking of the Bollandists, the *Acta sanctorum* (which gathered texts relevant to individual saints, especially texts of their lives, and arranged them in calendrical sequence), reached Sainte Foy's feast day of October 6. The Bollandists published miracle texts from the manuscript of Foy's miracles now in the Vatican Library. They introduced to the publication of Foy's miracles a basic principle of textual editing, that of collation. Comparing the text in the Vatican manuscript with that of Labbe, they selected what seemed to be the most accurate reading of each letter, word, and line of Latin. Introducing judgment into the editing process opened the way for a new kind of problem—a problem to which Bouillet has called attention: "In the transcription that they made of the miracles, the Bollandists, unaware of the work of the anonymous monk (which they nevertheless surmised) and noticing in three of the narratives some details and some particulars that seemed to them strange and inexplicable, suppressed these entirely. As for the others, they grouped them in ten chapters distributed among three books."[24] Although the overall value of the Bollandist project cannot be disputed, their reshaping of the *Liber miraculorum sancte Fidis* in accordance with their own principles of scholarship and propriety makes the version they published in the *Acta sanctorum* a product not only of the eleventh-century devotees of Foy, but of eighteenth-century Jesuits as well.

Scholarly purposes, but also the desire to validate texts about the saints as historical, motivated the first separately published edition of the *Liber miraculorum,* which was produced at the end of the nineteenth century by one Abbé Bouillet, a professor at the Petit-Séminaire in Paris. Bouillet had become interested in Sainte Foy through the narrative of her life in the early sixteenth-century stained-glass windows in the church of Sainte-Foy at Conches (Normandy). In his edition he describes the manuscripts containing Foy miracle texts that were known to him, takes the most complete surviving manuscript (Sélestat) as his base text, and records variants from three others at the bottom of each page. Footnotes identify people and places named in the text, and these are usefully arranged in an alphabetical index as well. Bouillet's attitude toward the *Liber miraculorum* as a text is revealed in the following comment: "Unfortunately certain scribes thought it appropriate to choose among the miracles; they truncated them, modified their original order, even confused those written by the anonymous monk with those by Bernard, and presented their compilation as the work of the latter." [25] Bouillet the scholar had a strong sense of respect for "original order" and for authorship.

In 1900 Bouillet, along with L. Servières, published a huge compendium of materials about Sainte Foy, which gathered between two covers all the information they could assemble about the saint: descriptions of cult objects and buildings, lists of all known cult sites, discussions of the events of Foy's life, and a translation into French of the Latin miracle texts that Bouillet had published in 1897. Bouillet and Servières's project participated in the goals of hagiography that had been set at the Council of Trent: "The lives of the saints may not remain content with spiritual truth, but must also take into account the teachings of History. However, they are not to be mere historical biographies, since the purpose of the life of the saint is to edify." [26] Articulated from within a Catholic Christian world view, this perspective sought to eliminate the obviously fabulous from hagiographic accounts.

The purpose of making such texts available was the edification of the believer, but Bouillet's edition of the Latin text reveals another, not entirely complementary goal; it appears in a series entitled "Collection de textes pour servir à l'étude et l'enseignement de l'histoire" (Collection of Texts to Enable the Study and Teaching of History). Bouillet assures the reader of the value of this text for history:

No chronicler gives us knowledge of the history of the provinces of the Midi of France and their social conditions during the high Middle Ages. The numerous charters of that region that have been preserved for us, as important as they are, nevertheless are powerless to fill this gap. Therefore, from this special point of view, the information furnished by the scholar of Angers and by his continuator are of high value, and their interest should not be dismissed in doubt. . . . The often brutal behavior of the lords, the oppression of the weak and small by the great and powerful, thousands of details about habits and customs, thousands of bits of information about institutions and about the practices of both private and social life, all these things pass before our eyes as we read the *Book of Miracles* of Sainte Foy.[27]

Bouillet's claim that the *Liber miraculorum sancte Fidis* brought the social conditions of the past to life revealed his desire to see this text appreciated and used by writers of history. His publisher also handled the publications of the Archives nationales and the Société de l'Ecole des Chartes, institutions dedicated to preserving and studying the documents of French history. Thus the *Liber miraculorum sancte Fidis* entered the twentieth century as a historical text.

Ambivalence if not deep skepticism characterized the historical use of hagiographic writing. In a study that has become classic for hagiography, *Les légendes hagiographiques* (The Legends of the Saints), Hippolyte Delehaye urged scholars to remember that "the work of the hagiographer may be historical, but it is not necessarily so."[28] Writing "Descriptions of Fortresses in the Book of Miracles of Sainte-Foy of Conques," historian Pierre Bonnassie is defensive as he argues the use of hagiography for his limited and specific purposes: "Hagiographical sources are, in fact, amongst the least reliable of those available to historians, and the traps they set are too well known to need emphasis here (uncertain dating of the stories, their constant rewriting, endless recourse to commonplaces drawn from models of the genre, etc.). These faults are not, however, general and there exist works whose authors and dates of composition are precisely known; amongst them is the Book of Miracles of Sainte-Foy, which will be discussed here."[29] Despite their misgivings, generations of historians have, like Bonnassie, continued to treat these eleventh-century texts of Foy's miracles as rich sources for historical data.

The success of this positivist historical approach can be easily demonstrated in the frequency with which historians of early medieval France extract nuggets of "fact" from the miracle narratives, a process that has continued into the 1990s. For a recent (1992) example of reading of hagiographic texts as transparent historical documents, one has only to examine the French collection *Les sociétés méridionales autour de l'an mil,* in which the *Liber miraculorum* of Sainte Foy provides one of the most frequently cited sources of historical data. As its editor, Michel Zimmermann, says in the introduction, the best source for "détails concrets" is the miracles of Sainte Foy.[30] A majority of the essays draw on Foy narratives for political and economic facts. The historical purpose to which hagiographic texts are put is illustrated by the inclusion of Foy miracle narratives in the documents appended to each essay. Among the donations, testaments, sale contracts, and legal appeals, the miracle texts are simply reprinted, as if the data they provide about eleventh-century history requires no mediating frame.

In spite of the persistence of such unreflective uses of hagiography, both the principles of textual editing and the attitudes toward hagiographic texts as historical sources have begun to change. Codicology has demonstrated the necessity of situating an individual text within its manuscript matrix and has thus created a respect for the integrity of each version of a text.[31]

As Felice Lifshitz suggests, there has been a move "from searching for the original version of each particular saint's biography to studying all extant versions, each in its particular compositional context. Instead of seeing 'legendary accretions' as dross to be sifted and cleared away, scholars have seen transformations in a saint's character as crucial indicators of many different sorts of changes over time."[32] Our study of the *Liber miraculorum sancte Fidis* is indebted to this new historical pluralism.

Further, a large number of contemporary historians has gone well beyond the positivist mining of hagiographic texts for facts, a method that Lifshitz aptly calls "bobbing for data." In tracing some of the approaches these historians use, we note that the *Liber miraculorum sancte Fidis* continues to serve as an important source of data for study of the high medieval period.[33] One group of scholars, taking as their subject what might be called the sociology of sanctity, seeks to delineate the institutional or class connections between a society and types of saints or cults. This approach is based on the assumption that, as Stephen Wilson puts it, "saints belong to and reflect the societies which produce and honor them."[34] For Benedicta Ward, who has written specifically about the cult of Foy, miracle narratives are "intimately associated with the society in which they take place."[35] Of the function of Sainte Foy's miracles at Conques, Ward comments, "They are miracles for the protection of the monks, the extension of their lands, and the aggrandisement of their church through their saint. They are set firmly in the countryside that housed the saint and take their colour from the needs and aspirations of the surrounding population."[36]

Ward's analysis of miracle texts emphasizes their direct response to social needs; however, the spectrum of critical methodologies within the social interpretation of sanctity is broad, ranging from phenomenology at one end to statistics at the other. Aviad Kleinberg, for example, wants to look at sainthood as a practice or lived phenomenon, "not a quality or a set of characteristics, but an attribution." Moreover, Kleinberg argues, as a "tacit 'pact' between saint and community," sainthood must be constantly renegotiated.[37] Thus, at the phenomenological end of the spectrum, primary attention is given to the fluidity of negotiations over sanctity.

In order to ground (and perhaps more firmly fix) their analyses of sainthood, a majority of scholars of the high and later Middle Ages have used institutional definitions found in canonization proceedings.[38] Michael Goodich, looking at the thirteenth century, and Richard Kieckhefer, studying the fourteenth, both focus on the canonization process. André Vauchez has traced the growing importance of lay persons in religious milieux beginning in the eleventh century, by examining canonization records of lay individuals. Since Foy was recognized as a saint before papal canonization procedures were instituted, study of her sainthood has not been influenced by approaches based on such definitions.

Institutional definitions of sainthood are usually supported by broad statistical surveys. Pierre-André Sigal's *L'homme et le miracle* boasts a huge data base of five thousand miracles drawn from seventy-six lives of saints and 166 collections of miracles or *translations*. From this mass of data from works written between 1050 and 1150 in northern France, he constructs a typology of the miracle. Referring specifically to Sainte Foy, his comparative analysis shows that the "curious type" of miracle in which saints extort offerings is well represented only in the *Liber miraculorum sancte Fidis*.[39] The numerical extreme of the statistical approach is exemplified by Weinstein and Bell, who, in surveying saints from 1000 to 1700, offer many pages of statistical profiles.

Although the sociological approach has yielded a wealth of information about categories of medieval saints, it tends to emphasize what is new within the period's data base and to ignore the earlier models of sanctity that continue through the period. As Michael Goodich points out, historical sociologists are often reluctant to acknowledge the influence of traditions inherited from early hagiographers because they may undermine the reliability of the period data.[40] Finally, the sociologically oriented historians are functionalists, arguing that saints' cults offer universal assistance, patronage, and other political functions,[41] and that their purpose is to sacralize or legitimize some form of social order or control.

For a recent group of cultural historians, however, hagiography is embedded not just in the political and economic but also the symbolic life of the community. Influenced by cultural anthropology, these historians read religious rituals and texts as social events open to multiple interpretations and uses.[42] One of the first historians to employ cultural models in the study of hagiography was Peter Brown, who reads the rise of the cult of saints in Latin Christianity as a manifestation of a profound cultural shift between the late antique and medieval periods.[43] By using anthropological concepts such as Victor Turner's "liminality," Brown is able to show that the liminal cult of saints cannot be explained by the prevalent two-tier model of elite versus popular religion.[44] Brown's analyses of the functions of symbolic forms like cults and rituals not only influenced historians of religion, but also modeled a new way of writing other kinds of history.[45]

The articulation of anthropological theory for historical analysis is even more pronounced in the work of Patrick Geary. Geary recognized in stories about thefts of relics an "underlying structural similarity" that raised questions which could not "be entirely resolved by traditional historical investigation." The scholarly approach Geary adopted moves beyond historical location of individual saints' cults to produce typologies of sanctity, since cults "display certain structural features which may be seen across cultures and across time." [46] In an important contribution to the study of texts about Sainte Foy, Geary analyzed the *Translatio* text in which the Conques monastery claimed that it had acquired Foy's relics in the ninth century. Geary concludes that "when the theft of relics is placed within the entire spectrum of practices, devotions, and uses of relics . . . it becomes evident that relics were perceived as the living saint, and that the translation account is really that of a ritual kidnapping by which the saint passed from one community to another." [47] By assuming that translations of relics are analogous to phenomena studied by anthropologists, Geary shows that the monks in effect saw themselves as having kidnapped their saint from the town of Agen.

Amy Remensnyder, another historian who has studied the cult of Foy and the *Liber miraculorum,* employs a variety of anthropological and French *mentalités* theories. Her important article on the reliquary-statue of Foy and the miracles identified as *joca* in the *Liber* concludes that, although there may be cultural strata inscribed in the miracle texts, both elite and popular cultures shared in one religious perspective within the cult of Sainte Foy. Historian Brian Stock even sees an anthropologist at work in the writing of Foy's miracles when he appreciatively describes author Bernard of Angers as "a systematic hagiographer and an anthropological fieldworker at once." [48]

And, finally, historians and art historians have begun to study the ideological functions of hagiography. Sharon Farmer refers to medievalists who have "directed their anthropological gaze not so much to the social and cultural worlds of peasants and marginals as to the ways in which elites— especially monks and aristocrats—employed legend, history, and ritual in order to shape the social world." [49] Thomas Head's *Hagiography and the Cult of Saints,* Sharon Farmer's *Communities of Saint Martin,* and Barbara Abou-El-Haj's *The Medieval Cult of Saints* all trace the networks of episcopal and monastic patronage that supported saints' cults and the competition among rival cults that instigated the production of hagiography.[50] Abou-El-Haj understands the cult of Sainte Foy in these terms when she writes that it "was not enlarged significantly until the late tenth and early eleventh centuries, when Conques and Figeac accused each other of murder and ambush. . . . At this point, Saint Foy was embellished with the jewels she now wears, translation stories were written, and miracles were recorded by Bernard of Angers." [51] Abou-El-Haj's analysis forwards our understanding of the circumstances in which specific hagiographic texts were written, although in our reading of cult politics an event does not lead quite so inexorably to one specific outcome. In "An Unsentimental View of Ritual in the Middle Ages," we conclude that rituals such as the exchange of valuable jewelry for a miracle to be worked by Sainte Foy provided a site for social negotiation (whether peaceful or contested) and that the outcomes of such negotiations could not have been predicted in advance.[52] Although we employ a number of concepts from symbolic anthropology, our work on the cult texts of Sainte Foy moves even farther away from cultural functionalism through the use of communication and reception theories.

Our analysis of gender constructions in the Foy cult texts draws on feminist theory. Women's history and feminist studies have been major forces in the increased visibility of hagiography in the last two decades. As Jane Tibbetts Schulenburg remarks of the genre of hagiography, it "holds a remarkable potential for social historians and especially historians of medieval women, for, unlike many other sources of the Middle Ages, saints' lives focus a great deal of attention on women: the *vitae* are directly concerned with female roles in the church and society as well as contemporary perceptions, ideals, and valuations of women."[53] Hagiography about women is now available in fine translations, owing to scholars like Brigitte Cazelles, Jo Ann McNamara, Elizabeth Petroff, Marcelle Thiébaux, Katharina Wilson, and Jocelyn Wogan-Browne. Materials about Sainte Foy in English include Brigitte Cazelles's translation of the thirteenth-century Anglo-Norman "La Vie seinte Fey, virgine et martire," Sheila Delany's translation of Osberne Bokenham's text about Saint Faith, and Pamela Sheingorn's and Robert Clark's translations of the eleventh-century texts about Foy in *The Book of Sainte Foy*. Patrick Geary's collection of translated primary documents for classroom use also contains several miracles of Sainte Foy.

Our analysis also benefits from the critical attention to the body and gender that has made hagiography central to its project. Caroline Walker Bynum's *Holy Feast and Holy Fast* opened up the interpretive study of this material to a feminist approach, demonstrating the power that holy women accessed through control of their bodies. For this scholarship, the male-authored text or image "presents a model of female sanctity that assumes a woman's essential, inescapable corporeality. Because a woman can never escape her body, her achievement of sanctity has to be through the body," as Elizabeth Robertson argues for the thirteenth-century *Life of Saint Margaret*.[54] However, within hagiography studies the focus has been further narrowed to only a few aspects of body. As Jocelyn Wogan-Browne puts it, "The hagiographic representation of virginity is one of the principal European narrative representations of women. In this vast genre, extending throughout the Middle Ages and beyond, the *passio* of the tortured and dismembered virgin is the dominant representation of female sanctity." [55] Hagiographic texts are regarded as voyeuristically fixated on the saint's physical body, a fixation that reaches its zenith in a kind of eroticization of the suffering female body in scenes of martyrdom. Thus medieval scholarship has combined with contemporary feminism to produce a prevailing model of how gender works within hagiographic contexts: males tend to display qualities of mind, will, or spirit, but females are described in terms of biology and sensory perceptions.

Perhaps because her supposed age at martyrdom was a prepubescent twelve, the Foy who appears in the *Liber miraculorum* (books 1 and 2) does not fit easily into the paradigms of the eroticized female body. In addition, this saint was not the victim of medieval misogyny, nor was self-imposed suffering her route to sainthood. Amy Hollywood's revisionist study of the female mystics renders problematic the link between suffering and power basic to the old paradigm,[56] and our study demonstrates that gender theories based in anthropology provide rich resources for analyzing not only the anomalous Sainte Foy but also the large cast of characters in her miracle stories.[57]

Our approach to the Foy materials relies heavily on literary analysis. For historically complex reasons that grow out of the way medieval language, literature, and culture have been defined as academic subjects, hagiographic writing is only now beginning to receive serious and sustained literary attention. The majority of hagiographic texts are in Latin, a language which until recently has been studied from a philological point of view by scholars in Classics departments. Peter Dronke's work on the composite text about the early Christian martyr Perpetua (in a study of medieval women writers) was an admirable exception to the general indifference to Latin hagiography.[58]

A second reason that hagiography has not drawn close literary attention is that construction of the field of Literature in the nineteenth and early twentieth centuries went hand in hand with a separation of this new discipline from religious and historical studies. Joaquín Martínez Pizarro, for example, comments that authors such as Gregory of Tours, Gregory the Great, and Paul the Deacon have been neglected by literary scholars since "their narrative works are histories and saints' lives, and literary scholarship has long treated these genres as if they belonged only marginally to literature." [59] Furthermore, as Gabriella Signori has pointed out, "Like penitential books and 'popular sermons,' miracle collections are primarily a literary product of clerical scribes. And it was their criteri[a], which were not uniform, that determined whether and in what form the religious thoughts and actions of the others, the laity, would be handed down." [60]

Because most Latin literature of the Middle Ages was written by clerics, their productions have held a stigma for "literary" scholars. As Lennart Rydén noted with regard to his study of a Byzantine hagiographic text, "Hagiography, in spite of its volume and importance has been treated very much like a stepmother in literary handbooks. . . . Hagiography still is very rarely studied and evaluated as a literary art."[61] This state of affairs was especially pronounced for literatures in the vernacular, which are normally studied in national literature departments by scholars trained in literary methodologies. From those disciplinary perspectives, true "literature" is secular; only recently, therefore, have works by major vernacular writers (such as Chaucer or Christine de Pizan) been acknowledged to be examples of hagiographical writing.

The literary approaches to hagiographic texts have tended to follow two paths. The first is the broad approach through narrative typology. For example, Alison Elliott in her *Roads to Paradise: Reading the Lives of Early Saints* reads hagiographic texts through models drawn from folklore and narratology. She traces two separate narrative structures: an agonistic one that shapes the accounts of martyrdom, and a set of motifs and themes drawn from romance that are used to interpret ascetic lives. Her interest is therefore in fundamental fictional types rather than specific or historically located literary reshapings.

A very different approach to martyr narrative is exemplified by Michael Roberts in *Poetry and the Cult of the Martyrs: The* Liber Peristephanon *of Prudentius*. Roberts does a literary analysis of one hagiographic text, a collection of martyr poems by one author, Prudentius. He attempts to answer some of the same questions that we have taken up with regard to the *Liber miraculorum* of Sainte Foy, namely: "What is the relation between martyr text and martyr cult in the *Peristephanon?* how are the beliefs about and the practice of the martyr cult embodied in the text? what is Prudentius' poetics of the martyr text?"[62] Using cultural theory and reader response criticism, Roberts makes a case for a kind of liminal polysemy as "an important constituent of Prudentius' poetics of martyrdom," since it appropriately expresses "the temporal and spatial indeterminacy associated with veneration of the martyrs."[63] Interestingly, however, in historicizing his set of texts as a response to the cultural milieu of a martyr's shrine, Roberts tends to ignore nonreligious cultural roles of the shrine. Our analysis of the cult of Sainte Foy recognizes that the cultural work performed by its hagiographic texts serves purposes that cannot be identified as solely religious.

Joaquín Martínez Pizarro further argues that early medieval historiographical and hagiographical works "document clearly and abundantly the specific features and patterns of narrative in the first medieval centuries."[64]

His discussion, however, focuses on the individual scene, not on "macro-narrative, which is more directly shaped by the historical purpose." [65] Our interest is not only in the close literary analysis of the microscene but also in relating these small units to the historical structure of the entire text, which we see as having an ideological function. The effect of Pizarro's method is to separate the literary from the historical, whereas we believe that any piece of writing may be interpreted as part of a historical process.

There has been relatively little work on the cult materials of Sainte Foy from a philological point of view. The most important for our purposes is the fine edition of the *Liber miraculorum* by Luca Robertini. A scientific edition according to the latest principles of textual scholarship, Robertini's book is immensely valuable, especially for its extensive notes and multiple indices. He demonstrates that Bouillet in his edition had not worked directly from the Sélestat manuscript, his base text, but had relied on a transcription made for him by the curate of the church of Sainte-Foy in Sélestat. In his notes, Robertini shows that the *Liber* was shaped by literary borrowings from numerous *auctors,* and he identifies especially the important classical sources. However, owing to his philological approach, he constructs a "book" different from any extant manuscript of the miracles and he pays little attention to the ways in which the *Liber* authors employ their classical borrowings for rhetorical and ideological effects. [66]

For our reading of the *Liber miraculorum* of Sainte Foy, we have put together a tool kit of methodologies that we found useful to illuminate features of individual texts and make sense out of the hagiographic ensemble, both as a formal structure and as a historical production. Those methodologies include the traditional literary ones of philology for close reading of the Latin language, stylistic analysis of poetry and prose narratives, identification of classical/medieval rhetorical tropes and genres, and study of sources and borrowings to understand the *Liber*'s intertextuality with other texts in the hagiographic tradition. We have also analyzed the internal structures of the *Liber,* looking at the ways groups of stories have been meaningfully arranged by various of its authors, both named and anonymous.

To these conventional literary methods, we have added an orientation from contemporary cultural and poststructuralist theory that emphasizes the semiotics of the text, and we have used the figure of the trickster from anthropology as an explanatory model for the Bernardian texts. We first emphasize the way that textual inclusions and exclusions make sense within a given interpretive frame, and then we historicize these conceptual frames by relating them to social discourses. We use internal contradictions and other traits to trace embedded ideologies in the various stages of production of the *Liber* and to hypothesize about the role of this book in the historical process of promulgating a monastic saint's cult. Our most ambitious goal has therefore been to situate this collection of miracle narratives culturally within the eleventh century without losing the nuanced and subtle differences inscribed in its textual subdivisions.

We have adopted the term "social semiotics" to characterize our project because it suggests the interdisciplinary nature of this study. As Bennetta Jules-Rosette comments, sociosemiotics is an area of study that has not yet been clearly charted, although it builds on traditional semiotics.[67] Robert Hodge and Gunther Kress argue in their book *Social Semiotics* that "mainstream semiotics emphasizes structures and codes at the expense of functions and social uses of semiotic systems," and, in particular, ignores "the complex interrelations of semiotic systems in social practice."[68] It is just this delineation of socially signifying systems interacting in hagiographic practice that we have sought to make through our analysis of Sainte Foy's miracle narratives.

We first trace a particular set of rhetorical codes we associate with the clerical author Bernard of Angers. Thus, although Bernard may be promulgating the cult of Foy, his narratives are also strongly inflected by his need to celebrate himself as a member of the northern intellectual elite class, which requires him to portray the saint, her monastery, and her regional culture as illiterate and folkloric. This sign system is specific to the Bernardian literary structure; its ideological underpinnings obviously have no appeal to the monk-continuator authors of later miracle narratives.

All of the post-Bernardian authors straightforwardly articulate a monastic point of view and monastic ideologies. They do this by elevating their patron saint to the celestial heights and celebrating her omnipotence over death, the devil, human error, and even other saints. In recording the miracles of their saint, the monk-authors make every attempt to employ the high style of recondite allusion appropriate to the subject matter. The narrative voice is anonymous because it represents the corporate persona of the monastery. Many of the miracles center on threats to the monastery or to someone or something under Foy's patronage; the miraculous resolution of the threat unambiguously demonstrates and unanimously celebrates Foy's power. Despite their overall similarities, the miracles written by monk-continuators form further subsystems of meaning.

In practicing a form of social semiotics, we have found two things to be of equal importance: first, understanding the system of signs which any set of texts engages, and second, situating that system of signs historically.[69] As we show in our discussions of the miracle narratives produced by Bernard of Angers and by the monk-continuators, there is a complex relationship between any individual semiotic system and its situatedness in history. To begin with, any producer of signs—in this case, writer of miracle stories— is constrained in what can be selected to a repertoire of possibilities pro- vided by the culture and historical moment. But at the same time it is clear that any semiotic system represents a meaningful and coherent but very radical selection from the huge range of options. In analyzing these miracle narratives as semiotic entities we must simultaneously attend to three as- pects of the texts; we must see them as rhetorical structures (a set of inter- nally related signs), as historically contingent constellations of signs, and as sign systems designed to have historical agency.[70]

Bernard of Angers's rhetorical production, especially his description of the monastery and the cult, is not literally historically accurate because he constructs a portrait of them that functions within his semiotic system. Bernard's techniques of verisimilitude have masked the extent of his his- torical manipulation from those who have read his texts. It is easier to see the reshaping according to a monastic agenda in the work of the monk- continuators.

But all of these texts—mediated though they may be by any internally coherent system of signs—of necessity have a relationship to larger histori- cal developments. The virtual absence of heretics and Jews, for example, in most of the *Liber miraculorum* narratives can be attributed to their produc- tion before the late eleventh century. After the middle of the eleventh cen- tury, when raids by "outsiders" like Muslims and Vikings had mostly been contained, Christian European societies experienced significant changes, including the growth of a market economy.[71] The latest miracle narratives frequently set their action outside the Rouergue; characters participate in this emerging money economy or engage in wars with the Saracens, all of which clearly indicate the historical location of these texts in the second half of the eleventh century.[72]

This introduction has situated the *Liber miraculorum sancte Fidis* within the context of medieval hagiographic production and has traced the study of this text and the saint's cult through the centuries. It has also described the approaches employed by scholars of hagiography and unpacked the tool kit of methodologies and theories that we use in our analyses. In chapters 1 and 2 we focus on the named author of the first two books of the *Liber,* Bernard of Angers. Chapter 1 uses the paradigm of the trickster to analyze Bernard's literary and rhetorical relationship to the hagiographic traditions he inherited. We position Bernard rhetorically relative to the dominant early medieval conventions of hagiography, demonstrating both his know- ing appropriation and creative rewriting of key tropes and narrative ele- ments. Chapter 2 historicizes Bernard's clerical liminality relative both to the Conques monastery and to the cultural shifts of the eleventh century. We situate Bernard's texts historically in the eleventh century, using our analysis of their contents and rhetorical strategies to illuminate the intellectual and cultural complexity of this transitional period (and thus to revise the current historiographical view that the major shifts took place in the twelfth century). Chapter 3 turns to the monk-continuators of the *Liber* who appropriated the Bernardian task of miracle redaction, and chapter 4 takes up the additional miracles composed at the Conques monastery in the later eleventh century. In each case we use comparative analysis to reveal narrative and ideological differences among the various layers of authorship. In chapter 5 we offer a semiotic overview of the complete *Liber* that draws attention to the multiple signifying systems within this complex text which—despite its internal differences—remains a striking example of male monastic literary production. Finally, in our Conclusion, we compare the Foy materials to the miracles of Saint Benedict written at Fleury in order to delineate the cultural work performed by the Conques miracle collection.

I BERNARD Of ANGERS AND THE TRICKSTER TEXT

Bernard of Angers, the named author of the first two books of the *Liber miraculorum sancte Fidis,* is not an unknown writer whom we have discovered. The miracle stories he produced and his responses to his hagiographic materials have already entered scholarly discourse. For art historians, Bernard's narratives offer a rare glimpse of contested attitudes toward three-dimensional sculpture in the crucial period of its reemergence,[1] while, as we have seen, historians consider the *Liber* to be one of the richest written sources surviving from early eleventh-century southern France. The *Liber*'s present position in historical discourses depends on its being read as a straightforward record of events and an accurate portrait of life in the region.[2] Christiane Caitucoli, for example, writes that the *Liber miraculorum* "is a true picture, lively and detailed, of life in the Rouergue and its surroundings around the year 1000,"[3] and Brian Stock also sees Bernard of Angers as an accurate recorder of the alien lifestyles of southerners.[4] By treating Bernard's manipulation of literary and religious genres as unimportant, historians have been able to regard his writing as a trustworthy portrayal of life in the Rouergue at the turn of the millennium.

Furthermore, few historians have acknowledged that they are drawing disproportionately on the two Bernardian books—they simply refer to the *Liber* as if it were a whole, internally consistent text. The "true" and "detailed" picture of "life in the Rouergue" that they perceive is mostly found in Bernard's part of the *Liber miraculorum* since, we argue here, he is a master of the literary "verisimilitude effect."

Underestimating Bernard's rhetorical sophistication, historians have also ignored the ideological dimensions of the miracle narratives; in our view, Bernard's ideological agenda always shapes his historical data.[5] He claims to be writing according to the conventions of the miracle genre, since his announced aim is to write a hagiographic text, to make known an unknown saint. The density of literary allusion and the deliberation with which the *Liber* is ideologically shaped, however, suggest that Bernard was playing with hagiographic conventions in ways that his literate readers might appreciate. Through artful descriptions of himself as collector and recorder of Foy's miracles, Bernard leaves the memorable impression of a sophisticated author dealing with popular materials. Further, in his uniquely autobiographical text Bernard becomes a major recurring character—as both collector of and witness to Foy's miracles. In the process of writing a spiritual autobiography of his conversion from skepticism to belief, Bernard vividly represents his own subjectivity.

Bernard's playfulness with hagiographic conventions and his generic experimentation prompted us to explore the variety of ways in which this author exemplifies the paradigm of the trickster—a paradigm we use as our lens for analyzing the Bernardian books 1 and 2 of the *Liber miraculorum*. The figure of the trickster is ubiquitous in world folklore and mythology, but we are not restricting the trickster paradigm to its folkloric sense alone. We are adopting the more general semiotic sense given to the figure in cultural theory where trickster has been theorized as demonstrating the contradictions and possibilities of the liminal zone between or at the margins of established social structures and norms. Cultural theorists of liminality like Victor Turner and Barbara Babcock have analyzed not only trickster figures but also what one might call trickster modes of cultural performance, production, and narrative, which employ contradiction, paradox, shifting identity, and reflexivity to define semiotic boundaries and to allow a measure of metasocial commentary.[6] Typically—through boundary crossing or flagrant violation of norms—the trickster figure of folklore and literature helps the community to better comprehend what those norms and boundaries are. Liminality is also seen as a site of experimentation from which innovation and even major paradigm change may be generated.

In accordance with trickster semiotics, Bernard crosses generic boundaries with ease and juxtaposes contradictory elements to challenge his reader's stylistic and generic expectations. His collection of miracle stories both is and is not an example of a saint's *Liber miraculorum* and must be read with attention to its complex textual dynamics. Moreover, despite its place of honor as historical source for the eleventh century, Bernard's text cannot be considered a reliable picture of the local culture in south central France.

Its verifiable "facts" are part of an ideological portrait of Bernard himself, the Conques monastery, and the Rouergue.

Bernard as Hagiographer

In this chapter we show the extent to which Bernard deliberately challenges the expectations of his readers, but we also demonstrate Bernard's profound intertextuality with hagiographic traditions that were well established by the eleventh century. Early in the Middle Ages, the miracles recounted in Sulpicius Severus's *Life of Saint Martin* and in the miracle collection of Gregory of Tours "had a standardizing effect and became authoritative for the genre."[7] Thomas Head has elaborated what such standardization implies: "Hagiographers borrowed phrases, themes, motifs, even verbatim passages from stories from earlier works, adapting them to the specifics of their story. The traditional and even repetitive character that such use of *topoi* creates is one of the most striking aspects of medieval hagiography."[8] In fact, as we will suggest, the effect of Bernard's experimentation could only be appreciated by a readership familiar with the highly conventionalized nature of miracle stories.

Bernard's collection of miracles signals its membership in the tradition of literary hagiography through the use of specific literary genre markers. Perhaps the most typical of these markers is an introductory letter or preface filled with rhetorical humility *topoi*.[9] Bernard addresses his letter to Fulbert of Chartres, with whom he claims to have studied and in whose company he says he first heard of the miracles of Sainte Foy. True to form, Bernard uses a humility *topos* as he confesses that he is "unlearned and ignorant in the art of composition."[10] He tells Fulbert that "if the truth in these stories has been corrupted by my bad style, readers will turn away in disgust and this best of subjects will have been debased."

Bernard is clearly imitating the rhetoric of Sulpicius Severus, whose *Life of Saint Martin* was one of the most widely read hagiographic texts of the early Middle Ages and, as a result, "became a virtual mine of topoi."[11] Although Sulpicius had declared himself "the weakest of creatures" and had bemoaned his "all too unpolished diction," Bernard acknowledges Sulpicius's hagiographic preeminence with the hyperbolic statement that, "for relating the life of Saint Martin it was not possible to find a better writer anywhere on earth than Sulpicius Severus" (1.34).[12] Working within this tradition, Odo of Cluny, who wrote the life of St. Gerald of Aurillac in the tenth century, also displays the generic humility codes. Odo's dedicatory epistle to Abbot Aymo expresses "trepidation" about writing the life and miracles of the saint: "On the one hand I fear to be presumptuous in undertaking something beyond my capacity; on the other hand in not doing it I fear greatly to be contumacious by being disobedient." [13]

Early medieval writers often used the humility *topos,* as Odo does, to set up their rationale for writing. Gregory of Tours, in his preface to the first book of his miracles of St. Martin (late sixth century), laments the lack of learning in Gaul and makes excuses for his own unlearned style, [14] but nevertheless claims to have been advised by three visions that he should write. He finally persuades himself that although he lacks eloquence he should perform the task of narrating Martin's miracles. In the preface to his "Glory of the Confessors," Gregory of Tours opposes to his own sense of unworthiness the conviction that he must record the testimony about the "miracles of the blessed" and turns his confession of ignorance in rhetoric and grammar back upon educated men whom he constructs as potential critics. He says that he plans to tell them, "I am doing [the same] task as you, and by my [literary] incompetence I will engage your wisdom. For I think that these writings will offer you one benefit: what I describe unskillfully and briefly in an obscure style, you will amplify in verse standing clearly and sumptuously on longer pages." [15] Hagiographic tradition thus offered Bernard the clever paradoxes of humble self-authorization.

In adopting the well-established humility ploy to address Fulbert, Bernard of Angers first acknowledges that his own "foul pen may have sullied his materials. If so, you will not offend me by adopting such a noble and glorious theme as your own; you will embellish with a noble and glorious style, since all agree that you stand alone at the pinnacle of wisdom." [16] Bernard justifies his own project of writing up the Foy miracles by saying he does not judge himself culpable for striving to the best of his ability "when the very scarcity of writers strongly insists that I do it." Later, as we shall see, he also uses rusticity to critique learning and associates belief in Foy's miracles with naive popular culture.

With regard to his writing project, Bernard invokes the brevity *topos* that was becoming fashionable in the rhetoric of letters and miracle collections, but at the same time he signals his potential divergence from this norm. [17] He claims that in Conques he has been overwhelmed with the great number of miracles pouring forth from various narrators. His solution is to note down "the more beautiful ones swiftly and with the greatest brevity." Then he will carry his notes back home and "make a fuller text for the future reader out of this material." And he says that these miracles will be "not abbreviated, but in a narrative long enough to satisfy my readers." Bernard thus indicates his familiarity with the prevalent idea of concise composition, while announcing his intention to compose at greater length. [18]

Bernard also clearly signals his acquaintance with the trope of the eyewitness to miracle, a means of authenticating extraordinary events.[19] In the dedicatory letter Bernard implies that he is writing down only miracles with eyewitnesses. He then goes beyond the minimum requirements of this trope by casting himself as chief among eyewitnesses. Rather than being just the redactor, he makes himself into one of the guarantors of the truth of these events, a maneuver related to his autobiographical strategies. So Bernard reports that when he is inundated with miracle narratives only his dedication to the task keeps him going: "If my mind had not been burningly eager to hear them my brain would have been overwhelmed with weariness."

In the conclusion of his letter to Fulbert, Bernard uses another well-known *topos* of such collections—the unusual or novel content of the miracles—when he refers to "the unusual novelty *(inusitata novitas)* of the miraculous content" which is potentially disturbing to his readers. In his explanation of the principles of rhetoric, Isidore of Seville lists five kinds of reasons or causes. The first, honorable causes, wins the sympathies of an audience immediately, but the second, strange or astonishing causes, provokes an unfavorable or hostile response.[20] As Amy Remensnyder has pointed out, hagiographers generally attempted to avoid extreme *novitas* in their miracle accounts,[21] fearing that it would generate incredulity. Bernard, while sensitive to the stigma of the *nova et inaudita* in a traditional genre, nevertheless defends his narration of unusual miracles such as Foy's replacing of eyeballs or resurrection of donkeys. He simultaneously acknowledges the traditional caution against novelty and uses it as an occasion to go beyond expected materials. In Bernard's rhetoric, the very outrageousness of Foy's characteristic miracles becomes an opportunity to logically demonstrate the saint's powers.

Other typical features of such hagiographic narratives include the motif of the skeptical searcher converted to faith in the saint. Odo of Cluny, who traveled to Aurillac in order to conduct investigations into Gerald's miracles, refers to his initial position as one of skepticism: "I too, formerly, hearing the fame of his miracles, was nevertheless in doubt, and for this reason chiefly, that stories get about here and there, through I know not what channels, and are then gradually discredited as empty."[22] Then Odo tells his reader that having investigated the behavior of Gerald, "having learned how religiously he lived and that God had shown this man to be in His grace by many signs, I could no longer doubt of his sanctity. I marvel rather, that in this age of ours, when charity is almost entirely grown cold, and the time of AntiChrist is at hand, the miracles of the saints should not cease."[23] Bernard seems to be following the convention of authorial conversion when he describes his initial response to stories of Foy's miracles:

"We put no faith in them and rejected them as so much worthless fiction."
In the narratives of Odo and Bernard, the skeptical investigator is eventually
persuaded by the truth of the stories he gathers. Both authors model in their
framing comments a transformation from skepticism to belief that their
reader should be inspired to follow.

Play with Hagiographic Conventions

As we have suggested, in his two books of the *Liber miraculorum sancte Fidis,*
Bernard does more than just appropriate hagiographic traditions; he deliberately expands the boundaries of the genre by manipulating conventions
for a variety of unexpected effects.

Bernard notably avoids allegorical interpretation, almost always preferring the literal level.[24] But although in most cases he eschews allegory, occasionally he demonstrates that he could use it, for example in 1.2 on Gerbert's restored eyeballs: "You who heal them in body are just as concerned
to heal them in spirit, and for this reason you removed light from the
exterior eye of the body, in order that the inner spirit might become
brighter." However, in many other cases where we might expect a spiritual
reading Bernard does not provide it, but makes literal details carry the sig-
nification. Thus, when a warrior named Gerald had borrowed and then
lost his lord's falcon, Bernard reports the exact circumstances of the falcon's
return during a meal, when a goose flew into the room and the falcon
followed in pursuit. Rather than allegorizing the falcon's return, Bernard
simply calls it "the sign of an excellent miracle, that, as if intentionally,
the winged creature returned from another district to a place that it didn't
know" (1.23).

Unlike Gregory of Tours, for whom there is one life of the saint reproduced endlessly in contingent history,[25] Bernard appears genuinely fasci-
nated by the minutiae of narrative and the specificity of locale. His narratives
effectively undercut transcendent patterning in favor of local specificity.
Despite their differences at the macro level in their conception of hagiography, Bernard does employ a technique also found in Gregory of Tours's
historical writing, the realistic detail (what Roland Barthes calls the "punc-
tum"). In analyzing "a rhetoric of the scene," Joaquín Pizarro describes this
new technique by comparing it to "the presence in photographs of those
unplanned, involuntary details that capture the viewer's attention as mani-
festations of the irreducible reality behind the picture . . . very 'lifelike' and
prominent details that seem nevertheless irrelevant." Pizarro says that this
technique is "a clear attempt on the part of Gregory to make us feel that
we are witnessing an unedited slice of life."[26]

Bernard often seems to adopt this scenic technique of mentioning a detail as if for its own sake, rather than for some larger symbolic or metaphoric purpose. For example, to aid a prisoner's escape, Sainte Foy provides not just a generic tool, but "a small hammer that was very old; its whole surface was covered with rust" (1.32). The rusty surface Bernard describes is a gratuitous detail that has no function in the episode other than to provide verisimilitude; it is not allegorized or otherwise interpreted, but simply offers an unforgettably vivid image of the physical object which, as we will show later, triggers a philosophical moment on the part of the author Bernard.

Bernard's descriptions are almost novelistic in technique; they create a sense of place, setting scenes at the monastery and in the surrounding countryside, and specifying time of year and day. Perhaps as a consequence of his commitment to verisimilitude, not every chapter offers a miracle; some simply fill in background information, setting, and character. For example, in 1.32, Bernard departs from his narrative project to offer generalizations about Foy's most renowned type of miracle, the freeing of prisoners. This leads him to describe how the great masses of iron chains and fetters that the freed prisoners brought to the Conques monastery were turned into iron grillwork for the church, and from this he moves to an unusually detailed description of the church itself, concluding: "There is scarcely any opening in this church full of angular passageways that doesn't have an iron door fashioned from fetters and chains. To tell the truth, they would seem to you more marvelous than the whole edifice of the basilica, with the exception of the beautiful furnishings, whose abundance, whether of gold, of silver, or of rich fabrics, together with precious stones, provides a pleasing variety." As in a novel, these descriptions of the church provide colorful settings for the miracles related in other chapters.

The chapter entitled "How Sainte Foy Collected Gold Everywhere for the Fashioning of an Altar" (1.17) also gives historical information about the monastery's former poverty and present wealth rather than recounting a miracle. The theft of Foy's relics from Agen had given rise to miracles, which triggered lavish contributions of land, buildings, precious metals, and precious stones. Bernard itemizes the "golden or silver reliquary boxes," the crosses, basins, candelabra, thuribles, crowns, chalices, altar cloths, and copes now to be found in the monastic treasury. He mentions Foy's body-shaped reliquary, which was refurbished to become a "splendid image" worthy of the now rich and prestigious monastery. He also describes the process by which gold and precious stones were accumulated for the "golden frontal of the high altar, which is not less than seven feet and two fingers in length—not in geometrical feet, but as the peasants are accustomed to measure, with both hands spread out and the thumbs linked at the upper joint." The saint is said to have extorted the materials from pilgrims and local residents—a form of miracle, perhaps—but the chapter functions more centrally to give a distant reader a visually detailed picture of the monastery and its dazzling treasures.

Ironically, given these vivid accounts of Conques's splendor, the reference to measurement according to "peasant" techniques in 1.17 shows how Bernard nevertheless manages to suggest the rusticity of Foy's cult. Bernard almost always describes the Rouergue as the antithesis of northern France: its topography and climate are alien, and the level of culture is lower. He strives to create the impression that he has discovered a rather isolated and primitive religious culture, one that has little to do with the written word and is totally naïve with respect to hagiography. In Bernard's portrayal, the cult of Foy is assimilated to popular religion.[27]

In keeping with his construction of Foy's cult as popular, Bernard tells his distant readers:

It has been a custom since the old days that pilgrims always keep vigils in Sainte Foy's church with candles and lights, while clerics and those who are literate chant psalms and the office of the vigil. But those who are illiterate relieve the weariness of the long night with little peasant songs and other frivolities. This seemed to ruin utterly the solemn dignity and decency of the sacred vigil. I addressed the monks in chapter about this matter, and I made and proved a variety of arguments that this detestable and absurd custom ought to be completely prohibited. But they maintained that all these practices were valid and did not deserve censure; moreover, they asserted that it was impossible to restrain practices of this kind, which, in any case, weren't contrary to divine will (2.12).

The monks reply to Bernard that their predecessors had attempted to keep "the swarms of peasants" with their "unruly singing" from vigils by barring both the outer doors of the monastery enclosure and the inner doors of the shrine; however, the doors miraculously opened for the peasant mobs and from then on "rough peasant songs" were allowed in the sanctuary. Bernard provides an erudite rationalization for these rustic practices, but his narrative gives the impression that this vividly portrayed religious culture of the Rouergue is very different from that of the north. We would argue, however, that the verisimilitude that creates the "Otherness" of Conques and the south must be regarded as one of Bernard's most successful rhetorical devices. What we call his "verisimilitude effect" is a deliberate if unusual technique that serves Bernard's ideological agenda by differentiating the elite cleric from his rustic surroundings.

Another unusual aspect of his miracle collection is Bernard's creation of a cast of recurring characters, including Guibert the Illuminated, Gerbert the warrior-turned-monk, the abbot Peter, and local villains. In the case of Guibert, Bernard gives us virtually a full characterization and a life story, for within the Bernardian miracle collection Guibert is featured in five different chapters. Guy, the villain responsible for blinding Gerbert in 1.2, dies memorably in 1.8. The vividness with which the Conques region is portrayed, the creation of this cast of recurring characters, and the foregrounding of Bernard himself as a controlling intelligence give Bernard's miracle collection a unique narrative coherence. Rather than functioning as exempla within an abstract moral or allegorical frame, the individual miracles always relate to the story Bernard is telling about Foy and her devotees in the Rouergue.

Judging only from the types of miracles Bernard recorded, scholars can easily demonstrate that most of Foy's miracles fall into conventional types.[28] For example, Foy is especially renowned for miracles that restore eyesight. The basis of these narratives is quite traditional, since blindness was commonly seen as a punishment for lechery.[29] For example, in the tenth-century life of Saint Gerald of Aurillac, Gerald lusts after a beautiful girl and, although he does not succumb to the temptation, God punishes "his concupiscence" with blindness "so that the eyes which had looked on unlawful things should not for a time be able to see even that which was lawful."[30] Foy similarly punishes Guibert with blindness for finding "a like-minded and unchaste woman" and the saint must repeat the punishment more than once. When Guibert repents, Foy cures his blindness, but further lapses into lechery provoke Foy to inflict renewed bouts of blindness.

However, close comparative study suggests that Bernard anticipated the easy familiarity of his sophisticated readers with such hagiographic conventions and worked to retain their interest through manipulating convention. Even the miracle stories (such as the healing of blindness) that we might see as conventional types tend to verge on the parodic. Far from being a mark of closure in a Bernardian narrative, the miracle itself often gives rise to further "business," and in some stories is part of the effect of comic excess. Guibert, for example, although healed by the saint, keeps lapsing into lechery again and again, and he lives an utterly unexemplary life as a pauper supported by the monastery. Bernard wryly comments: "For every time this happened, I would have been able to write a little chapter of miracles, if I hadn't avoided a taste for redundancy." Gerbert, another beneficiary of an eyeball replacement, actually becomes a monk after his miracle. Rather unexpectedly, Foy prevents him from returning to the life of a warrior by re-blinding him in one eye. As Bernard notes with reference to Guibert and Gerbert: "For when they begin to sneak off to worldly affairs, divine power immediately hinders them. Either by blinding an eye or by disabling a limb, God forces them to stay where they are" (1.7). The two men are joined at the monastery by one of the most unlikely of miracle-recipients, a donkey who had died on the route to Conques and was about to be flayed by peasants when Foy brought the animal back to life. Its owner eventually sent the donkey to the monastery of Sainte Foy and "for many years afterwards he dispatched many donations to her."

In Bernard's presentation, Guibert, Gerbert, and donkey thus function as a series of exhibits maintained by the monastery to demonstrate the authenticity of its saint's miracles. All three are represented as grotesques, whose visible scars witness both to their trauma and to supernatural healing. Bernard does not "pretty up" their physicality but seems to enjoy their burlesque of hagiographic decorum — of who might be expected to receive a miracle and even of the miracle event itself. These episodes playfully exaggerate the expected norms, at times going to the limit of absurdity in a mode of hagiographic writing Ernst Curtius identified as typical of rewritings of the saints' lives.[31]

Bernard's thinking through the logical consequences of a miracle also results in humor. In book 1 Bernard reports several miracles in which deafness, muteness, or blindness is healed by "a sudden and violent discharge of blood" that both signals and effects the cure. The same feature occurs, for example, in a miracle of Gerald of Aurillac, where "blood burst forth" from a deaf child's ears in the middle of the night.[32] But by the time he reaches book 2, Bernard selects three miracles out of the thousand that were worked during a procession of the saint's reliquary-statue because each is a jest *(ludus)*. The first subject is a deaf-mute boy, cured when "spouts of blood" (Bernard uses a medical term from pseudo-Soranus: *ebullitio*) from his ears, "along with a bloody stream that rose up from his throat, broke through the obstacles that were blocking his voice and his hearing" (2.4). In response to the cure, the monks began their usual celebratory ritual: chanting praises to God and Foy, ringing bells, and blowing trumpets. Quite logically, the boy who had never before heard a sound was driven into a frenzy by the racket and "seemed to have become insane." Bernard opines, "It would have been better for him to have remained a deaf-mute but with a rational mind than to be cheated of the gift of human intelligence and turned into a madman in circumstances like these." He then reports that the boy "recovered his senses," but leaves the reader to wonder about the mental condition of all the other former deaf-mutes healed by the saints.

In addition to ironically reframing familiar types of miracles, Bernard also seems to parody specific hagiographic texts that his educated audience knew well. For example, in his *Miracles of the Bishop St. Martin,* Gregory of Tours writes of a man named Ammonius who was thrown from a two-hundred-foot cliff by a demon. "And when he was whirling from the height of this precipice and was flying down without support of wings, each second of his descent he kept calling on the aid of St. Martin." The saint deflected his fall toward some trees so that he fell "little by little, from branch to branch," and thus survived the fall, though he suffered an injury to his foot.[33]

Bernard's exaggerated imitation features a prisoner in a castle tower to whom Foy appeared in a vision, urging him to jump out the highest window. Understandably reluctant, the man did not comply until Foy's third chiding appearance. Then, according to Bernard, "never did his own feather bed caress Sardanapalus more softly and more sweetly than those very rugged cliffs caught the prisoner. Divine power supported him so well that this man to whom nature had denied wings seemed not to fall but to fly. Gaining confidence from this miracle, he did not hesitate to make a leap to a far lower cliff. And then he made a third leap from the very high cliffs upon which the whole structure of the fortress rested and, rushing past the lower parts, he glided along to the firm earth" (1.34). If the passage from Gregory of Tours is "mock-heroic" and has a "humorous tinge," as translator William C. McDermott suggests,[34] then Bernard's parody pushes the humor to a new level of outrageousness. He inserts a Juvenalian reference to Sardanapalus, and he has his protagonist descend to the ground in three giant leaps. Thus Bernard does not simply replicate a hagiographic trope, but explores its limits in a reflexive and often overtly humorous mode.

Foy as Trickster Saint and Her *Joca*

Sainte Foy herself stands out as one of Bernard's most unusual and memorable characters. According to her legend, at the time of her martyrdom Foy was a female child of about twelve years, an anomalous age for an early medieval saint.[35] Bernard links her age to capriciousness, a central trait in his characterization of the saint. His Foy employs her powers to trick people into giving her their glittering jewelry, a type of behavior that he attributes to Foy's "girlish mind, [which] took pleasure in the things that girls of a youthful age usually want and try to get for themselves" (2.10).

Picking up on Bernard's rationalization, Amy Remensnyder has attributed the saint's playfulness to the need to give Foy a personality that would appeal to the lay worshipper.[36] Remensnyder argues that for the most part eleventh-century saints were not lay persons but monastic or episcopal authorities; as a female and a child Foy deviates from these hagiographic norms. To Remensnyder, the saint's unusual characterization arises from her function as mediator for the laity, and the playfulness of her miracles is a logical extension of a nonclerical cult. Another scholar, Jean Wirth, sees popular elements beyond mere "plaisanteries." He argues for a general inversion of values resulting in confusion between saintliness and fooling ("anerie") in pilgrimage cults.[37] Although scholars like Remensnyder and Wirth attribute the trickster elements in Foy miracle stories to folklore influences or popular functions,[38] this trait appears primarily in Bernard's two books. It is important to note that it is the author Bernard of Angers who portrays Foy as trickster saint, a characteristic that fits well into the rhetorical strategies of Bernard's trickster text.

One of the unusual features of Bernard's miracle collection is its organization around clusters of miracle stories on similar themes rather than by chronology, since chronological structure was followed in the vast majority of miracle collections.[39] Two roughly contemporary hagiographers, Aimo of Fleury and Letaldus of Micy, chose to follow the usual chronological order.[40] Bernard acknowledges his innovation in his prefatory letter to Fulbert: "The miracles will be grouped not in chronological sequence but by the similarity of their subject matter." These subjects include the freeing of prisoners, the acquisition of jewelry and other precious objects, punishment of those who insult the saint's reliquary-statue, and protection of pilgrims and monastic property.

One miracle cluster (1.23 – 1.28) has drawn special attention, since in these stories Foy exhibits a variety of behaviors whose common feature is their joking quality. Pierre-André Sigal, who has analyzed the corpus of eleventh- and twelfth-century southern French miracle collections, considers this a type of miracle unique to the Foy collection.[41] The miracle stories in this cluster share the distinctive linguistic feature of repeated reference to Foy's miracles as *joca*—tricks or jokes. Bernard of Angers associates this term with peasants twice in book 1. He introduces 1.23 by saying, "Even in regard to the smallest of problems a great many miracles were performed, and such miracles the inhabitants of the place call Sainte Foy's jokes, which is the way peasants understand such things." Likewise in 1.26 Foy teases the warrior-monk Gimon as he sleeps, and Bernard identifies this as a miracle of the kind "that the inhabitants of the place call Sainte Foy's jokes, which is the way peasants understand such things."

Although not as explicitly identified as *joca,* the miracle stories of 1.16 to 1.22 also demonstrate the saint's trickery and violation of decorum. In these narratives, the saint extorts gold and precious objects; for example in 1.18, a woman setting out on a pilgrimage to Conques tries to trick the greedy trickster saint by leaving her ring at home with her chambermaid:

"'Hold this,' she said, 'and keep it safe until I return, for Sainte Foy may snatch it away from me if I take it to Conques.'" The saint sees through the ruse, appears to the woman in a dream to demand the ring, and strikes her with a fever until she complies. Similarly, in 1.22 a local castellan named Austrin attempts to thwart Foy's lust for jewelry by withholding a ring his dying first wife had bequeathed to the saint. Austrin instead uses the ring to marry his second wife Avigerna, but Foy causes her ring finger to swell in unbearable pain. Recognizing the folly of tricking Foy, Austrin and Avigerna go to the saint's shrine and pray there for relief. On the third night "when the sorrowful woman happened to blow her nose, the ring flew off without hurting her fingers, just as if it had been hurled from the strongest siege engine, and gave a sharp crack on the pavement at a great distance." Bernard's description of this scene highlights the grotesqueness of the suppliant-wife and the dynamic details of her deliverance from pain, as if authorizing the reader to respond to the humor. Bernard's Foy is a practical joker. Whether specifically called *joca* or not, the narratives are appropriate to a trickster saint who outwits those trying to trick her.[42]

Since some of these trickster narratives attribute the term *joca* to "peasant understanding," French cultural historians have assumed that the saint as trickster is a popular element in the text, one opposed to the seriousness of Bernard, as clerical recorder of the events. Sigal, for example, sees in Bernard's narrative "an opposition between one more popular, more folkloric conception and another one that is more intellectual."[43] Historians have tended to emphasize the cultural oppositions between elite and popular views inscribed in these texts. Amy Remensnyder, however, stresses the compatibility of popular and elite conceptions of this female child saint. Remensnyder argues that Bernard uses the word *joca* instead of *ludi* precisely because this was the term illiterate peasants used for a category of miracles. (Monks, presumably, would have employed the more learned *ludi*.) For Remensnyder Foy's jokes are based in lay peasant culture; ultimately she argues that elite and popular traditions do not clash in the text, but converge.[44] Most significantly, no one who has closely analyzed the Foy miracle collection has ever suggested that the jocular element in the text is other than a contribution of popular culture.

Our own reading of these distinctions between the popular and the elite understanding insisted upon by Bernard is that—far from being transparent signs of cultural stratification—they are themselves literary codes within the best-known classical rhetorical scheme, the Virgilian wheel. Bernard identifies the story in which a falcon miraculously returns as an example of "the smallest of problems" *(de minimis causis)* that Foy dignifies with her miracle-working powers, and he refers to the return of a pilgrim's lost ring as an example of "Sainte Foy's power even in trifling matters" (1.21). In both cases, Bernard signals the lowest category of literary material within the Virgilian wheel. This tripartite scheme of medieval rhetoric included the *humilis stilus, gravis stilus,* and *mediocris stilus.* Thus in the large cluster of miracles worked by a joking trickster saint (1.16–1.28) the common thread is not just the saint's sense of humor, but more tellingly the narrative's humble or trivial subject matter. As Bernard says in 1.23, "I am going to speak about the least important matters, or, if it is permissible to call them this, Sainte Foy's jokes."

The *Rhetorica ad herennium* (IV.ix.14) describes the "simple type of style" as employing "the most ordinary speech of every day," that is, colloquial terms and body-centered actions. It gives the example of a bathhouse scene of conflict between a crude, abusive stranger and a more refined young man.[45] A number of the Foy trickster stories share these slapstick qualities. One example features a dishonest and greedy entrepreneur who wanted to make a killing in the wax market (1.24). Having purchased a large amount of wax at a very low price, he "slipped [a huge candle] into his clothing in such a way that the larger part of it projected below his belt and the smaller part jutted up towards his beard through the opening in his garment." The vivid image Bernard creates of the huge, erect candle is both sexually grotesque and broadly humorous. Foy punished the merchant's greed with miraculous ignition of the candle; the merchant's hair and beard caught fire and the flames encircled his entire body "and burned his backside as well." Bernard caricatures the frenzied actions of the enflamed merchant ("You would have been astonished at his horrible bellowings as the flames drove him mad, at the noises he emitted as he kicked, at the grating of his teeth, at his wildly rolling eyes, and at the uncontrolled contortions of his whole body") as if in accordance with classical rhetorical schema of the *humilis stilus.*

According to medieval rhetoricians, the low style *(humilis stilus)* was defined by social criteria. It was used to speak of low topics associated with low people (the shepherd or peasant), whose utterances were blunt and based in the senses rather than being metaphorically elaborated. Eugene Vance describes the low style as "centered in the infliction of bodily pain and, more precisely, in stark gestures of sexual retribution and emasculation by a club-wielding peasant," a style he finds in the late medieval fabliaux.[46] Details like the wax merchant's phallic burning candle lead us to conclude that the rhetorical strategies of the low style inform Bernard of Angers's hagiographic narratives as well. Bernard's references to *joca* and to "peasant understanding" are the purest of textual effects, which he implicitly contrasts with his own elite sensibility. Such references to trickery and the low style thus cannot be read as offering unmediated access to folklore materials or peasant culture; they are signs in the construction of Bernard's trickster text.

Features of the Trickster Text

In Bernard's two miracle books not only is the saint herself a trickster, but others among the recurring cast of characters share this quality. Before his eyeballs are restored in the cult's foundational miracle, Guibert is a liminal character who lives literally on the margins of the monastery as an itinerant musician, a *jongleur*. Unlike many latter supplicants at Foy's shrine, Guibert didn't care that he was blind. He was making so much money as a *jongleur* that, from his point of view, Foy's miraculous healing of his eyesight was unnecessary. The founding miracle of this cult, then, is a healing worked by a trickster for a trickster.

Another anomalous character is Gimon the warrior-monk (1.26), an almost mythical figure from the earlier history of the monastery that Bernard chooses to describe much more fully than any of the monks he actually encountered at Conques. Paradoxically, Gimon embodies both contemplative values and their opposite. For the early Middle Ages the monk and *miles* were construed as mutually exclusive categories. To be a warrior was to participate in a set of values and activities that contrasted to monastic values and practices. It is striking, then, that Bernard assigns an important role in his narrative to the figure of Gimon, who had remained a warrior even after he became a monk:

When he lived in the secular world Gimon had a fierce and manly heart, and he didn't leave it behind when he entered the monastery, but applied it entirely to vengeance against evil-doers. In addition to his other garments, which were suitable for clothing a monk, Gimon kept in the dormitory a cuirass, a helmet, a lance, a sword, and all kinds of instruments of war. These were placed above the foot of his bed within easy reach for use, and to the same end he had a fully equipped warhorse in the stable.

In flaunting Gimon's violation of monastic expectations, it is almost as if Bernard has playfully made the tough old monk an antitype to St. Martin, who had totally rejected the military life.[47]

Even as he explores the anomalies of the Gimon character, Bernard devotes considerable energy to justifying the monk's military predilections: "I've heard his deeds described as irreproachable in every way, except that he used to go on expeditions armed. But if people understood this behavior of his correctly, they would be able to ascribe it more to moral excellence than to an assault on the monastic rule." Especially concerned that Gimon might even have slaughtered enemies of the monastery, Bernard argues, "That man will not be regarded as a murderer whom the Lord Saboath and King of Armies and Powers destined to be the sole protection of his own monastic community, as if he were another defender-angel." The rhetoric of Bernard's portrait of Gimon employs paradox, emphasizing the transgressions at the same time as they are rationalized, with the result that neither term is subordinated.

Bernard's strategic ambivalences structure his Foy miracle stories, but his ambiguous characters and rhetorical paradoxes are not extensions of folklore or popular culture. They are best understood as features of the semiotic paradigm of the trickster. According to this model, the trickster represents a mediating position that combines traits from different categories. In folklore, tricksters are characters who are often both wise and foolish, violent and funny, sources of both order and disorder. In world religions, tricksters are the anomalous figures—incarnated gods, virgin mothers, and other divine paradoxes.[48] In ritual, the trickster is the sacred clown who is both the transgressor and the policer of boundaries.[49] Gimon, the fighting monk, trangresses the Rule of Saint Benedict but also defends the monastery and its holdings. He functions to give Bernard's text a nonnormative perspective on monastic ideology, simultaneously inside and outside the institution.

The ultimate expression of the logic of this trickster paradigm may be found in Bernard's portrayal of the saint herself as murderess (2.5). Bego, bishop of Clermont and external abbot of Conques, intended to "plunder Sainte Foy's treasures" from the monastery in order to ransom his nephew, who was being held prisoner in Gourdon Castle. The first attempt to steal Conques's valuables was thwarted when the mule laden with treasures plunged off the cliff; "Marvelous to report, it did not appear that the mule was injured, or the vessels battered or crushed, or the altar cloths even dampened by the river. It is clear from the height of the dizzying fall that these things were preserved by heaven," and the sacred objects were miraculously transported back to the monastery. The evil bishop planned a second raid the next day; that night, however, one of the laymen who guarded the monastic church received a visitation from Sainte Foy in a dream. The saint told him: "I come from Gourdon Castle, where I myself have killed Hugh, the one whose ransom was to be paid today with my treasures. But it won't be possible to take them anywhere." She then informed the dreamer that she planned three more murders.

This astonishing portrait of Foy as serial killer is difficult to reconcile with any expectation that a saint must exemplify good behavior. We can understand it as an extreme representation of the trickster paradigm in its combination of good and evil. Paradoxically, this holy figure can perform acts which by human norms would be unacceptable, violating these norms of human behavior in order to protect the monastic community. In the extremity of this portrayal Bernard explores the furthest limits of his semiotic paradigm and shows his willingness to challenge hagiographic conventions. Perhaps it is significant—as a sign of his awareness of just how far he has gone with his hagiographic experiment—that he does *not* put himself into either the narrative or the framing comments of this miracle account.

Trickster Narration

Bernard's miracle narratives feature outrageous liminal figures, as well as a trickster narrator who delights in juxtaposing materials and concepts from mutually exclusive categories. We say "juxtaposing" to emphasize the often-jarring paradoxes that are insisted upon in the text. Even where harmonious synthesis could be narratively achieved, the author calls attention to incongruity. This gives the miracle stories a tone of jest or irreverence that undercuts straightforward praises of Foy's power.[50]

The narrator's irreverent tone is particularly in evidence in a "very renowned" miracle about the freeing of a prisoner (1.32). In a vision Foy appeared to a prisoner to bring him the rusty old hammer mentioned earlier. The prisoner freed himself with this unexpected implement and, as part of the ritual of thanksgiving, delivered it to Foy's shrine at Conques. Bernard concludes his account with a personal comment: "The little hammer had hung in that place about three years, and as the sign of such of a great miracle it was an attraction to pilgrims. I was extremely angry that it had been destroyed in the making of the iron grillwork. But what a wondrous thing! Where do you think Sainte Foy got a physical hammer? But we shouldn't judge divine work with human reason; we should firmly believe that it was done."

Bernard's final question—"Where do you think Sainte Foy got a physical hammer?"—undercuts the miracle he has just recounted. Ostensibly miracle narratives were told in order to increase the devotion of the faithful. Bernard's comment, however, opposes divine miracles to human reason. Paradoxically, Bernard uses reason to question miracles with the very statement in which he claims to be doing the opposite: "But we shouldn't judge divine work with human reason; we should firmly believe that it was done." By calling attention to the anomaly of a physical hammer brought by a disembodied saint, Bernard effectively raises the issue of the epistemological status of miracle stories, and in doing so problematizes his whole narrative enterprise. This paradoxical approach to miraculous material functions as a kind of trickster's rhetoric.

A trickster does not always call attention to his own maneuvers. For example, Bernard describes Gerbert, who has suffered the violent excision of his eyeballs, as "now despising his life" (1.2). In his despair, Gerbert went into the countryside ("rus") in search of goat's milk since, as Bernard relates, "people say that if anyone who has recently been wounded drinks goat's milk the person will be undone by death on the spot. But no one would take the responsibility of giving Gerbert goat's milk." Bernard's narrative firmly locates the action in a rural setting and implies a folk knowledge of the milk's effects. Although he does not explicitly employ the terms, this situation is analogous to Bernard's use of the words "peasant understanding" in its signal that we are in the realm of popular culture.

Bernard's depiction of the rural populace is, however, a rhetorical trick. The source of the information about medical uses of goat's milk is not medieval folklore but Pliny the Elder. In his *Natural History,* Pliny exhaustively describes the uses and effects of goat's milk in treating a variety of ailments.[51] Bernard's trick is to recast as folklore the materials he has gathered from his classical education. Examples like the goat's milk anecdote reveal the constructedness of Bernard's text—the way in which textual effacement of his own learning enables the construction of an "other"—the rural peasant culture of southern France.

Text as Autobiography

In contrast to this rural and popular milieu of Conques, the portrait Bernard gives of himself as northern cleric emphasizes his education and his sophistication. Though both the images of Conques's rusticity and those of Bernard's urbanity are textual constructions, the autobiographical dimension deserves further discussion, for it is one of the anomalous aspects of this miracle collection. Indeed, Bernard's redaction of Foy's miracles consistently functions as a representation of his own complex subjectivity.

We might go so far as to say that the author's subjectivity *becomes* the subject of his text. Bernard is always explaining himself; he is consummately reflexive of himself and his making of the collection.[52] His foregrounding of his own decision-making process goes far beyond the usual hagiographical *topos* of the collector faced by miracles too numerous to recount. For example, in describing his criteria for selecting from the large numbers of miracles available to him, he explains: "I have concentrated on the miracles that were worked to take revenge on evil-doers or on those that are in some way new and unusual, and have greatly abridged them in order to bring out a small but precious volume" (1.9). As we have seen, he also gives detailed description of his composition process from note taking to final distribution.

In his experiments with reflexivity, Bernard appears to have blended the genre of the miracle story with another genre, the spiritual autobiography. One of the most striking differences between his miracle text and those he clearly knows well is the development of an autobiographical mode beyond the framing preface and the passive role of witness and redactor. Bernard creates for himself the role of chief protagonist. His collection is framed by address first to his audience in the north of France and then to his audience at Conques. In both of those roles he is the writer of the miracles, but even that role is dramatized far more vividly and persistently in his text than in any of his models.

Bernard tellingly signals both his deliberately literary strategy and his autobiographical performance when he writes in his prefatory letter that the entire miracle collection will be structured around the founding miracle of the cult, Guibert's eyeball restoration. Thirty years before Bernard set foot in Conques Foy had miraculously healed a certain Guibert, whose eyeballs had been ripped out. Bernard reports elsewhere that this miracle inaugurated Foy's miracle-working reputation (1.17). In the letter to Fulbert, Bernard depicts himself as the chief authenticator of this foundational miracle:

But I myself have been fortunate enough to see the very man whose eyes were violently plucked out by the roots and afterward restored to their natural state, intact and whole. And I can see him even as I write this. Since he himself asserts that this really happened and the whole province attests to it, I know that it is true. Therefore I think that his story ought to be introduced first as the basis for reading the rest of the miracles, and not just my interpretation of his meaning, but word for word as I hear it from his lips.

Bernard portrays himself not only as a collector of miracle stories but as a skeptic who comes to jeer and is persuaded to belief. His letter to Fulbert presents his entire miracle collection as the outcome of a spiritual journey. The description of cultic practices in south central France is framed by his personal responses, beginning with his encounter with body-shaped reliquaries.

The propriety of three-dimensional cult images was a highly controversial issue in the intellectual circles of northern Europe in the ninth and tenth centuries, where the prevailing opinion rejected such images as idols. Thus when Bernard first sees the golden reliquary-statue of Saint Gerald above the altar at Aurillac, the opportunity would seem to present itself for a philosophical or theological excursus. However, Bernard portrays his theological scruples in autobiographical terms as spiritually foolish responses. He both identifies himself as a learned person who thinks this type of statue is superstitious and condemns himself as "foolish, for I also thought this practice seemed perverse and quite contrary to Christian law" (1.13). Bernard and his companion Bernier mock the reliquary as the "very old, incorrect practice and the ineradicable and innate custom of simple people," that is, they initially construct themselves as both different from and superior to southerners who venerate body-shaped reliquaries.

Bernard and Bernier also sneer at the statue of Sainte Foy when they arrive at her shrine in Conques. Representing the saint as crowned and frontally enthroned, Sainte Foy's reliquary-statue (which is still extant) enshrined what medieval Christians considered to be the most important relic of a saint, the skull. The trunk of the statue is formed of a roughly hewn wooden core over which silver and gold sheets were nailed, with the skull housed in a cavity hollowed out of the core. Wooden arms are jointed to the core, but all visible surfaces are gold or silver, encrusted with stones, antique cameos, and precious gems. The golden head, apparently representing an adult male, is a Gaulish production, late Roman in date, and may well have been an imperial gift. Presumably fashioned shortly after Conques first claimed to have acquired the relics of Sainte Foy, the appearance of the reliquary-statue changed frequently as new gifts to the saint were incorporated into its fabric and old ones removed for other uses.[53] Bernard reports his first reaction to this reliquary-statue: "With a sidelong smile I looked back at Bernier, my scholarly companion, thinking it absurd, of course, and far beyond the limits of reason that so many rational beings should kneel before a mute and insensate thing." Bernard uses his small-minded response to reveal his own spiritual deficiencies.

The incident sets Bernard up as ignorant in his educated superiority and very much in need of a change of heart that would come from experiencing the faith of believers firsthand. He contrasts himself to "a certain cleric named Odalric who was considered a prig and carried himself somewhat above the others." Odalric derided the statue as it was being carried in procession and was visited the next night in a dream by a "lady of terrifying authority" (Foy) who beat him with a rod so that he survived only long enough to report this experience.[54] Bernard comments, "After that no room was left for argument as to whether the shaped image of Sainte Foy ought to be held worthy of veneration, because it was manifestly clear that he who criticized the statue was punished as if he had shown disrespect for

the holy martyr herself." Bernard suggests that "the statue is to be understood most intelligently" as "the pious memory of the holy virgin," implying that he himself has changed his mind. Bernard's physical journey to
Conques is also a spiritual journey from foolish skepticism to intelligent
veneration of Sainte Foy's image.[55]

In coming to Conques, Bernard takes on an unexpected role not just as
the outsider listening to miracle stories but as the reformer of local monastic
practices and impresario of the cult of Foy. He writes that "one kind of
miracle above all others is specifically associated with Sainte Foy, for which
she is best known and most highly renowned. This miracle is that she frees
prisoners who cry aloud to her and orders the freed prisoners to hurry to
Conques with their heavy fetters or chains to render their thanks to the
Holy Savior" (1.31). The monks, however, have failed to commemorate
their own place in sacred history. Bernard depicts himself as the intrusive
and critical outsider, who impatiently lectures even the senior monks "because they had not kept written records on the freed prisoners—their
names, families, homes" (1.31). He clearly sees his composition of miracle
narratives as the solution to their inadequacy.

With his sense of liturgical decorum, Bernard, the sophisticated northern
cleric, finds the noisy and frivolous lay practices so offensive that he again
inserts himself into the life of the monastic community by addressing the
monks in chapter to chide them for allowing laity to spend the night in
the church (2.12). When the monks explain to him that their practice is
the result of a miracle worked by Foy (affirming the lay right to be in the
sanctuary), Bernard reassesses his own attitude and accepts the practice as
God's will. This would seem to be an example of the learned sophisticate
humbled by the rustic illiterate—a transformation implied by the spiritual
autobiography.

However, a further maneuver by Bernard undercuts his humility and
recuperates the superiority of his learning. He arrogates to himself the role
as interpreter of God's viewpoint, telling the monks that although there are
probably pragmatic reasons for tolerating these practices, still it isn't the
songs that please God but the hardships of the vigil. He returns to his old
position that the songs are unworthy in themselves, but he concedes that
since singing these songs is the best simple people can do, their song must
be acceptable to God. He continues, "Nevertheless no one should think
that with these assertions I wish to conclude that God wants these songs
purely and simply because they are rough peasant songs. Rather, in the way
I have said, God turns his gaze to the devotion of our hearts and shows
good will toward human ignorance and simpleness." Bernard turns this explanation into an internal debate—"For where I thought to refute I was

refuted by my own thoughts"—and thereby manages to salvage his position. At the end of the chapter he can return to his superior stance, ironically via a humility *topos:* "My responses, which were based on the limited ability of my small store of knowledge, were very helpful to those who had doubts about this issue. And vice versa." Whether humble or critical, Bernard portrays himself as an important agent in this monastic milieu.

Although he had expressed disdain for local reliquary practices when he first arrived in southern France, after Bernard narrates his own conversion to belief in Foy's miraculous powers he construes Foy as his personal patron. He personalizes the *topos* of the eyewitness report to a miracle by fashioning his own immediate experience of a healing miracle into one of the more charming stories of his stay at Conques (1.9). He reports that shortly after he arrived in Conques on his first visit, a widow came on pilgrimage with her blind daughter to invoke Foy's special powers on the girl's behalf. During the night vigil, the miracle occurred. Bernard chose to understand the event as an episode in his autobiography: "The Lord favored me by letting me see something that had a divine cause." He recounts that "the monks who watched over the relics and some of the monks who were taking their turn officiating at night, . . . saw what had happened. At once they all began to run swiftly to my lodgings. And because they knew that I longed to witness a new miracle, they exhausted one another in their eagerness to report it to me. "'Look! For you, fortunate Bernard, a miracle, a miracle from Sainte Foy!' they said. 'This is what you have been praying for, what you wished would be shown to you before your departure. You thought it wasn't fair that, when you came so far intending to write miracles, you weren't seeing any yourself.'" Bernard thus personalizes his miracle collection by inserting himself as eyewitness.

Far from being the neutral writer who is content to remain in the frame of the preface, Bernard casts himself as a pivotal character in his own narrative—the person for whom events take place. The last three miracles in book 2 heighten Bernard's autobiographical appropriation of Sainte Foy. In recounting the miraculous healing of his brother, Bernard reveals his autobiographical motivations for his composition of the miracles (2.13). The miracle is cast in the most personal terms as a special favor the saint has extended to him, but also as one he deserves. Bernard frames his account with the comment, "Very recently through Sainte Foy's intercession the mercy of the highest Father deigned to work a miracle for me, though I am most undeserving. It won't be a burden to me to relate this miracle, though some may think me full of empty pride if I do so." He also makes it clear that his collecting of Foy's miracles should have gained him her favors: "'Sainte Foy, how does it help me to praise your powers everywhere, if when I am myself engulfed by sorrow I am left a stranger to your beneficent aid?'" Likewise, in 2.14, Bernard's personal secretary Sigebald was cured of a swelling of his brain and chest suffocation by a vow to Foy, and, in 2.15, two of Bernard's pupils who were traveling near Angers recovered their lost psalter. In both cases, Bernard stresses the protagonists' relationships to himself, implying his special intercessory position in relation to Foy.[56]

His commitment to writing up Foy's miracles was Bernard's ostensible reason for making his first return visit to Conques, but the description of this visit reveals increasing emotional involvement with the monastic community. He opens his second book with the second miracle about Gerbert, which had occurred in Bernard's absence. Since Gerbert died shortly after the miracle, Bernard didn't see him on the second visit, but he was able to enjoy a reunion with Guibert the Illuminated, the first recipient of an eyeball replacement, now an old man. The old man "wept profusely" and called Bernard "my lord father."

Bernard makes Guibert into his mouthpiece to express Bernard's own sense of satisfaction at his accomplishments, as well as the depth of his personal involvement: "May God and Sainte Foy reward you, for you alone undertook the task of coming here from far away to hear and record her miracles." Bernard reports that he responded by kissing Guibert's eyes

warmly three and even four times and, saying farewell to him, I left. I was no less struck by compassionate emotions than a person who travels across the sea, leaving behind sweet children or a dear spouse, uncertain as to whether he will ever see his own once again. If only God would ever, through His mercy, let me come back to Conques again and Guibert should still be living then! Only if I now held him in low regard or didn't care about him at all, could I be prevented from handing down the record of his very celebrated miracle to perpetual memory and making him memorable to every generation.

The affective depth of this interaction between miracle recipient and narrator is highly unusual in hagiography and an index of Bernard's particular autobiographical project.

Finally, in 1020, "motivated both by love for Sainte Foy and by the desire to see Guibert the Illuminated again," Bernard made a third trip to Conques and "took it very hard" that Guibert had died (2.7). He had no intention, he claims, of writing further miracles; his personal involvement thus outlasted his professional interest. Moving from supercilious critique to sentimental attachment, Bernard's text dramatizes the transformation of the protagonist–author in accordance with the techniques of medieval spiritual autobiography.

In shaping his miracle collection to the demands of this other genre, Bernard exploits the potential for liminal fluidity since, typically, the spiritual autobiography reveals its narrator's change of heart. As cultural theorists have argued, liminality (and trickster phenomena) by paradoxically bridging mutually exclusive semiotic categories may give rise to new possibilities.[57] The *Liber miraculorum,* books 1 and 2—Bernard's trickster text—dramatizes the author's own conversion to belief in Sainte Foy's miracles and invites his readers into their own liminal engagement with these challenging hagiographic materials.

2 BERNARD OF ANGERS BETWEEN TWO WORLDS

furdum de
de aho . necesse
mauditum fi mis
timode pfpren c

This chapter moves outside the textual dynamics of the *Liber miraculorum,* books 1 and 2, to historicize Bernard's trickster strategies and social ideologies. The reflexive quality we have identified in so many of the Bernardian miracle narratives often characterizes the end of a tradition.[1] Writing in the eleventh century, Bernard is, first of all, a product of the earlier Middle Ages, and his text gives us a portrait of the clerical, monastic, and feudal mentalities of the period. At the same time, Bernard engages intellectual topics and employs persuasive techniques usually associated with twelfth-century thought and the "new men" of the period's emerging institutions. Writing Foy's miracles from this position, he articulates a complex dialectic, both promoting and critiquing the older ideology of monasticism.

The End of a Tradition

In significant ways, the miracle stories by Bernard of Angers are recognizable products of early medieval cultural systems. His depiction of morality, spirituality, theology, and social ideology belongs to the era before 1100. For example, Bernard portrays his subject Sainte Foy as an agent whose power is independent of morality; in her miracle stories, there is no correlation between a person's moral status and Foy's favors. As we are told, she frees prisoners solely in response to their ritual invocation of her and their acknowledgment of her power—regardless of whether they are guilty or innocent (1.31). The saint represents a system in which one accesses the centers of spiritual power through correct ritual actions rather than through moral rectitude.

In Bernard's miracle stories the monastery, too, is portrayed as a source of power rather than as a center of holiness. Bernard's rendition of the monastic life has little or nothing to do with spiritual perfection or living according to the Rule of Saint Benedict; rather, the monks' possession of Foy's relics means that others must perform the right actions toward them and their property. Thus it is significant that the recipient of the acknowledged foundational miracle of the cult's fame, Guibert, is characterized by moral turpitude and never successfully reforms. In his repeated backsliding, Guibert exists not to model correct behavior but to be a living witness to Foy's power. He represents a world still focused on cults of local saints, each reigning supreme over a circumscribed area.

From the twelfth century on, local cults were increasingly subsumed within the ideological structures of a centralizing Church. Saints of the universal Church came to predominate, chief among them the Virgin Mary, who is virtually absent from the *Liber miraculorum.* The invention of expiatory concepts such as Purgatory and elaboration of the penitential system begin to shift religious emphasis from external rituals of power to internalized notions of accountability for sin. With regard to such characteristics of later medieval practice, Bernard's miracle narratives look quite old-fashioned.

In another attitude typical of the earlier Middle Ages, Bernard represents himself as suspicious of three-dimensional representations of the sacred. Justifying his initial negative response to the reliquary-statue of Saint Gerald of Aurillac, he writes: "For where the cult of the only high and true God must be practiced correctly it seems an impious crime and an absurdity that a plaster or wooden and bronze statue is made, unless it is the crucifix of our Lord. The holy and universal Church accepts this image, in either carved or modeled form, because it arouses our affective piety in the commemoration of Our Lord's Passion. But the saints ought to be commemorated by displaying for our sight only truthful writing in a book or insubstantial images depicted on painted walls" (1.13). Bernard's attitude reveals that he is still enmeshed in the theology of the *Libri Carolini,* the response of Charlemagne's theologians to a misleadingly poor 787 translation of the decrees of the Council of Nicaea. Both in preferring word to image and in making an exception of the crucifix, Bernard follows the *Libri*'s tendency toward iconoclasm.[2] By contrast, the twelfth century will witness an explosion in the production of religious sculpture, with the Church as eager patron.

In his social thinking, Bernard accepts the schema of functional roles prevalent in his era; his narratives ideologically follow the three-estates model. By the eleventh century one of the most common ways of classifying society was according to three orders of *oratores, bellatores,* and *laboratores,* that is, those who prayed, those who fought, and those who worked.[3] Bernard understands the roles of peasants, warriors, and clergy in society, but has no place for the entrepreneur or the money economy.[4] In his text money-making functions as a sign of avarice, so he disapproves of a wax merchant's scheme for making himself a wealthy man.[5] After describing the merchant's spectacular fiery punishment, Bernard concludes, "Since things like this happen, I don't think I would offend anyone by asserting that Sainte Foy's goodness is praiseworthy and marvelous also for this: that to prevent vile commerce from weakening her pilgrims, she punished greed and avarice" (1.24).[6] Likewise in 1.4, when the warrior Gerald's mule dies and he offers to sell the hide to the innkeeper, "the wicked innkeeper offered a price to Gerald that was as low as possible, reckoning that even if he gave nothing he would still get the hide." Bernard later characterizes the innkeeper as "perfidious," but offers no reason for the innkeeper's wickedness. Rather, he stigmatizes the very position of innkeeper, who, like the merchant, belongs to a social class still without a firm positive identity.

The one person Bernard calls a "townsman" or burgher he also characterizes in negative terms as drunk, bad-tempered, verbally abusive, and so violent that he wields a meat spit to hack up a monk's eye (2.1). In 1.15 too, a young woman who had been healed by the saint and remained in the settlement near the monastery working as a weaver provides a portrait of an urban artisan who does not fit the tripartite social estates model and must therefore be represented as deviant. Bernard's narrative describes her as continuing to work at her loom when she should have honored the saint's reliquary-statue passing in procession. The saint's response was swift and dramatic: the girl "became so mishapen that it was just as if she had never been healed but had remained bent and crooked, wholly deprived of the function of her muscles. Her body was completely drawn together and she didn't have the strength to let go of the tools of her loom — the very shuttle was held fast in her clenched fist." Her grotesque punishment symbolizes her marginality as an artisan to the traditional estates.[7]

Ernst Curtius has pointed out in discussing the comic elements in hagiography that a technique of comic exaggeration is especially found in descriptions of pagans, devils, or other evil men who, despite their violence or threat, are conceived of as fools to be treated by *reductio ad absurdum.*[8] In chapter 3, we fully discuss the technique of comic exaggeration as Bernard uses it in 1.12. In general, however, the Bernardian descriptions that employ caricature and exaggeration tend not to concern devils or pagans but to refer to people in those social categories—the artisan, bourgeois, or commercial classes—which do not fit into a tripartite social order. In fundamental ways, therefore, Bernard's social views mirror the dominant models of the early eleventh century, and the same might be said about his educational training.

Bernard's Classical Education

Bernard of Angers was a product of the classical liberal arts education whose importance was at its peak in the eleventh century. In the course of the twelfth and thirteenth centuries, under the influence of Aristotelian science and the new scholasticism, the liberal arts would cease to be the mark of the educated man that they had been since the time of Cicero.[9] At the cathedral school of Chartres, Bernard presumably had a traditional liberal arts education, which began with the reading of dialectical treatises (Porphyry, Isagoge, and others by Aristotle, Cicero, and Boethius). The structure and sequencing of the curriculum at Reims, about which we have some knowledge in this period, was paradigmatic of the educational curriculum Bernard also completed. Master Gerbert at Reims, "knowing that his students could not advance to the oratorical arts until they had mastered the kinds of speech, which are learned from the poets . . . had them read the 'poets' Virgil, Statius, and Terence, the 'satirists' Juvenal, Persius, and Horace, and the 'historian' Lucan. After this they studied the art of rhetoric. . . ."[10]

Fulbert, whom Bernard names as his intellectual mentor at Chartres, may have studied at Reims under Master Gerbert late in the tenth century before taking up a position as instructor in the cathedral school at Chartres.[11] Some scholars are suspicious of Bernard's claim that he studied at Chartres and was an intimate of Fulbert's circle. His writing reveals, however, that he has the kind of education typical of a cathedral school like Chartres or Reims in the north of France during the tenth and eleventh centuries.[12] Further, in the prefatory letter to Fulbert, Bernard demonstrates his knowledge about the existence and precise location ("outside the walls of the city") of a small church in Chartres dedicated to Sainte Foy, which suggests more than a passing familiarity with the town. It seems reasonable to accept Bernard's claim of an affiliation with Fulbert and Chartres, but the real evidence for this claim lies in his deep familiarity with classical writers.

Very occasionally Bernard cites a classical *auctor* by name—as in 1.5 where he refers to Prudentius's *Psychomachia* and the allegory of pride—but for the most part he does not reveal his textual sources.[13] With the exception of Luca Robertini, no scholar has recognized the extent to which Bernard's text is laced with classical allusion. This is not entirely surprising, since, as we have indicated above, Bernard's trickster technique centrally involves the obscuring of his learned sources. In the goat's milk example, Bernard totally erases the literary source in Pliny the Elder in order to create the impression that the source is rustic folklore. Bernard's construction of popular culture requires the disguising of his high culture allusions. Likewise, the caricature of the wax merchant, whose fiery predicament Bernard treats comically in the low style of narration, is actually rife with phrases that Bernard adopts from Terence, Virgil, and Horace.[14] In 1.33, he silently drops a whole line from Virgil's *Georgics* (1.88) into his minutely observed and richly detailed description of the climate and topography of the region: "Of course in the summer on account of the nearness of the sun it blazes up excessively with torrid heat. But just as the south wind rules with a free rein in the summer, in the winter, on account of the altitude of the land, it is stiff with ice and snow because of so many cold spells. Therefore, the more the contraries of nature weigh upon that soil, the more 'faults are burnt away and harmful moisture sweated out'" *(excoquitur vitium atque exsudat inutilis humor)*. Later in the same chapter, Bernard uses a phrase from Sedulius in his description of a lord and his household asleep in the upper story of a castle tower: "enjoying quiet slumber and placid dreams."[15] Bernard's educated audience in northern Francia—the audience he specifically describes in his letter to the abbot and monks of Conques—would presumably have appreciated the artistry of his classical allusions.

Bernard promises in his letter to Fulbert to give more than just an interpretation of the meaning of the founding miracle; he will relate it "word for word" as he heard it from Guibert's lips. Nonetheless, the elaborate vision of Sainte Foy *(prosopographia)* that Bernard records as Guibert's echoes Boethian language: "Her clothing was very flowing and interwoven with the most elegant gold throughout, and delicate, colored embroidery encircled it. Her long sleeves, which hung down to her feet, had been delicately gathered into very tiny pleats on account of their fullness" (1.1). The inclusion of Boethius's *Consolation of Philosophy* in the liberal arts curriculum doubtless influenced Bernard's imagery,[16] so he shaped Guibert's description of Foy's clothing and his dialogue with her to conform with Boethian formulations about the appearance of Lady Philosophy.[17] He also appears to have drawn on Plato's *Timaeus* (widely available in the Chalcidius translation, as Barbara Boehm has suggested) for his comments on Foy's head: "And, rightly, on the principal part of the body, that is, on the head, four gems were seen, through which we are able to observe clearly the quadrivium of the cardinal virtues: prudence, justice, fortitude, and temperance" (1.1).

One of Bernard's favorite techniques is rhetorically to exploit paradox by making two contradictory statements. In the letter that concludes book 1 (1.34), which is addressed to his internal monastic audience at Conques rather than to his external clerical audience at Chartres, Bernard describes his "new edition" of Sainte Foy's miracles as simultaneously worthless and highly valuable. He claims that the miracles have both literal and oral origins: "I myself took them down from you or from the inhabitants of this village in your own words. . . . The narrative sequence of those who told me these miracles has been faithfully observed to demonstrate clearly that they were actually present at so many miraculous deeds." At the same time, Bernard acknowledges his own redaction of the stories "into some feeble sort of Latinity," noting that his "humble little additions to this book" have been vetted by the master of the school of Tours and others. In the course of a long, contorted explanation of how highly these eminent and learned men regard his version of the miracle stories he brags that another learned contemporary, John Scotus, "displayed such favor toward me that he asserted I was not inferior to the writers of antiquity."

In fact, despite his disclaimers, Bernard's text is a highly literary composition, rich in allusions to the writers of antiquity. In his text, Bernard both disavows and claims his place among these ancient writers. While we might read the rhetorical contortions of his letter simply as an unconvincing attempt at humility by someone who clearly wants to be recognized for making his literary mark, we can also see them as telling clues to his literary technique. Bernard's rhetorical sophistication allows him to reach various readerships with at least three different messages.

The first readers will be the monks at Conques, his explicit audience for the epistle (1.33) and its attached Book of Miracles. Bernard assures them that the cult of Foy is now spreading in northern Francia: "Many respected people have heard of Sainte Foy for the first time through my writing, and through me her previously unknown miracles become known to many." The expansion of the cult is obviously the message the monastic authorities want to hear.

A second message appears to be that Bernard, as hagiographer, has simply provided the literate vehicle for oral reports about firsthand experience of "miraculous deeds." The authenticity of "unadulterated truth" is conveyed through "the unlearned way of speaking." The *topos* of authenticity through illiteracy forms a stylistic analogue to Bernard's depiction of an unlearned monastery and peasant culture in the region of Conques, a rustic setting which nevertheless has been witness to amazing, divine miracles.

Within this religious rhetoric, unlearnedness and rusticity themselves become the signs that prove the authenticity of the miracles and foster the cult's appeal.

Bernard's statement that his compositional task required putting the miraculous events into some literate style covertly signals a third level of reception. This message appears to be aimed at those *literati* who would recognize the density of classical allusion in his prose, since it was aesthetically valuable to be able to mask one's sophistication. Bernard's achievement could be fully appreciated only by others trained as he was in the liberal arts. The trickster elements of Bernard's style are, therefore, authorized by the aesthetic norms of the Latin literary tradition going back to Augustine and beyond.

In Augustinian rhetoric, as Rita Copeland points out, "meaning can be expressed ambiguously, so that it is up to the reader to judge carefully and to be equipped with the fundamentals of doctrine (signs and things, *caritas*) and with the *techne* of exposition." Explaining the difference between Augustinian and classical rhetoric, Copeland says: "Classical rhetoric deals with ambiguities of meaning from the perspective of the orator, of the producer of the utterance," while Augustine's sacred rhetoric "takes up ambiguities of meaning from the perspective of the reader."[18] Interpretation thus gains authority and status after Augustine, as "textual power shifts from authorial intention to 'affective stylistics,' to what the reader can do with the text."[19] In *De doctrina christiana (On Christian Doctrine)*, Augustine writes, "But many and varied obscurities and ambiguities deceive those who read casually, understanding one thing instead of another; indeed, in certain places they do not find anything to interpret erroneously, so obscurely are certain sayings covered with a most dense mist. . . . [N]o one doubts that things are perceived more readily through similitudes and that what is sought with difficulty is discovered with more pleasure. . . . Thus the Holy Spirit has magnificently and wholesomely modulated the Holy Scriptures so that the more open places present themselves to hunger and the more obscure places may deter a disdainful attitude."[20]

Martin Irvine has recently described Augustine's "grammar of allegory" as a "reinterpretation of [classical] *grammatica* as part of a general theory of signs."[21] Classical theory of tropes "provided Augustine with the model for understanding the semiotic principles underlying interpretation as well as a methodology for exegetical practice."[22] A key point of Augustine's commentary is that "authoritative interpretation is a matter of the interpreter's competence in handling the cultural encyclopedia with its ideologically encoded discourses."[23] The possibility of multiple interpretations, indeterminacy, or polysemy in the sacred texts—rather than provoking "semiotic anxiety"—lead Augustine to posit semiosis as "the necessary condition of all interpretation. Indeed, Augustine states that writings of the highest authority would be written in a way that would allow someone to find reverberating in the words whatever truths he may, rather than in a way that would impose one true meaning and exclude others."[24]

In our reading, Bernard of Angers's texts employ these Augustinian principles. Copeland argues that "Augustine's transformation of rhetorical invention had no bearing on the 'academic' study of rhetoric from the Carolingian period onward. The study of rhetoric as a trivium art in the monastic schools, and later the cathedral schools and universities (especially of northern Europe) was a conservative tradition." Whereas Copeland sees Augustinian principles coming into practice with twelfth-century *artes poetriae,* we would argue that Bernard is already using these principles to create a text designed to be challenging and therefore to be received in different ways by different audiences.[25] As Cassiodorus puts it (giving "classic expression to the Augustinian position"): "The holy profundity of the divine Scriptures has common expression *(communes sermones)* so that everyone may receive it, but its meaning is hidden *(arcanum)* so that it must be sought for. It hides its mysteries in many ways, making use of definitions and syllogisms and figures."[26] Bernard's literary technique puts the burden of interpretation on the reader.

A comparison of his prefatory letter to Fulbert with his concluding letter to the abbot and monks of Conques clearly reveals Bernard's shape-shifting rhetoric. Writing to his revered teacher, Fulbert, Bernard insists on his poor writing skills and the need for Fulbert to improve Bernard's style. There Bernard's characterization of himself as "the least of scholars" (an example of a humility *topos*) is appropriate for addressing a distinguished superior. But in his letter to the monastic community at Conques, where Bernard employs the same humble self-characterization, its formulaic nature quickly becomes evident. Before he is far into the letter, Bernard has dropped the humble tone and assumed the role of hectoring schoolmaster. He invokes his familiarity with the classics: "I have paid attention to the long tradition of ancient writings," and his association with Master Fulbert, "most learned of almost all mortals in this our age," as he proceeds to correct the Latinity of his audience at Conques. Admonishing the monks to abandon their own practice and accept his superiority in matters of Latin grammar, Bernard insists that the name of their saint is a noun of the third declension, not the fifth, and should therefore be expressed in the genitive case as "Fidis" not "Fidei." Paradoxically, one effect of Bernard's humility *topos* is to denigrate the monks at Conques, the primary recipients of his letter. The voice of the classically educated northern cleric comes through loud and clear.

Virtue Made Visible

All of this internal literary evidence clearly demonstrates that Bernard had enjoyed the elite liberal arts education offered by top cathedral schools of his day. Bernard's description of his encounter with one Abbot Peter affords an excellent example of Bernard's concern with cultural status. In 2.7 Bernard reports that he had first heard about Peter when the monks flattered him by describing Peter's admiration of Bernard's writing: "A man named Peter, a cleric from Auvergne, a man of very distinguished family and of great power because of the high offices he held, had come a little while before to Sainte Foy. When they had shown him the new little book containing the first miracles I wrote and had mentioned the author by name, he lamented greatly that he had not known of my arrival and that I had not made a detour so as to cross his own borders." Subsequently, on a journey to Rome in 1020, Bernard "by chance" met Abbot Peter, who was also on his way to Rome, "surrounded, as always, by a company of his own noblemen, seated on the best mule, saddled with regal opulence." Both 2.7 and 2.8 present Peter as a member of the social, political and economic elite; he has status, power, and wealth.

In addition to Peter's elevated social status, it becomes clear, the abbot is a cultured man. As Bernard relates the encounter, the two men have a kind of meeting of minds when, "because Abbot Peter noticed a level of culture in my conversation, he began to discuss a variety of topics with me learnedly and with great courtesy." Bernard then discovers that Peter is not only a cleric but holds high office in the Church. The two men realize they had heard of each other from the monks at Conques and "joined in a single thought, we rejoiced at our mutual recognition." The specific clue to Bernard's education is the way in which his description of Abbot Peter as both learned and courteous fits the ideal promulgated by the cathedral schools of combining liberal arts with virtuous conduct.

When Bernard describes Peter's "flowing blonde hair; he was of medium height and broad-shouldered, and the lines of his limbs accorded with his nobility," he employs a trope well known in his academic milieu, that of "virtue made visible"—wherein the beauty of the body and the elegance of gesture offer reliable guides to interior virtue and cultivation. Stephen Jaeger provides a full description of the "virtue made visible" *topos* in tenth- and eleventh-century institutional contexts, including monasteries and cathedral schools. In particular, he notes that it becomes a structuring idea in various saints' lives of the eleventh century, including Jotsald's life of Odilo of Cluny (ca. 1051) and Odo of Cluny's life of Gerald of Aurillac (ca. 975).[27]

Jaeger argues convincingly that this culture of the body documented in various eleventh-century texts is "directly connected with the cultivation of virtue, since bearing makes virtue visible. The cathedral school practiced a pedagogy aimed at creating the balanced, restrained, decorous, 'well-tempered' human being." [28]

"Virtue made visible" was more than a formula of praise. It registered a pedagogic practice, one in many ways central to the cultivation of virtue. . . . The cultivation of virtue began with the body, with training in gesture, gait, motions (emotions, impulses) of the body, attitude of body and mind, facial expression, voice and speech. . . . The man who walks, talks, stands, and carried himself perfectly is the *magister morum*. He shows in his every gesture what harmony reigns within him; the composition of his body shows the composition of his soul. [29]

Jaeger traces the source of this trope to Cicero's *De Officiis*.

In his chapter on what he calls "the old learning" Jaeger treats the concept of "ethics colonizing the liberal arts." He points out that a "fundamental feature of the intellectual life of the schools of the eleventh century" was that "the person of the teacher is the curriculum." [30] When, therefore, Adelman of Liège writes a poem in praise of his teacher (and Bernard's), Fulbert of Chartres, he elides *mores* with knowledge. Explicating sacred text for his pupils, Fulbert exemplified the virtues of dignity, gravity, and sweetness in words. In him, style *was* substance. [31] Bernard, by describing the scene in which he and Abbot Peter recognize each other, demonstrates that he considers himself to be a model of "virtue made visible," and that one learned and humane man recognizes another in this way. He also reveals himself to be a product of tenth- and early-eleventh-century schooling. [32]

Bernard as Rationalist, Philosopher, and "New Man"

But while Bernard is signaling his learned readers about his familiarity with the traditional liberal arts and cathedral school curricula, he also demonstrates his abilities to reason about issues that have rarely been recognized to have been current at the beginning of the eleventh century. Most intellectual historians posit a cultural shift beginning in the mid eleventh century at the earliest, which they correlate with numerous factors including the growth of cities, the rediscovery of Greek science via Arab philosophers, the development of new forms of religion based on the human nature of Christ and the cult of the Virgin Mary, the establishment of the university with new scholastic methodologies, the displacement of rituals by administrators in government, the rise of a money economy—in short, the twelfth-century renaissance. [33]

Bernard's intellectual approach as he justifies belief in Foy's miracles seems to have more in common with what we expect in the twelfth century than what we know of the late tenth.[34] That is, Bernard is extremely adept at debating issues of proof and evidence and takes genuine delight in his logical skills, an attitude that would seem more at home in a later university setting. As we have suggested, Bernard constructs himself as the skeptic who will be converted to belief in Foy's miracle cult, a self-representation consistent with his autobiographical aims. In addition to portraying himself as doubter who must be convinced, Bernard describes within his narrative numerous other skeptics who supply a fictional audience for his arguments and proofs.

This fictional audience of skeptics allows Bernard as narrator/redactor to rehearse the arguments that will persuade them, and thus it functions as a mechanism for processing skepticism. He pauses in his recitation of miracle stories to devote 1.7 entirely to the refutation of such a skeptic. He reports that some of his fellow Angevins went on a pilgrimage to Le Puy where they met

an impious and heretical man who said that he lived near Conques. When he had learned that they were Angevins he said, "You must know that Bernard who came to Conques this year. Bah! How many lies about Sainte Foy he wrote down there! For how could any reasonable person believe things about eyeballs torn out and afterward restored, and animals brought back to life? I have heard of other kinds of miracles that other saints and—rarely—Sainte Foy worked now and then. But mules! For what reason, for what necessity, would God bring them back to life? No one who is mentally stable can or ought to expound such things."

This supposed attack becomes the occasion for Bernard's hyperbolic denunciations of "this blind and foolish man," a "liar with a depraved and perverse mind." Bernard denounces his object of attack as an "empty-headed little man," likens him to the Jews, and calls him "a son of the Devil, an enemy of Truth, a minister of Antichrist." Finally Bernard attributes the man's skepticism to the Devil, who was working through the skeptic in an attempt to deflect Bernard from his plan of writing the miracles. Since Bernard condemns him as "a peasant, a stranger to all wisdom, and . . . illiterate," the preceding hyperbole scarcely seems necessary.

Bernard, however, uses this scoffer as the occasion to offer lengthy explanation as to why the resurrection of a donkey is justified. This allows him to deal with the resurrection of the body, a burning issue in the twelfth and thirteenth centuries.[35] He rather elaborately explains the reasons for this kind of miracle on behalf of a brute animal, which might seem to be "a lesser concern to the Creator" than humans: "But it actually seems to be much more necessary and reasonable that animals, which were created only for human use, should live again, but that men, who have been called for the purpose of earning eternal life and for whom the present life is nothing other than death or a passage to the future, should rest after death in the hope of the Resurrection."

Bernard then piles up a number of reasons that animal resurrection will build faith in human resurrection. He gives several analogues drawn from other authorities, including the argument from God's omnipotence. Finally he comes back to his own authority as a firsthand witness: "Whoever does not believe the stories that I, a Christian, have told about people whose eyes were torn out by the roots and that I saw restored in the same faces, let them go and see. After the beneficiaries have described the events and the whole province has corroborated them, let such people put aside all their unbelieving arguments then and there." Bernard's reasoning ultimately comes down to autobiographical assertion: "I saw those men who were healed myself, I invited them to meals, I gave them money, and there will never be a day when I am dissuaded from the truth of this opinion. If I wished, I would be able to keep on writing a great many miracles about them."

In this anomalous chapter Bernard thus rehearses a set of arguments that come from not one but several medieval philosophical/theological milieux. The argument against disbelievers is of course an early Christian ploy; the defense according to eyewitness experience is found in hagiography and scholastic argument; and the appeal to divine omnipotence, God's power to contravene the laws of nature, anticipates nominalist argument. This chapter is the epitome of a Bernardian moment where the narrator runs a gamut of the emotional and philosophical positions. Felice Lifshitz assigns to the twelfth century the scholastic examination of "the miraculous" and makes the claim that miracles were "very much taken for granted by all levels of society before that century."[36] It was the scholastic philosophers of the twelfth century who "increasingly carved out a sphere of inquiry in which proto-scientistic modes of analysis were used to narrow the concept of the 'miraculous.'"[37] Bernard, however, already demonstrates the "epistemological reorientation of scholasticism."

Bernard is obsessed with processing through his own intellectual machinery the amazing events told to him, so that he can present convincing arguments to the elite for whom he is writing. The uneducated believe the miracles, and the eyewitnesses Bernard interviews are "prepared either to swear on the holy martyr's relics or to undergo ordeal by fire" (1.2). So important to Bernard are eyewitnesses that he returns to them in the last passage in his last chapter; he knows a "very beautiful [miracle] story and one succinct enough even for exacting readers," he claims, but he refuses to include it in his book because "two of my witnesses had . . . disagreed on some points" (2.15). Bernard implicitly asserts that his standard of proof is much higher than that of past writers, who, as he says elsewhere, "were content to skillfully describe marvelous events much previous to their time, when the source was only one oral informant who wasn't even present when the thing happened" (1.1).

In addition to eyewitness, Bernard searches for other kinds of evidence. He makes expected and traditional arguments; for example, he harmonizes his material with biblical types when he compares the appearance of a magpie that carries away Guibert's excised eyes with the ravens God sent to feed Elijah (1.1). But it still troubles him that one of the witnesses saw a magpie whereas the others saw a "snow-white dove." The explanation that he offers correlates physical perception with degree of guilt; he argues by analogy that each may have seen differently "just as God will seem terrifying to the wicked but gentle to the just." Here Bernard is not satisfied to cite Scripture; he must frame the authoritative reference with rational explication.

His preferred mode is that of the materialist for whom identifying patterns congruent with sacred history does not suffice. In the case of the second eyeball restoration miracle, Bernard reports that he "tracked down so much evidence that it is too boring to go over all of it," but regarded as especially powerful the physical evidence that he experienced for himself: "You may still see the old marks of Gerbert's scars and the horrid disfigurement caused by cuts in the skin around his eyes. The deed was done as night was falling and it was growing dark. Gerbert was rolling his head back and forth and trying to pull away from the hands of his tormentors. Therefore the wounds that he received then, before his eyes were gouged out, lend greater credence to the words of the witnesses I mentioned above." Old scars also demonstrate the veracity of the next miracle (1.3), the resurrection of a mule when it was already in the process of being skinned: "So that the firm belief in the truth of the miracle might be based on more than the oral testimony of those who saw it, there was also a certain kind of clear writing to banish every wavering uncertainty, for on its two hind legs the mule had the furrows of fresh wounds. And as long as the mule lived it possessed evidence of its resurrection, for in that very hour the wounds healed and were soundly joined together. Like the oldest of scars they even had grey hairs" (1.3). It is quite surprising to find an empirical scientist in the early eleventh century.

In historically situating Bernard of Angers, who appears to bridge an earlier and a later medieval period, we can use the concept of the "new man." There has been much discussion among historians of the "new man" of the fifteenth and sixteenth centuries,[38] and Richard Southern has made the term current for an earlier period.[39] Although Bernard is clearly a product of the earlier period's educational system, he exemplifies the new social type. The new man has clerical training, but he is not identical to the *clerus* as defined by the tripartite social model of the estates. The earlier medieval model of the three estates of society was predicated on monasticism, where the role of the Church was to pray for society. The new clerical man belongs to a new educated class—he tends to be an intellectual who works for a bureaucracy. This new man has no old wealth, no roots; he succeeds by exploiting new opportunities as they arise, taking risks, using his intelligence to gain access to power. Typically, such a man, both early and later in the Middle Ages, staffs an administrative class that supports centralizing monarchies. The education in literature and manners offered by the cathedral schools in Bernard's time was the foundation of a courtly style associated with this new administrative class, as Jaeger shows.[40]

The cluster of traits and social positionings brought together under the term "the new man" is usually assigned to the twelfth century, but Bernard of Angers, writing at the beginning of the eleventh century, exhibits these characteristics as well. Analysts of the new romance genre of the twelfth and thirteenth centuries have also connected the ethos of the romance protagonist—an appreciation for *engin* or ingenuity, and an ability to manipulate circumstance that verges on trickiness—with the ethos of this emergent class.[41] Seeing Bernard as an early example of the "new man" makes sense out of the rhetorical strategies in his trickster text, where trickster author, trickster saint, and a cast of liminal characters are celebrated.

Bernard and Monastic Ideology

The *Liber miraculorum sancte Fidis* is Bernard's deliberate portrayal of a popular religious cult in southern Francia as "Other." Bernard uses the "otherness" of Conques to heighten his self-representation as sophisticated and educated outsider. A product of the clerical culture of the cathedral schools, Bernard is not a member of monastic society. There remains a deep contradiction built into his text, which always looks at monastic culture from the outside. Although Foy is the feisty protectress of her monastery, and some miracles present a monastic point of view, the whole of Bernard's production is framed by a different viewpoint—that of Bernard as intellectual "new man." It is significant that Bernard's conversion is not to monasticism but to a belief in the saint, in her powers, and in a certain kind of evidence.

Despite the fact that Bernard's clerical viewpoint clearly frames his miracle stories, the narratives he relates often articulate monastic ideology. Foy, after all, is the patron saint of the dominant monastery in the region, so miracles celebrating her powers tend to reinforce the values of monasticism. Bernard of Angers's miracle texts thus juxtapose monastic ideology to various alternatives—the warrior life, the family, the secular church, commercial society. These juxtapositions enable Bernard both to support and to criticize the Benedictine monasticism of his day.

Opening the first of a number of miracle narratives that vividly represent Foy's punishment of the monastery's enemies, Bernard introduces models of proper and improper actions relative to the monastery. He begins with a narrative about property donated to Sainte Foy as part of the process by which its owner became a monk at Conques: "There is a monk named Bergand who is a member of Sainte Foy's monastic community. Before he took up the sacred monk's habit, Bergand turned over to God and Sainte Foy his hereditary rights in his share of the family property" (1.5). Bergand models the ideal sequence of events; economic donation followed by spiritual commitment. Many of these early miracles address issues either of property donated to the monastery or of what it means to become a monk.

Those who threaten the monastery's holdings are usually colorfully punished by the saint. Introducing a "miracle of divine vengeance" (1.11), Bernard becomes a spokesperson for ecclesiastical institutions, including the monastery. This chapter begins with a lengthy diatribe against those who "steal goods from God's holy Church, or those who appropriate, as if it were legally their own, property that the saints have inherited, and unjustly claim the rents and services due its owners." Bernard personalizes his diatribe with the comment, "I have seen canons, or even monks and abbots, driven out of their positions, deprived of their goods, and violently slaughtered. I have seen bishops, some condemned by being outlawed, some driven from their episcopal sees without cause, others slaughtered by the sword and even burned to death in cruel flames by Christians for defending the rights of the Church." The narrative concerns a noble woman named Doda, who had "unjustly seized one of Sainte Foy's manors" but who, on her deathbed, "returned the estate to the abbey of Conques." Acting out of family ideologies, her grandson reappropriated the manor, but Bernard explicitly rejects those values and celebrates the saint's revenge. One of the grandson's men who occupied the property insulted the saint:

Then suddenly the air resounded with the fearful din of a windstorm sent from heaven. With an abrupt crash the solarium of the house was completely destroyed, the structure of the upper story collapsed, and the whole fabric of the building, both above and below, fell in ruins. Nonetheless not one of the multitude of people perished except that shameless man and his wife along with their five household servants. . . . Hear, you plunderers and ravagers of Christian property, how inevitable are the scourges and just judgments of God!

Bernard here expresses with rhetorical intensity a monastic point of view according to which the Conques monastery competes with local families for resources.

In other miracle narratives, Bernard paints the monastery as a victim of predatory local castellans. A lord named Hugh, for example, who ruled over a castle named Cassagnes, eight miles from Conques, "seized an opportune moment and ordered two of his servants to carry off the monks' wine, which was kept at the country estate called Molières" (1.6). One of the servants, searching through a local peasant's barnyard for a cart to convey the wine, was warned by the "simple peasant" not to pursue this "evil task," but he replied blasphemously, "Does Sainte Foy drink wine? What foolishness! Don't you know that whoever doesn't drink doesn't need wine?" For his blasphemy and assault on the monastery's storeroom, this man was disgustingly and appropriately punished: "At that very moment his muscles lost their ability to move and stiffened completely; the wretch lay paralyzed on the ground, his arms and legs drawn up to his body. In addition, his mouth was stretched back to his ears and gaped obscenely, and the filth that streamed foully from his entrails manifestly revealed how harshly and distressingly he had been afflicted." In examples like this Bernard shows considerable relish in wholeheartedly adopting the monastic point of view that enemies of the monks' property should be cruelly punished.

Historians tend to see the Foy miracles as almost exclusively concerned with maintenance of monastic power, but Bernard's point of view is far more complex. Bernard both is and is not "of" the monastery. He witnesses miracles firsthand and champions the saint, but his view does not completely coincide with that of the monks. Precisely because of his outsider status, Bernard can reflect upon and even critique monastic life. He creates portraits of characters like Guibert, who tries and fails to become a monk (1.1); Gerbert, who succeeds in transforming himself from a warrior into a monk (1.2); and Gimon, who remains both a warrior and a monk. In constructing these almost mythical figures Bernard draws on the model provided by Sulpicius Severus's account of St. Martin, a soldier who renounced his warrior life for religion. Even more tellingly, Martin, though rough and uncouth, was holy—a kind of fool for Christ who communed with spirits as Gimon also does. A straightforward exposition of monastic values is provided in Bernard's account of Gerbert, a fighting man whose eyes were "violently cut out of their sockets" and restored by Foy. Gerbert tries to return to his life as a mounted warrior, but the saint and her human allies dissuade him. Eventually Gerbert "completely abandoned his resistance and made no further efforts to thwart the divine will. Therefore he serves God and His saint now in that very monastery with the most devoted obedience, content with a monk's daily allowance of food. He is a man of calm character and a simple way of life, measured by our times and our ways of doing things. Thus the authorities of the monastery have treated him well up to the present time, and he obeys them in all things and cherishes them with a deep affection." Here Bernard represents approvingly the simple monastic lifestyle with its rations of food, rule of obedience, and rejection of violence. Gerbert embodies a norm of monastic life.

In the character of Gimon, however, Bernard rejects the straightforward exposition of monastic norms for a far more complex exploration of monasticism. As we have shown above, Gimon is anomalous in combining categories usually regarded as mutually exclusive: the warrior and the monk. Yet Bernard praises Gimon as "a person in whom no impurity of body or mind could dwell. He was always prepared to undertake every labor for the advantage of his monastic brothers and he was second to none in the virtue of obedience. . . . But how much he truly excelled in the preeminence of virtues can be judged from this: that he would tame everyone, not only the other monks, but even the abbot himself, as if they were under the yoke of discipline; and this was due not to his erudition in letters, but to his fortitude of spirit." In other ways, Gimon violates monastic norms. For example, he was minimally socialized, tending to outbursts of anger and harsh words, but Bernard devotes long passages in 1.26 to rationalizing those defects.

God did not consider the harsh words to be sinful, since in all other things Gimon's mind was sound and filled with moral excellence. For God does not judge people by their manner of speaking, but by their intentions or actions. . . . Therefore it is my considered opinion that Gimon ought not to be blamed for his harsh manner of speaking when I've heard his deeds described as irreproachable in every way, except that he used to go on expeditions armed. But if people understood this behavior of his correctly, they would be able to ascribe it more to moral excellence than to an assault on the monastic rule.

Indeed, Bernard uses this anomalous warrior-monk to criticize monasticism itself: "If only lazy monks would put aside their cowardly sloth and act as bravely to the advantage of their monasteries! Instead they parade the handsome habits of their order on the outside, while making a hiding-place for iniquity on the inside!" [42]

Gimon's liminal purity of motive becomes a vehicle for attacking the vices of monastic life, and Bernard shows Gimon to be a favorite of the saint herself. One of Foy's joking miracles is directed affectionately at Gimon, who was the guardian of the sanctuary. Occasionally he would fall asleep and the candle before the high altar would go out. When this happened, the saint would appear to awaken him by "gently touching his cheek,"

but, before he could reach the candlestick and touch the candle itself, which he could see had gone out, he would see that it had been lit again at that very moment from heaven. Or if by chance, as happened frequently, he carried it to the fire, before he reached the coals the light would revive by divine power right there in his hands. Again, when he had returned to his bed and was already beginning to sleep, the same vision returned three and four times, as if she were playing with him. This would force the old man to rise up reluctantly from his bed and hurry back to the candlestick. By this time he was thoroughly enraged, for he had a fiery temperament. He would rail against Sainte Foy just as if she had been disturbing him and making sport of him. He scolded her and called her names in his native tongue (1.26).[43]

Gimon was clearly on intimate terms with the saint. His conduct may violate decorum of various kinds, monastic and secular, but Bernard does not see it as reprehensible. In fact, Bernard uses Gimon's rough manners to attack not just monastic hypocrisy but also, more tellingly, the clerical trope of virtue made visible. Gimon's behavior demonstrates that one cannot draw simple conclusions from external appearances—that what matters is moral integrity.

Bernard draws Gimon's story from a time before the monastery's accumulation of wealth; for a critique of monastic riches he turns to events of the early eleventh century:

And with a great abundance of material riches, the monks showed greater boldness in sinning. And so the wicked lives of the monastery's inhabitants, caused by over-indulgence in debauchery and by great wealth, drove the miracles of the saints to cease. This example demonstrates that for the preservation of a morally upright life nothing is better than a mediocre talent for worldly matters, because then one is neither saddened by harsh poverty nor bloated with immoderate excess. But I am speaking of an ordinary way of life, because there is a more powerful opinion that judges the highest perfection to belong to those who have absolutely nothing in the world (2.5).

Tracing a causal chain from monastic wealth to sinful monks to a cessation of miracles, Bernard issues a devastating critique and presents absolute poverty as the ideal. The miracle story that follows illustrates his point that monastic officials are only stewards of Sainte Foy's wealth, not its possessors.

Whether Bernard praises or criticizes, he never totally identifies with the monastery but always represents himself as speaking from an external point

of view. The Foy miracles he redacts are thus complexly and even contra-
dictorily layered. Bernard's clerical intellectual voice interacts, often ironically, with monastic perspectives. The monastic writers who continued his
collection of miracles after Bernard's death, evidently using notes he had
taken, initiate a process of muting the contradictions and moving toward a
monological presentation of monastic ideologies.

3 THE MONASTIC APPROPRIATION Of BERNARD'S TEXT

 The prologue of the third book of the *Liber miraculorum* informs readers that Bernard of Angers has died and that a new author has "taken up the business of continuing Bernard's text." The author-continuator voice shaping books 3 and 4 presents itself as a spokesperson for the interests of the monastery at Conques, whereas Bernard had primarily represented a class of cleric-intellectuals. Book 3 was probably written from about 1030 to shortly after 1035, and book 4 (with the exception of the last chapter) was added before 1050.[1] Throughout the prologue to book 3, verbs in the first-person plural signal the corporate ideology that this monastic authorial voice articulates. By contrast, Bernard's letter to Fulbert, which functions as a prologue to his books 1 and 2, employs the first-person singular. Furthermore, from this point forward authors of the miracle narratives remain anonymous. It would be extremely difficult, if not impossible, to determine how many individual monks wrote the miracle narratives in books 3 and 4. Unlike Bernard—the self-promoting author who wishes to be recognized for his literary labors—the monk-continuator voice subordinates personality to the glorification of Foy, powerful patron of the Conques monastery. The erudition embedded in these texts demonstrates a level of learning and literary expertise to be attributed to the whole monastery rather than to any individual monk.

The writer of the prologue to book 3 appears to be employing a particular type of prologue structure that was considered "modern" in the eleventh century, according to A. J. Minnis. The "ancient" schema, which probably developed out of Virgilian commentaries, called upon the author of the prologue to give seven rhetorical circumstances *(circumstantiae)*—who, what, why, in what manner, where, when, and by what means—information that was considered to provide "the basis for a comprehensive and informative prologue."[2] The "modern" exordium reduced the number of elements to three: the name of the author, the subject of the work (indicated by its title), and its relationship to extant texts.[3] The monk-author of the prologue, as we will see, expends some effort discussing authorship, analyzing how he has acquired the materials for the work, giving it a title, and indicating the purpose for which he is composing the miracle narratives.

Although in the prologue to book 3 the continuator voice praises Bernard as "that man imbued to no small extent with both practical and theoretical knowledge," and clearly appreciates the magnitude of Bernard's legacy for the monastery, the relationship between this project and Bernard's is complex. Books 3 and 4 maintain a dialogue with Bernardian books 1 and 2 through continuities in methodology, but also through resistances. For example, the prologue itself functions both to situate its monk-author in relation to Bernard—adopting his mantle—and to enact rebellion against Bernard's practices.

Book 3: Intertextuality with Bernard

In his lengthy and fascinating letter concluding book 1 (1.34), Bernard addresses Abbot Adalgerius and the monks at Conques, reporting that he has finished his edition of Foy's miracles "just as you asked." With a characteristic mixture of self-abasement and self-aggrandizement, Bernard describes the process of oral collection of Foy's miracles and their revision into a Latin book that he has circulated among many influential friends and churchmen in northern Francia. He further claims that his volume is responsible for extending the cult far beyond the Conques region.

The monk-continuator voice, in taking up "the business of continuing Bernard's text," implicitly acknowledges that Bernard's volume has put Conques on the hagiographic map; the monks want to capitalize on and continue Bernard's successes as composer of miracle narratives. In this respect they participate in the rich hagiographic tradition of the Midi. As Pierre Bonnassie observes, from the Merovingian era on Aquitaine produced numerous hagiographic texts, but it was especially the tenth and eleventh centuries that saw the great flowering of hagiography. The most prestigious sites, in addition to Sainte-Foy at Conques, were Saint-Martial of Limoges and Saint-Victor of Marseille, but there were also scriptoria at Périgueux, Figeac, Mauriac, Mende, and Saint-Michel de Cuxa where the miracles of local saints were collected.[4]

The implication of the monk-continuator's prologue is that in "continuing Bernard's text" the author will work from Bernard's notes and rough drafts. He has assembled the "accounts of Sainte Foy's miracles left after Bernard's death," but which are presumably in a form not literarily elegant enough to be disseminated. This sounds as if the monk-author planned merely to revise a text that Bernard had been primarily responsible for drafting. The monastery must have either kept or acquired Bernard's notes, which may have resembled the "little booklet . . . made from several scraps of poor-quality parchment, several of which had been scraped down after previous use as charters" used at another monastery in about 1074 to note down a miracle of Saint Maximinus. As Thomas Head observes, "It is impossible to determine how many similar booklets were kept in the archives of religious houses, which probably consisted of little more than a wooden cupboard or chest, waiting to serve as source material for later authors."[5]

It may appear that in appropriating Bernard's notes the monk-continuator was doing something new, but a careful reading of Bernard's two books provides a picture of the many ways the monastic authorities had enabled and even controlled Bernard's project. For example, Bernard says that when he returned to Conques in 1020 he had come to visit old friends and had no intention of writing any more miracle stories. The monks, however, saw Bernard as a convenient agent for their saint's cult, and they had a different agenda in mind for him, as he reveals in the following anecdote:

When the customary services of prayers had been properly completed, I wished to return at once, but they began to interrupt me insistently and to implore that I should add a third book of Sainte Foy's miracles. I very strenuously refused to do this, and said that it was not necessary. Not only was it the case that more powerful miracles than those I had already written could not be found, but, further, there were none even equal to those. But they insisted that it was absolutely necessary, and in order to ensnare me for their cause, they said they knew such a wondrous miracle that I myself would judge that nothing in divine works would be preferred to it (2.7).

Evidently the monks' cult agenda coopted Bernard's personal agenda, for he did continue his collection (2.7–2.15), and in addition he compiled the notes and rough drafts that the monk-continuators inherited.

We also discover that the monks used Bernard's miracle collection to attract more miracle stories and publicize Foy's reputation as a miracle worker. Bernard reports to his satisfaction that when the monks had shown Abbot Peter Bernard's book of miracles, the abbot was inspired to tell one of his own. "Peter told them a remarkable miracle that deserves to be included among the most excellent" (2.7). Bernard recounts this incident as if it enhances his reputation as hagiographer, but it also shows that the monks employed his book as an artifact encapsulating *their* authority as custodians of Foy's cult. We can, in other words, read through Bernard's egocentrism to an insight about the ways he was manipulated by monastic agendas.

Even in the prologue, the monks begin to revise Bernard's approach to the authorial task. In the letter we have been discussing (1.34), Bernard places himself intertextually relative to Sulpicius Severus's *Life of Martin*. He notes that Martin's hagiographer chose not to name himself on the title page ("the silenced page announces . . . the book's subject and does not announce the author")[6] and acknowledges that Sulpicius Severus did not want to be called "a conceited person." Bernard then presents his rationale for including his own name "at the beginning, and in the middle and at the end" of his text of Foy's miracles. He argues that the practice of naming the author provides some authority where "materials so unknown" are being published; he fears unknown miracles would be doubted and the "great works of Sainte Foy would be held in contempt." In a final reversal, the monk-continuator rejects Bernard's rationale and returns to Sulpician anonymity, "lest I inflict some harm on this work because of the inadequacies of my manner of writing." In a kind of authorial one-upmanship, this author reveals his mastery of the humility *topos* that Bernard had brandished.

Although for Bernard, Foy's miracle stories formed *the* text for his ideal textual community back in northern Francia, the *Liber miraculorum* was for the Conques monastery merely one of the texts about their patron saint that functioned as the basis of their cultic community. It appears that not long after Bernard's death the monks of Conques were consciously compiling a collection of texts about their saint, a type of manuscript called a *libellus*.[7] This monk-author does not simply plan to add to Bernard's books as a humble if rebellious continuator. He ends the Prologue to book 3 by announcing that he has reconceived the whole project and sees himself creating a volume he entitles "*Panaretos,* by which I mean the book of all her powers," adding to Bernard's miracle narratives and his own the text of Foy's *Passio* as he has rewritten it.[8] In effect, then, the *Panaretos* or the *Book of Foy's Powers* has subsumed and subordinated Bernard's two books, and its compiler has attempted to subdue the personality of the author Bernard. The anonymous monastic voice ends the prologue with a gesture that is ostensibly humble but functionally an authoritative appropriation: "In the place where one would expect to find the author's name only silence will be found. I have decided that the title I assigned it is the one by which it should be known forever."

With due acknowledgments but a kind of lethal efficiency, the monk-continuator dispatches his predecessor. After the opening lines of 3.1, there is no further mention of Bernard of Angers in the narratives of Sainte Foy's miracles composed at Conques. Further, this appropriation transforms the conception of Sainte Foy for books 3 and 4. No longer the trickster-child who appears and reappears in the monastery itself or to her devotees—as in Bernard's two books—Foy is now the celestial virgin-martyr, a powerful player in the politics of the court of heaven. In naming the volume *Panaretos* the monk-author explicitly announces the chief theme of virtually every miracle story in books 3 and 4: they are to demonstrate Foy's extraordinary powers.

Even though this monk-author wishes to remain anonymous, which we link to his corporate monastic task, he is no less literarily aware and committed than was Bernard. As he takes up his task of continuing the miracle collection, he offers a lengthy justification of the need for another preface in addition to Bernard's, indicating his awareness of reader response in the situation where a shift in author takes place:

Had it been written by one person, then it certainly would have been appropriate that the whole work follow behind an ascription to a single author and that the beginnings of the other books be left without such ascriptions. But because it has been necessary to burden the work with a change of author, another prologue, set in its proper place, is required. Once this has been carried out as it is here, all doubt about authorship is removed and the work of each individual follows its appropriate ascription. Had this not been done, uncertainty about authorship not only would have been sure to confuse readers, it might even have annoyed them so much that they would have neglected to read the work itself.

Although this explanation is almost comically labored, it does reveal a fairly acute awareness of the affective process of reading a book, and rhetorically it acknowledges the death of Bernard, whose production of books 1 and 2 of the *Liber miraculorum* was proving so crucial to the fortunes of the Conques monastery.

Brief as it is, the prologue sets up the hagiographic task as more than just a simple matter of celebrating a powerful saint. For both the monk-continuator voice and for Bernard, the central task is a literary one. As the monk says, "We have collected the accounts of Sainte Foy's miracles left after Bernard's death, miracles that deserve to be widely known and written up in elegant style." He implies that the aim of disseminating the saint's reputation hinges upon the difficult task of writing in an appropriate style. This authorial voice is no less reflexive than Bernard about his hagiographic task. He plans to add Foy's passion narrative to the volume but he points out that he has rewritten the existing version: "Since it was clumsily composed on the basis of early descriptions of her torments and is highly confusing and far too short, even to the point of obscurity, it has been my task to straighten out some of its confusions and correct it by casting it in a more highly rhetorical style."

Bernard's rhetorical interests were served by presenting the Conques monks as virtual *illiterati* (neither good Latin grammarians nor committed to keeping adequate records of the miracles) and himself as the author-intellectual. However, as the monk's discussion of rewriting the *Passio* reveals, the monastery's rusticity is very much a Bernardian construction; he does not give a reliable description of the monastic culture at Conques. There is much external evidence for the monastery's sophistication and cultural preeminence in south-central France, and the internal evidence from books 3 and 4 of the *Liber miraculorum* also reveals Bernard's shortcomings as historical source.

Learning and the Conques Monastery

Its earliest documentation, a charter dated 801, indicates that the Conques monastery followed the Rule of Saint Benedict. The adoption of the Rule may well have had to do with the reforms of Benedict of Aniane, as a number of scholars have suggested; Benedict was especially active in Aquitaine.[9] As a major beneficiary of Carolingian patronage, Conques presumably participated as well in the educational initiatives of Carolingian reformers like Alcuin, which included the revival of the *ars grammatica* of antiquity.[10] Conques's membership in the Reichenau prayer confraternity, one of fifty-six monasteries and churches listed in the years 826–34 and the only one in south-central France, indicates that it had relations with many of the major Carolingian religious institutions of its day. M. M. Hildebrandt notes that this confraternal network promoted education and created "a social and religious milieu that fostered contacts and friendships among the people who belonged to the associations."[11] Hildebrandt sees this educational network as providing training for monks who were to become priests: "The most talented among them traveled as externs through the confraternal network, getting the best theological training that the system had to offer and then returning to their own monasteries to undertake the important business of training other monks and secular clergy or stepping into abbeys and/or bishoprics where they functioned as secular clergy. This scholarly exchange seems to have slowed down after the middle of the ninth century when individual monasteries had improved their programs sufficiently to undertake the advanced training of their best scholars." [12]

Since Conques did not suffer from the invasions that disrupted learning in the late Carolingian period in so many parts of Europe, there is no reason to assume that either its adherence to the Rule or its level of education declined during the later ninth and tenth centuries. Certainly in the early eleventh century Conques was building and staffing churches with monks who must have been priests as well (see 4.21 [4.22]). Its school would have taught Latin grammar, using classical authors, and both poetic and prose composition.[13] Of the liberal arts, the focus was on the *trivium:* grammar, rhetoric, and dialectic. In speaking of monastic education in the tenth century, Heinrich Fichtenau observes, "To master the classical form of poetry and of artistic prose was a fine reward for all the misery of the school lessons. Here monks had a certain freedom for personal development and here too was that lightheartedness that young people need in their lives. A playful element sometimes asserted itself; style became artistry. Monks were proud of learning and proud also that they could understand artfully constructed sentences." [14] Education at Conques probably did not extend to the *quadrivium,* which was not very widely taught. It is noteworthy that the parts of the *Liber miraculorum* written by monks show no evidence of special knowledge of arithmetic, geometry, astronomy, or music.

Conques had a scriptorium in the eleventh century, and probably well before. Robertini concludes that the entire manuscript tradition of the *Liber miraculorum* can be traced to Conques. Furthermore, Benedictine scriptoria produced classical texts. From his census of classical manuscripts produced in medieval scriptoria, Birger Munk Olsen concludes that "classical textbooks of Benedictine origin are relatively numerous for the eleventh century, amounting to about fifty." [15] Fleury, another Benedictine abbey known to have produced hagiography, had an impressive classics collection: "By . . . 1004 the major literary works of Latin Antiquity were to be found on the shelves of the Fleury library, several of them in multiple copies." [16]

Further evidence of a literary atmosphere at the Conques monastery comes from the "Chanson de sainte Foy," which was most likely composed between 1060 and 1070. One of the earliest texts in Occitan, the "Chanson" tells the story of Sainte Foy's *Passio* and *Translatio,* and refers briefly to her miracles. In its evocation of a society characterized by the personal bonds usually called feudal, the "Chanson" anticipates by several decades the "chanson de geste." The one surviving copy provides no evidence of authorship, but studies of its language confirm Rouergat origins. Frédéric de Gournay recently argued that the author belonged to the aristocratic world and had been formed by the abbey school of Conques.[17] The "Chanson" confirms the existence of a school whose students aspired to the composition of literary texts.

Bernard himself acknowledges the existence of the school in 2.4, when he writes about a miraculous healing as "a clever joke" Foy played "on students," that is, "some mischievous young men who belonged to the community of monks." There is material evidence for a school at Conques in the form of a lintel still surviving at Conques (though not *in situ*). Calvin Kendall has published a photograph of the lintel and transcribed its inscription, which begins: "ISTE MAGISTRORVM LOCVS EST SIMVL ET PVERORVM" ("This is the place of the master and the boys").[18] Its date of circa 1100 attests to the existence of the school at that time. For Kendall, this and other inscriptions associated with Conques in the late eleventh and twelfth centuries are the work of a single author who "was an accomplished Latinist and a thoroughly competent versifier who could express himself clearly in meter and rhyme. He must have known a little Greek."[19]

There is evidence even within Bernard's own miracle collection that the monastery was not as unlettered as he implies in his address to Fulbert. Bernard composed part of one of his chapters in hexameter verse (1.6), and in the subsequent chapter he attempts to rationalize this anomaly by telling the reader: "A monk named Arseus persuaded me to write [the hexameter verses] with his insistent pleas." If Arseus actually existed and was a monk at Conques (which is implied but not explicitly stated),[20] then this detail reveals a literary culture at Conques that Bernard otherwise ignores.

Extensive and disparate types of historical documentation from Conques itself also reveal various ways that the monastery formed a textual community with other sectors of society. A chief example is the cartulary compiled at the monastery in the early twelfth century, which records charters of donation from the previous three centuries.[21] The cartulary testifies to the importance of Conques as a pilgrimage site and to the monastery's economic and political power in south-central France; it also suggests the monastery's status as a representative of a community including both the laity of many classes and the monastery—a community textualized by the cartulary.[22]

As we discuss below, a variety of other evidence also points to the monastery's enjoyment of literary experimentation and to its poetic self-awareness. Numerous passages in the non-Bernardian continuation of the *Liber miraculorum* written in highly elaborate metered verse with classical allusions testify to a textual community based not just on miracle stories but also on the antique poetic tradition.[23] By identifying unattributed quotations in books 3 and 4, Robertini shows that their authors were familiar with the *Aeneid* and *Georgics* of Virgil; the *Satires, Letters,* and *Odes* of Horace; *Metamorphoses,* the *Epistolae ex Ponto,* and *Tristia* of Ovid; and some of Juvenal, as well as Prudentius, Venantius Fortunatus, and Sedulius. Pierre Bonnassie (who believes that there was only one monk-continuator) comments, "It is remarkable to verify that the anonymous monk of Conques was at least as cultivated as Bernard of Angers. Here is sufficient evidence to sweep aside all the assertions that actual historiography continues at times to convey about the supposed 'crass ignorance' of the southern clergy before the Gregorian reform."[24] It is quite clear that not just a general textual community of monks existed at Conques but, more specifically, one formed around classical poetic texts, an identity which was then displayed in an efflorescence of metered verse in the non-Bernardian narratives.

Organization and Function of the Miracle Book

The continuities between the monk-continuators' project and Bernard's are nowhere more visible than in the clusters of miracles that have a similar subject in books 3 and 4. We noted earlier how unusual Bernard's organizational principles are in the corpus of medieval miracle collections. In his letter to Bishop Fulbert, Bernard had addressed "future readers," alerting them to his organizational principles. They are not to look for "a chronological sequence of events," rather the miracle stories will be grouped "by the similarity of their subject matter."

Obviously the model left by Bernard was a powerful one. Thus in book 3, chapters 11 and 12 both deal with miracles affecting horses' eyes, and in book 4, chapters 4 through 9 form a group about the freeing of prisoners. The narrator in many of these miracles acknowledges this attention to sequencing; for example, he frames 4.9, writing at the beginning, "There still remains one miracle that belongs with those I have just related," and concluding with, "And now I have said enough about the freeing of captives." The beginning of 4.10 picks up this idea: "So that my narrative will be arranged in the best sequence, I must follow these astonishing and great miracles of liberation with the wondrous miracle related in this chapter." The authors of books 3 and 4 seem to be adopting Bernard's unusual organizational principle.

Not all of the continuators' inheritances from Bernard are fully understood by the narrators of books 3 and 4. For example, 3.2 is introduced with the term "unheard-of" *(inaudita),* which is employed by Bernard several times to flag miracles that raise issues of epistemological interest and literary decorum. The monk-continuators appear to have adopted the term from Bernard, but show no understanding of the way Bernard uses it to raise a set of questions both about miracles as events and about the hagiographic task. In 3.2 the "unheard-of miracle" is a very dramatic story of a pilgrim's fall into a churning river in a deep gorge and his eventual escape from what appears to be certain death. The narrator's interpretive frame is that "if we didn't believe that nothing is impossible for God, this miracle would seem entirely incredible." And at its conclusion all the onlookers on both banks of the river who had earlier "blamed Christ's holy martyr Foy, from whose abbey church the pilgrim had been returning," now "proclaim Sainte Foy's omnipotent power with splendid declarations of praise."

The shaping of this narrative reveals that "inaudita" for this monk-author means sensational or unbelievable in its extremity, which is the conventional rhetorical use of the term. His purpose for recounting the story is to bring all internal participants as well as readers to the same point of acknowledging Foy's power. The narrator, the authorized voice of the Conques monastery, articulates a sense of unanimity and closure in the last sentence: "They spoke truly when they maintained that the pilgrim had been plucked out of death's abyss by her sustaining right hand." With this pronouncement he has created the appropriate uncritical response to Foy's "unheard-of miracle," one of faith rather than (as in Bernard) one of philosophical exploration.

The monk-continuators also adopt the theme Bernard sounds about the expansion of the cult outside the Conques region. In the closing letter to book 1, Bernard gives a very autobiographical version of the spread of Foy's cult into the northern French region centered on Angers and Chartres. He takes credit not only for popularizing the saint but also for writing the book that motivated powerful friends and patrons to establish new cult sites in the north. The monk-continuators reinterpret these events for their own purposes, using Bernardian data to demonstrate the expansion of the cult beyond southern France and its transformation into a universal cult. We read in 3.1: "It is by the power of this same Spirit that the prodigious miracles of the renowned virgin and glorious martyr of Christ were shimmering through the vast reaches of the world. As is quite clearly evident in the preceding pages written by Bernard, Sainte Foy's power was traversing the farthest regions of the universe and was leaving behind no one untouched by her gifts." The narrative that follows, the very first miracle in book 3, takes place in Normandy and narrates the founding of a church of Foy there in gratitude for the healing of the noblewoman Goteline. This monk-continuator has adopted the Bernardian principle of using a thematically key miracle story for an opening chapter of the book.

To epitomize Foy's local reputation as miraculous healer Bernard had employed two miracles set in Conques; however, the monk-author of 3.1 wants to portray the cult of Foy as universal, so he puts into the mouth of a Norman bishop the following words: "We have just learned the quickly spreading news that in Aquitaine a very holy virgin and martyr named Foy shines brightly, working miracles completely unheard-of and full of wonder." When completed, the book compiled by the monks of Conques (the *Panaretos*) formed the basis for the cult's extension to the Alsace, Germany, England, Italy, and Spain, with Normandy signifying the internationalization of the cult.

The monks' concern with internationalization is clearly revealed by comparing a story involving Spain in book 4 with one of Bernard's. In 2.2 Bernard offers a highly literary rewriting of elements from the *Odyssey* in which a man named Raymond, a pilgrim to Jerusalem, is shipwrecked, captured by pirates, taken from them by Berbers, and eventually reaches Spain, where he fights with Sancho the Great on the side of a Muslim force that is attempting to claim the caliphate. In Bernard's narrative, Spain functions as one of several exotic locales for a fantastic adventure story in which Foy has only a small role and Conques none at all. But Spain, specifically Catalonia, has an entirely different function in 4.6, written by one of the monk-continuators. First, the cult of Foy is already established there, for the narrative concerns Calonge, where there had been a church of Sainte Foy "for a long time" when the leading citizens of the town contacted the monastery at Conques for protection against Saracen raids. The lords of the castle of Calonge "pledged it to Sainte Foy, to be held outright by her. And because there was a great distance between them and the holy virgin's monastery, they established as tribute to her that they would send every year a certain weight of gold to be used in the decoration of her sacred church. And if they were successful in the wars through her intercession, in recognition of the triumphal victory they would send her one-tenth of the spoils taken from the conquered Saracens." The response at Conques was enthusiastic: "The monks rejoiced greatly that love of their great patron saint had grown up in such a remote part of the world." They decided to send a banner to the embattled Christians, promising that "when this standard was carried before their troops it would invoke the holy virgin's power and the fierce enemy forces would be so afraid that they wouldn't break through the lines." Not only does this miracle illustrate the extension of the cult's reach into foreign lands, it also models a norm of behavior vis-à-vis the Conques monastery: the saint's effectiveness and therefore Conques's importance as the site of her relics should be acknowledged through appropriate donations.

Another indication that spreading the cult of Foy was of more central concern to the monks than to Bernard (in spite of his rhetoric) comes from their narratives about Rouergat pilgrims to Rome or Jerusalem. Bernard writes in 2.3 about a pilgrimage to Jerusalem made by a Conques monk who subsequently became abbot. When there was a shipboard miracle worked by Foy, the witnesses thought about their own safety: "Those on board were deeply moved, as much by recovered life as by the joy of a miracle." Bernard does not include a communal celebration of thanksgiving and recognition of Foy's powers, and his conclusion suggests that he found the story ill-suited to his own particular agenda: "I wouldn't have bothered to write this miracle if I hadn't been exhorted by many a petition from that same lord abbot." By contrast, the monk-author of 4.18 (4.19) uses the occasion of an animal resurrection among a group of pilgrims on their way to Rome to demonstrate the spread of Foy's reputation. As they are passing through Lombardy, a Rouergan tells his traveling companion from Poitou about Sainte Foy. After the miraculous events, the innkeeper and the pilgrims all recognize the cult of Foy: The innkeeper exclaims, "Oh how fortunate you are to have such a great virgin as your patroness! Through her omnipotent intercession, not only do you gain the salvation of your souls, but even your bodies are cared for by her great medicines. This virgin, holy in deed and power, does not permit you to suffer misfortunes even if it comes to the resurrection of animals." Then the whole column of pilgrims bursts into cries of praise, "their voices rivaling one another and making the air resound with the cry of 'Sainte Foy!' "

In spite of their zeal to promote a universal cult, the monks of Conques did not forget the need to document the saint's effectiveness in southern France; most of the miracles of books 3 and 4 are in fact located either in the immediate region of Conques or a slightly wider region including Quercy, Albi, Cahors, and Agen. The writers of these books seem eager to convey the impression that those living in the region recognize the saint's growing reputation; for example, in C.4 (4.26) the inhabitants of a castle "midway between Albi and Cahors" who benefited from a miracle thanked and praised "their own highly renowned martyr Sainte Foy." In their selection and organization of miracles the monk-continuators univocally promoted the fame of their saint at home and abroad.

Narrative Voice in the *Liber miraculorum*

The difference between the subject position of Bernard and that of the monk-continuators may be revealed by a comparison of their narrative techniques. One of the striking qualities of Bernard's narratives is the attention he gives to modes of validation of the miracles; he recurrently asks what kinds of proofs will be believed. Bernard is especially fond of the authority of the eyewitness; he has seen miracles firsthand, or has interviewed eyewitnesses, or has seen the results of a miracle—there is a whole rhetoric of evidence and proof in Bernard's chapters. The monk-continuators also use the device of the credible eyewitness, but their eyewitness is a community of believers rather than the exceptional individual, as closer examination of the narrative voice in the Latin texts reveals.

Another method Bernard uses to validate miracles is the construction of a doubter. He creates and exploits opportunities to play out a variety of interpretive points of view by including a set of internal characters that require the narrator to explicate logically how a particular miracle could have been performed. The monk-continuators, however, address an audience that already accepts Foy as a worker of powerful miracles. The ultimate message in almost every chapter is that the public who witnesses the miracle rejoices and celebrates Foy as the celestial and powerful virgin. These chapters culminate in a moment of ritual affirmation when everyone is of one mind; narrator, internal cast of characters, and readers agree entirely about the standing of Foy and the interpretation of her miracles.

Bernard betrays his singularity and his self-promoting agenda through his choice of pronouns. Although he uses the plural in many places as the formal and expected mode of narrating serious material and signaling a communal task, his tendency to report autobiographical anecdotes often returns him to the individual voice and experience. As we have noted, his autobiographical approach to the miracles dictates this. For example, in recounting his meeting with Abbot Peter (2.8), Bernard not only uses first-person singular verbs repeatedly, he further intensifies the individuality of his perceptions and his participation in the action through the frequent use of the pronouns "me" and "ego."

During the time that I heard these things at Conques, and in the same year, I was going back to Rome. By chance Abbot Peter was making the same journey, surrounded, as always, by a company of his own noblemen seated on the best mules saddled with regal opulence. He caught up with me as I was riding with companions and asked who I was and where I was from. But indifferently, as a stranger answering a stranger, I said only that I was from Anjou. Nevertheless, I was delighted with the society of Aquitaneans, so I began to ride at the same pace and to chat.

(Eadem tempestate, qua hec apud Conchas *audieram,* in hoc videlicet anno, *me* Roma redeunte, redibat forte et idem Petrus, nobiliorum suorum, ut semper, vallatus comitatu, mulis optimis regalique luxu stratis insidientium. Cum *me* assecutus tendentem post socios, qui et unde sim regat. *Ego* vero *me* solummode Andeca-

vinum esse, ita tenuiter ut extraneus extraneo responens, delectatus tamen in Aqui-
tanorum collegio, *coepi* equitare pariter an *fabulari.*)

Obviously Bernard is one of the two main characters in this story. Its
only relevance to the ostensible purpose of the *Liber* comes at the end,
where Bernard reveals that one result of this highly satisfactory encounter
was Abbot Peter's narration of two miracle stories. This is an example of a
repeated pattern throughout Bernard's books. An episode that could have
been recounted with a different focus is turned into a mirror of the narrator. His inability to remain in the first-person plural is symptomatic of Bernard's general tendency to work himself into his writing and make his own
subjectivity the subject of the narrative.

In contrast, the narrative voice of books 3 and 4 is, with rare exceptions,
the corporate first-person plural. Even where the narrator claims to have
been present at the miracle, he uses the plural. For example, 4.3 is framed
as an eyewitness account, but (unlike Bernard) the writer does not separate
himself out from the other monastic witnesses. The chapter begins: "With
our own eyes we saw a miracle at that same time which frightened us not a
little" ("Oculorum credibili intuitu *didicimus,* quod sub eadem tempestate
mire actum non mediocriter *expavimus*"). After the prisoner-release miracle
has been worked, the freed man delivers his fetters to the monastery at
Conques, a ritual action which the narrator witnessed as a member of the
monastic community: "*nobis* cernentes." Where Bernard tends to privilege
his idiosyncratic interpretation of unusual events, the writer here submerges
his individual witness into the corporate entity and returns to the communal perspective. The narrative concludes with a statement that is one of the
basic assumptions of the miracle cult: "for it was due to her compassion—
so readily available to those who importune her—that he was heard, and
due to her counsel that he took the action that gained him freedom from
his enemy's oppression."

In a Bernardian passage that ostensibly does the same work—that
is, summarizes the belief system undergirding a miracle-working saint's
cult—the contrast between Bernard and the monk-continuator voice is
striking. After hyperbolically extolling Foy ("Oh, the great merit of one
girl! Oh, the wondrous gift granted to one woman! Oh, the wondrous and
ineffable grace invested in one virgin!") and in the process of recapitulating
Foy's *modus operandi,* Bernard manages to insert himself into the account
both as the redactor of the miracles and as a beneficiary:

For Sainte Foy works miracles, not only there, where her body rests, but also, as I
have learned from those who witnessed her miracles daily, on land, on the sea, in

prisons, in infirmities, in many dangers, and, as I have also learned partly through my own experience, she responds to all kinds of needs. If anyone appeals to her with a pure heart, that person feels her presence. And wherever Sainte Foy is named, there her power is also, to the praise and glory of Christ Omnipotent, Who controls all things with the reigns of His own omnipotence, and rules with the Father and the Holy Spirit, in co-eternal unity that endures forever and ever. Amen (1.33).

The formulaic language of praise and of credo here is subverted by Bernard's autobiographical interjection. He simply cannot resist bringing himself into his accounts of Foy's miracles, always highlighting his role of privileged interpreter.

Unlike Bernard, the monk-continuator who composed 3.5 has no difficulty fusing his individual perceptions with communal response, or his individual agenda with the corporate task. Even where the narrator discusses the act of composition, which would seem to be a very singular one, the voice adopts the plural so that writing itself becomes communal: "Another miracle that demands deep reverence was also brought to completion during that same time. Since we have just related a similar story, we will compress this one with as much brevity as we can. But we will moderate the brevity somewhat, lest the story become too obscure for readers to follow" ("Aliud quoque sub eadem tempestate patratur valde terribile, quod, ut supra *retulimus,* quanta *poterimus constringemus* brevitate; quam tamen brevitatem tali mediocritate *temperabimus,* ne obscuritatem ingerat lectoribus," 3.5).

Bernard, by contrast, emphasizes his own particular agency as miracle writer in his letter to the abbot and monks: "And as regards these miracles, I myself took them down from you or from the inhabitants of this village in your own words. They should be returned to you in recompense, so receive these miracles back again with kindness toward the poverty of my talent" ("Atque hec miracula, ut a vobis ipsis vel ab huius vici incolis *ego ipse* verbotenus *accepi,* rursus hec eadem pro parvitate *mei* ingenii, digna vicissitudine referendi, qualicumque mandata latinitati, ipse cum benivolentia recipite," 1.34).

The conflicts and contradictions built into Bernard's text may be seen in 1.30 where Bernard describes his working method as miracle collector, switching pronouns from singular to plural: "Among all the other miracle stories that were told to me about Sainte Foy so far, while I was energetically pursuing various informants as if I were hunting with the greatest desire, everyone was speaking joyfully and very often about the miracle I begin now. After it had been verified more certainly by consulting those who were present, we record it so that it will be remembered" ("Inter cetera que *mihi* de sancta Fide, adhuc *pergenti* a diversis relatoribus sicut summo desiderio *indaganti,* dicebantur, istud quod nunc *aggredior,* in ore totius populi festivo atque celeberrimo resonabat preconio. Quod postea certius ab his, qui rei geste interfuerant exquisitum, alte memorie *tradidimus*").

Bernard's position as an outsider effectively prevents him from consistently identifying with the monastic community. He occupies an ambivalent position, both inside and outside the monastic community. His liminality is clearly signaled in the closing passage of 1.30, which takes up Bernard's repeated theme: how he can establish the credibility of the miracle. It is only Bernard who can weigh the oral accounts of the common people *(plebeio),* confirm the accounts with the monks *(concors monachorum sententia),* and even receive the testimony of the first cousin of the miracle recipient. The account ends with Bernard regretful that he has not been able to speak with the recipient Hadimar himself, an observation that has the effect of shifting the focus back to Bernard and his authorial task. Many of the Bernardian miracle stories in books 1 and 2 are framed by Bernard's role as the redactor of miracles, so that the focus remains on his processes of collecting and assessing the data and on his hagiographic task. Although subtle, this strategy contributes to the strong sense of Bernard's individual personality that permeates his books.

The narratives of books 3 and 4 only infrequently frame the miracle stories with comments about the monk-author; they rather tend to set the individual miraculous event into a larger cosmic context. The focus of these books is not on the individual activity of the writer but on the role of the cult and the ultimate power represented by the saint. Each narrative thus serves the larger purpose of enhancing Foy's fame. Most of the accounts of books 3 and 4 either end with an appropriate response by the miracle recipient or state a moral. Miracle after miracle concludes with a statement that "these events had happened through Sainte Foy's power" (3.13), which by extension is understood to be the monastery's power. This clearly reflects a corporate ecclesiastical ideology designed to reinforce the cult.

The monk-authors always speak from the point of view of the monastery, referring to it as "this monastery" (4.1), speaking of "the brothers in our monastery" (3.9), and referring to a castle near Conques as one that "many of you know" (3.12). Unlike Bernard, who must travel to collect stories from others, the monk-authors are part of the community and take it for granted that they are at the cult center. Most of their miracle texts end with a moment of ritual affirmation in which the miracle recipients celebrate Foy as celestial and powerful virgin. All—speaker, audience, and internal cast of characters—share an interpretation of Foy and the meaning of her miracles with the result that books 3 and 4 propound a monologic message about the cult of Sainte Foy.[25] Bernard of Angers's texts, on the other hand, play out conflicting interpretations of the saint and her actions, emphasizing alternate views and constructing doubting characters. A cast of internal doubters challenges and critiques the cult verities and requires the Bernardian narrator to rationally explicate the significance of Foy's miraculous acts.

All Roads Lead to Conques

For the miracles collected in the *Liber miraculorum,* Foy's home is Conques, site of her shrine, the place where "the clay of her body" is found. Bernard understands that only at Conques can he investigate the validity of the miracle reports he has heard back at Chartres. However, Bernard is primarily a pilgrim to Conques, who makes three journeys and whose two books have a double function: both within his life in northern Francia and as a redaction of the miracle stories for the monastery itself. Because of this dual role, Bernard's books give Conques a contradictory identity: it is both numinous center and cultural margin. For the continuator-authors no such contradictions obtain: Conques is the center of their world and the cult is universalized in their texts without challenging the priority of the home site.

Virtually every miracle in the post–Bernardian books represents a return to Conques as the appropriate conclusion to a miracle happening anywhere in the universe. In some cases, especially healing miracles, the petitioner must go to the shrine for the cure to take place; thus a warrior named Gozmer developed the habit of taking a mute man with him on his annual pilgrimage to Conques, trusting that Foy would respond each time with a miraculous cure (3.23). In other cases, for example the release of prisoners, the freed men must make a pilgrimage of thanksgiving, bring their chains and fetters to Conques as offerings of thanks to the saint, and the expectation was that the story of their miraculous liberation would be retold there.

The epitome of the theme that it is necessary to go to Foy's shrine at Conques may be found in 3.24. It begins with a warrior from a castle in the region of Albi who was coming as a pilgrim to Sainte Foy's abbey church when he was taken captive by a priest named Hadimar. In order to complete his trip to Foy's shrine, the warrior pledged that he would return to captivity after Christmas, and he fulfilled his pledge. The narrative then shifts its focus to Hadimar, whom Foy punished with running sores from head to toe. Since these sores made it too painful for Hadimar to walk on the stony footpath, he "went on horseback to the holy virgin's church."

There he confessed all his sins and was subsequently cured. After a success-ful pilgrimage to Jerusalem, Hadimar returned to Foy's church, "faithfully pledged himself to her and to all the monks, and from then on he honored his pledge by visiting there frequently." In its surplus of returns to Foy's shrine, this narrative models the appropriate attitude toward the cult site of Conques, a model that is reproduced in a large number of the other miracle stories in books 3 and 4.

The centrality of Conques itself to the ideological geography of the miracle stories is also evident in the large number of stories about Foy's punishment of anyone who threatens to deprive her monastery of property. Typically someone who tries to appropriate her lands, refuses to give to her a piece of property that she claims, or threatens her peasants is punished by the saint. This theme of Foy's protection of the monastery is certainly pres-ent in Bernard's books 1 and 2, although, in keeping with the social con-ditions of the time, its focus seems to be the local castellan as marauder or threatening force. Bernard's interest is in the personality and performance of the saint as she deals with threats to her desires. For example, in the miracles in which Foy demands jewelry, we can read indirectly the actions of the monastery to increase its wealth by extorting precious metals from owners of jewelry in the vicinity. But Bernard uses these stories primarily to explore the playfulness of his trickster-saint protagonist.

In books 3 and 4 the theme of Conques's centrality has become a *topos,* now infused with the need to retain and buttress territorial authority and possession. In this starkly black and white world, anyone who threatens the monastery is bad and will automatically be punished by Foy; anyone who recognizes the monastery's authority is good and receives a reward. The theme of the monastery's property rights is explicitly articulated in 3.14, the story of a certain Reinfroi who has the opportunity to reconsider his wrong choices.

In Quercy there was a piece of property that had belonged outright to the holy martyr for a long time. Because its tenants had long held it, they had come to think of themselves as its legal owners. The brothers of Sainte Foy's monastery agreed that control of this property should be regained by the community. They unani-mously decided that the golden image in which the blessed martyr's glorious head is enclosed should be carried there. When they arrived, they set down the sacred treasure in a church called Belmont, which is near the disputed land. The next morning they carried it to another of Sainte Foy's manors, which a warrior named Reinfroi was claiming as his own because he had occupied it for so long.

As Reinfroi with his fifty horsemen was planning to take vengeance on the monks, he and all his men were struck blind. Not a fool, Reinfroi sent a peace-making delegation to the monks, and with his men he approached the sacred relics on bare feet. Asking her pardon for his ill-considered action, Reinfroi fell to the ground before the sacred image, completely prostrating himself. He said that after his death possession of the manor would be relinquished to Sainte Foy, and agreed that his sons would not succeed him in holding it unless the brothers of the sacred community should wish it. As soon as he had made this vow, his sight was restored.

We then discover that Reinfroi had no intention of fulfilling his vow, and Sainte Foy appears to him on three succeeding nights, threatening him unless he cedes the property to her: "She declared that unless he took immediate action to give up the manor she would condemn him to eternal punishment and would pursue all of his future posterity until the end of time with a cursed hatred. Totally crushed by fear, Reinfroi immediately went to the holy martyr's abbey church. There he completely appeased all the glorious virgin's rancor against him. He relinquished without condition the possession of that manor for himself and abandoned the claims of his sons and grandsons." According to the narrator, Reinfroi's reward for handing the manor back to the abbot and the monks was that "in the end the holy virgin who is beloved of God would allow him to have full enjoyment of His heavenly mansions." This is a fairly naked representation of the appropriate behavior by landowners when confronted by the property demands of the monastery.

Even where the rights of workers on her lands are concerned, Foy is represented as pro-active. For example in C.5 (4.27), a certain warrior had left a horse in one of her fields, where it wreaked havoc on the monks' crops. "The peasants were deeply offended by the way their neighbor was injuring them, and began a constant clamoring for Sainte Foy's help. . . . One day when the horse was standing in the middle of a grassy meadow it bloated so badly that its belly burst and its entrails fell to the ground. . . . When the peasants saw this astonishing miracle, they recognized that it was the work of Sainte Foy's avenging power, which doesn't allow the arrogance of criminals to rejoice very long." In its unambiguous condemnation and punishment of those who defied the political reach of the Conques monastery, this miracle is typical of many in books 3 and 4 of the *Liber miraculorum*.

Authorship Issues in Books 3 and 4:
One or More Monk-Continuators?

Current scholarship on the *Liber miraculorum* argues that one monk was responsible for producing the individual stories that comprise both books 3 and 4. An important piece of evidence is the authorial promise at the end of book 3 to write another book, which is taken in conjunction with the opening of book 4 in which the author claims to be resuming a long-interrupted task.[26] Bonnassie and Gournay, in fact, would like to identify this monk-author with the abbot Odolric, who is thought to be the primary impetus behind the new church built at Conques beginning in the mid eleventh century.[27] And even if it isn't Odolric, they cannot imagine more than one monk with the cultural and literary repertoire to produce books 3 and 4 of the miracles: "If it is not him, it must be a Conques monk with numerous contacts, with broad horizons, and uncommonly cultured." [28]

In "What Is an Author?" Michel Foucault analyzes the need for authorial attribution as a way of producing meaning in the interpretation of texts.[29] Our own close reading of the narratives in books 3 and 4 accumulates a fair amount of strong evidence that there was more than one monk-continuator. In particular, we see a dividing line in style and in the conception of Sainte Foy between books 3 and 4 that we will bring into our discussion as we proceed. In the absence of a named author like Bernard of Angers, we must work from internal evidence provided by the texts to determine if there might have been more than one hagiographer at work. However, with a bow to Foucault, we might say we do not share the concern with assigning authorship to a historically significant individual, especially since these texts emphasize their authorial anonymity. We are more interested in the ideological role played by the texts and the function of the narrative voice in conveying ideological messages.

The overriding conclusion from our point of view is that whether there were multiple monk-authors or not, they all deliberately adopt a common persona. This persona, which we have already described, is anonymous because it is the voice of the monastery articulating its interests with regard to the cult of Sainte Foy and the institution's religious, political, and economic power. Despite the differences that we will outline, the overall project of the monk-continuator persona is one and the same: to represent Foy as a universal saint (as opposed to Bernard's local trickster-child), to show the expansion of the cult across the known world, to simultaneously reinforce the central position of the Conques monastery in cult activities, and to express moral authority by reading good and evil in the world. Whatever individuals were the actual writers, they share a common vision of the role of the Conques monastery.

It does seem to us, however, that the stylistic and cultural materials of book 4 differ substantially from those of book 3, just as both differ from the Bernardian books 1 and 2. Although ideologically we see books 3 and 4 forming a monologic monastic narrative unit that has profound differences from the mixed ideologies of books 1 and 2, we think it interesting that there are less profound but very real differences between books 3 and 4. One likely possibility is that the content of book 3 was more influenced by the materials inherited from Bernard. But in any case, book 4 contains significant innovations that clearly differentiate it from the previous books in the *Liber*.

The Constructions of Foy

Along with their project of raising the cult to international status, the monk-authors of books 3 and 4 transform the portrait of the saint, replacing Bernard's local trickster-child with a celestial virgin-martyr. In Bernard's books, the saint appears in numerous visions where she is described in elaborate physical detail. The sense of her psychological presence is profound; she engages in dialogue, berating, encouraging, cajoling, threatening, giving commands, promising rewards, interacting with each suppliant as an individual person whose character she knows. Often she addresses the person by name, as, for example, when she appears to Guibert in the first miracle. With Gimon and other monks she can be teasing. In 1.33 she helps a prisoner escape, "going in front of him as if to show him the way" and stiffening his weak resolve: "Have confidence! Quick! You won't escape any other way." In 1.25 she "rather severely" demands that a watchman return stolen gold, and becomes increasingly "terrifying" when he fails to comply.

Commonly in books 3 and 4, Foy is represented not as a little girl but as an authoritative adult who is repeatedly called a "physician" or "medicus."[30] In 4.17 (4.18), for example, Foy cures a warrior who has a shriveled hand caused by a wound. The warrior addresses her as "most gracious patroness," and the narrator assigns Foy a virtue conspicuously lacking in Bernard's books when he calls her "the most patient of physicians." She addresses the warrior as son, behaving like a mature adult rather than like a fooling child. In 4.18 (4.19) Foy does not permit her devotees to "suffer misfortunes" but provides them "great medicines."

In these later books, Foy has become a universal saint rather than one specific to Conques; she is a much more conventional virgin-martyr; and she mostly dwells in the rarefied heavens: "Our glorious virgin and martyr had already become a heaven-dweller and had joined the choirs of angels when she prevailed and gave the same gift to those praying to her. Because of the sanctity of her earthly life and because of the merits of her Passion, there is no doubt that after her departure from this life she went to live in heaven" (3.8).

In comparison to the engaging portrait of a trickster-saint in Bernard's books, the Foy of book 3 seems very bland. In a prisoner's vision in 3.4, her mode is "gentle encouragement" rather than cajoling and scolding. Similarly in 3.5 and 3.7, Foy appears in order to effect a miraculous rescue, but rather than taunting, teasing, and harassing (as is her wont in the Bernardian visions), she simply gives her helpful message and departs. The human recipient of the miracle occupies an ontologically distinct category from the saint, who appears in a vision and then disappears back to her celestial reality. By contrast, Bernard is obviously using Foy to explore the liminal boundary between the sacred and the human, the subjective and the objective, and to test the petitioner.

The authorial voice of book 3 has no such interests; there Sainte Foy is efficiently omnipotent and to-the-point in her dealings with needy humanity. She appears to provide solutions as if by formula: the ritually correct action guarantees a happy ending. The narratives construct a morally simple world in which one can easily know and should distinguish good and evil behaviors. Naturally, Foy is represented as devastating when she punishes the violators of her property, but in book 3 the saint has the ruthless efficiency of a Mafia hit man. In 3.17, for example, a warrior named Siger who occupies a castle in Conques itself is a threat to the saint and her monks: "Puffed up with arrogant pride and enflamed by the fires of avarice, he stole everything he could from the holy martyr's property. He never ceased harassing her monks with vile insults, and he mutilated the men who worked on her lands." Since the monks did not have armed men for defense, they prayed to Foy for help, and they displayed in the public square of Conques the banner, a cross, reliquary boxes, and the image of the saint.[31] In response to this ritualized petition for vengeance on the marauder, Foy destroyed Siger and, for good measure, killed four of his sons. Even his daughters were punished by loss of rank and goods, and, finally, "the very tower that had given shelter to this destructive group of people was shaken in all directions by a strong wind; it fell with a great crash and was completely leveled." The narrator concludes with some satisfaction that "thus through the holy martyr's power all that pride collapsed; thus the root of evils was torn out and destroyed; thus divine vengeance delivered the holy monastery from the assault of the impious." The authorial voice of book 3 has created a saint strictly keyed to the needs of the Conques monastery, with no gratuitous personality traits.

Book 4 initiates a fully developed treatment of Foy as celestial virginmartyr and bride of Christ. The language with which she is introduced in the very first chapter of book 4 heightens the universality of her fame:

Though she has been united with the angelic hosts in the heights of heaven, the remarkable great works of her miracles shine brightly and make her power known to the whole world . . . . For even if she can't show herself to people as a corporeal being, still she manifests herself perpetually through the revealed signs of her miracles. There is no land from one pole to the other where her fame and the praise of her name are not known. And this fame and praise are well deserved, for from her very early youth she had an outstanding character.

Distinctive to book 4 (4.1 and 4.8) is the language of the Song of Songs, language which is stereotypically used of the virgin-martyrs elsewhere, but introduced here for the first time to characterize Sainte Foy:

She was distinguished by the goodness of total chastity, and in all her actions she shone purer than gold. . . . Truly the fragrance of her sanctity and of her chaste life breathed out a sweet scent to the supreme king sitting on the high throne of the heavens, because she was wholly 'the good odor unto God,' to use the apostle's phrase. When finally she was burned in the searing fire of her Passion, when the alabaster perfume jar that was her body was shattered by the harshest punishments, she became choice myrrh. The court of God was filled with her most pleasing fragrance and sent forth pillars of smoke scented with her most delightful sweetness to all the earth's wide regions.

Martyrdom is the direct source of Foy's miracle-working power in book 4, a point on which neither Bernard nor the authorial voice of book 3 places much emphasis.[32] The author of 4.1 insists that "when she was tortured by excruciating pain for love of Him, she wasn't afraid to suffer with patience the final insult of death"; therefore God "enriches her" with the "great rewards and honors" that are her miracles. Books 1, 2, and 3 present Foy's powers as primarily residing in Conques and associated with her relics at the shrine, but without making an explicit connection to her martyrdom. However, in book 4, Foy is emphatically a celestial being *because* she is a virgin-martyr. Her appearances on earth are only one aspect of her activity and interventions throughout the universe. "She moves unconfined through the upper air surrounding the earth, and whenever a perilous situation reaches crisis she is present," according to 4.1.

Book 4 is especially preoccupied with Foy's position in the celestial hierarchy. In several miracles Foy responds to those in need not by a personal appearance but by deploying other saints to do her rescue work. In 4.8, for example, Foy is distant from the human realm, all her actions mediated by other celestial beings. When Raymond of Montpezat, a noble youth, is languishing in prison, rather than appearing herself to him in sleep, Foy prompts God to send Saint Stephen. In a dream, the protomartyr Stephen takes Raymond to the bridge over the Dourdou River at Conques to stage a vision of Foy's power and status in heaven. Stephen says to Raymond:

O my son, direct your gaze above this mountaintop wrapped in clouds and regard the bright light of God that you see shining there. For in the midst of that great splendor the most holy virgin and glorious martyr Foy shines forth, surrounded by the outstretched hands of the angels. This reveals very clearly the honor owed to her on her own merit. This is she of whom what was said in the Song of Songs can truly be believed—that she is beautiful among the daughters of Jerusalem, filled with charity and love; when the queens saw her they praised her in the citadel of heaven. When she climbed up to the heavens, crowned with the triumphal laurel, the heavenly citizens admired the marvelous gleam of her sanctity and spoke in this way: "Who is she who ascends like the glistening dawn, fair as the moon, bright as the sun, awesome as an army ordered in ranks? She is chosen for her excellence, truly sanctified, truly set at the head of the virginal choirs next to the mother of God, who alone has no equal."

Both the narrative situation and the rhetoric of the description explicitly elevate Foy beyond the mundane and human in a way that the saint's portraits in books 1, 2, and 3 never contemplate.

In this description of Foy, we are very far from either the trickster-child of Bernard or the efficient miracle worker of book 3. As Raymond listened to Stephen's description he saw Foy as the center of "a fiery globe sparkling with intense brightness." Foy's position next to the Virgin Mary, which places her above the other saints, is also emphasized in the Epilogue to book 4: "Without doubt she is an intimate acquaintance of the mother of God, because the dazzling whiteness of her virginity places her in the forefront of the virgin saints and the laurel-crowned glory of her Passion places her at the head of the chorus of martyrs." In another miracle (4.20) Foy in fact takes on qualities of the Virgin Mary, including "nurturing breasts" and "a cloak of compassion," which may suggest that by the time this miracle was drafted the author was aware of competition from the rising cult of Mary.[33]

In book 4, considerable energy is expended in delineating the politics of heaven and clarifying Foy's rank in that milieu. Bernard, by contrast, is far more interested in the politics of the Rouergue or his clerical milieu in northern Francia, deploying the saint as a player in those terrestrial power struggles. In book 4 the monk-continuators are careful to show Foy as superior to other saints, for example, Michael and Stephen. Even where Bernard has materials for that construction, he simply ignores their implication. For example, when Foy sends Gerbert to Saint Michael's altar in

2.1, Bernard does not use the incident, as a monk-continuator might have, to emphasize Foy's elevated place in the celestial hierarchy. According to book 4 (4.8), Foy has more status than Saint Stephen. Awakening from his celestial vision, Raymond realizes that he has been liberated from captivity. The protocol would require him to make a visit to Conques to thank Sainte Foy. On the way, he stopped in the city of Cahors at Saint Stephen's cathedral, since "he was eager to offer the thanks he owed to the protomartyr Stephen, who has, as it were, led him to his escape. And because he had been weakened by the long period of fasting and by his flight, instead of going on to Conques Raymond sent a candle to Sainte Foy, as large as he could afford, in gratitude for the rescue she had afforded him." Foy however does not accept the substitute offering and appears to Raymond to insist that he offer thanksgiving personally at Conques. In this version of Foy there must be no doubt: Foy outranks Stephen.

One of Foy's celestial powers that is only exercised in books 3 and 4 is the resurrection from the dead of human beings. Bernard avoids this kind of miracle in books 1 and 2, and tells his readers why. In rationally justifying Foy's resurrection of animals, Bernard argues that to include human resurrection miracles would imply a theologically incorrect view of life on earth. The monk-continuators, however, ignore Bernard's reasoning. For them, Foy is "the equal of any citizen of heaven in every kind of miracle" (4.24 [4.29]). The resurrection of the dead, one of the most powerful miracles, therefore had to be in Foy's repertoire.[34] Book 3 opens with a miracle story in which Goteline "lay at death's door." When she was revived, her body "already lay limp in death," that is, rigor mortis had not set in. In 3.8, Foy "poured breath back into" a body wrapped in its shroud as it was being carried to the church for burial. Book 3 introduces the resurrection miracle and book 4 develops it.

It is the lengthy first miracle of book 4 that most thoroughly explores Foy's power over death. This narrative recounts the death of Hunald's son and his subsequent resurrection after his father and funeral participants had all prayed to the holy martyr Foy. The dramatic climax of the miracle is the son's narrative of his soul's experience in the underworld. Saint Michael, the commander of Paradise, functions as Foy's emissary in this miracle. He scolds the torturers of the underworld: "You contrivers of evil, why are you raving so furiously and cruelly in tormenting this new arrival? . . . Stop mangling him now, because God has permitted through this very holy virgin Foy that his soul will be snatched from your power and restored to his body." The resurrected boy tells his spellbound audience that the blessed virgin Foy "rushed fiercely into the midst of the torturers' ranks and firmly dragged my soul from their hands. She delivered it to my body lying on the ground and poured it back in to work the miracle that you saw." Foy's field of action in book 4 shifts to the otherworldly venue where she partakes in eternal struggles and exercises her celestial powers on behalf of her devotees, both living and dead.

Not surprisingly, given the monastic authors' interest in Foy as cosmic player, the miracles of books 3 and 4 give the celestial virgin demonic antagonists. Bernard has relatively few allusions to a personified Devil (with the exception of his framing letter to Fulbert, which uses the language of diabolical intervention). But for the monastery, the demonic is an active power, and, in this feature, the monk-continuators return to the model of earlier hagiography, such as Sulpicius Severus's life of Saint Martin or Athanasius's life of Saint Anthony, where demonic attacks are a regular occurrence. There are only passing references to demons in book 3 of the *Liber miraculorum*. In 3.2, the mist in a dangerous gorge near Albi is said to be due to the presence of "malignant spirits" that had been driven out of the city, and in 3.18, Fredol's wife is stolen by "a man who had fallen prey to demonic enthrallment." However, the activity of demons *per se* is not of interest in book 3, nor does the saint confront demons directly.

As we have seen above, in 4.1 where Sainte Foy rescues the soul of a dead boy from Tartarus, book 4 exploits the drama inherent in cosmic confrontation. The narrative of 4.1 is structured by the battle between Sainte Foy and the forces of darkness, both in the boy's account of his soul's afterlife experience and in the subsequent action. Foy is portrayed here as leading the cosmic forces of good against the cosmic forces of evil. The narrative gives further examples of Foy's battle with demons as the resurrected boy and his father journey to Foy's monastery in order to offer the saint the praise due to her. When his horse slips on the steep mountain path above the Dourdou River, Foy saves the boy from a lethal fall. Then, while he was on his way to "celebrate holy vigils in front of the holy virgin" the boy "found the Ancient Enemy lying in wait to capture him, for, in an unforeseen calamity, when he was in the hall he tumbled down a gaping hole that had been covered over by wooden flooring. His companions ran down to him swiftly and found the accident-prone youth safe and uninjured; the holy martyr had placed her hand beneath him, and it was as if he had landed on soft cushions after a short fall." The battle between Foy and demons that structures this miracle takes place both in the next world and in this one.

As we noted in our discussion of the Bernardian books of miracles, the miracles called *joca* have been considered characteristic of that author's construction of Foy. A number of the miracles in book 3 have ludic qualities that resemble the joking tone of many of Bernard's narratives, with one significant difference: it is not the saint that is the trickster. Or, perhaps more accurately, in the Bernardian miracles the *joca* are presented as evidence of the low style, the grotesque, and the liminal. His Sainte Foy is associated with liminality; she is deviser of tricks in the low mode. In book 3, however, there seems to be a kind of decorum preventing Foy's feats from being conceived as *joca*. The very events that Bernard would have described as *joca* are in book 3 opportunities to demonstrate the saint's control and omnipotence.

Even where book 3 uses humor, it tends to be sentimentalized rather than put to the service of philosophical inquiry. In 3.12, for example, an ancient horse that often carried Foy's reliquary-statue in ritual procession has its eye torn out by a young man "waving a stick in play." The owner reminds the saint that the horse is her "old reliable servant" and, despite general ridicule and loud laughter from other people, he leads the horse home. In the morning the master finds his horse completely healed, its eye "in such perfect condition that there wasn't even a scar anywhere around it." Such an animal-healing miracle in the Bernardian books would have instigated a philosophical debate about the propriety of wasting saintly attention on animals, since they represented low material on the Virgilian wheel of literary treatment. No such issues are raised here. The joking neighbors are revealed to be misguided and the horse, despite its advanced years, is dignified by a role in the rituals of the cult. Immediately after recording the healed eye of the horse, the narrator says, "In this way the prodigious feat accomplished through Sainte Foy's power became known to all." The gentle humor of the narrative supports the ultimate miraculous act rather than qualifying or critiquing it, and in any case does not apply to the saint herself.

Foy as Trickster in High and Low Modes

In book 4, however, Bernard's term *joca* is employed to characterize both the saint and her actions. The miracle in 4.23 (4.28) appears to be directly intertextual with Bernard's joking miracles and his representation of Foy as trickster-saint. In this, the author is distinctly bolder than the monk-continuator voice of book 3. However, the development of the trickster motifs in 4.23 (4.28), although related to Bernard's, takes new directions. Only in books 3 and 4 is the saint referred to as a divine physician and thus becomes available for parody as a trickster-physician. What can be differentiated from Bernard's portrait of the trickster-Foy is the use in 4.23 (4.28) of the Virgilian high mode of elite poetics and theology.

"How a Warrior Was Tormented by the Irregular Shifting of His Intestines" (4.23 [4.28]) demonstrates both the high style of elevated rhetoric dealing with the elevated subject of Foy's "celestial cures" and the low style of slapstick violence dealing with the low subjects of a hernia and a black-smith. The monk-author, like Bernard of Angers, appears to be invoking the well-known categories of the Virgilian wheel from medieval rhetoric. In making a flamboyant shift between high and low styles, the narrator manipulates rhetorical categories as if they were distinct and then, by a kind of sleight of hand or narrative trick, deconstructs the binary system. Unlike Bernard, for this narrator Foy is not just a trickster in the low mode, "which is the way peasants understand such things." She is also a trickster in the high style, which is this author's elaboration on the Bernardian materials.

Foy, a high culture trickster in the guise of a goddess,[35] is lauded in the poem that opens 4.23 (4.28) for her "brilliant remedy" which is at the same time a "remarkable joke." The introductory poem refers to medical traditions that range from Asclepius, the classical god of healing and son of Phoebus Apollo, and Chiron, the centaur well-known as a physician, to the lowest popular remedies alluded to in the lines:

She doesn't scrape away diseases with an iron hook
Or twitter old witch's songs over rotting wounds.[36]

Her miraculous powers are shown to reverse natural processes:

Prison-caves stand open, breached strong-rooms gape,
Iron fetters melt like ice in the sun,
Scourges have no power to harm, at the advent of this virgin.

Implicitly, Foy, who is called "celestial physician" elsewhere in book 4, is being compared to Christ, physician of the soul.[37]

Not only is Foy a miraculous physician, but she also is compared to Christ as the conqueror of Death. Images associated with Foy's power in this poem come directly from the theological language describing Christ the trickster who outwits Satan and death in the abuse-of-power theory of the atonement:

Even fierce Death, now frightened, takes cowardly flight,
And sighs at the loss of the prey snatched from its jaws
And restored to life, and at the return of the ancient ones after they had lived their
  last day,
When they had been carried off at the appointed time.
I believe that Tartarus itself will not lack these endless tears
Because of unwanted and frequent plunder,
For the esteemed virgin snatches them away and leads them to the light.

The metaphors of "prey" snatched from the jaws of Death and the leading of the "ancient ones" to the light are obvious references to Christ's role
as trickster-redeemer in the medieval theory of atonement known as the
"Abuse of Power."[38] Patristic theology, to the extent that it offered a supreme deity who used divine trickery to outwit Death or the Devil, differs
from later scholastic theology, which emphasized human will and choice.
When the cult of Foy was developing in the ninth to eleventh centuries,
the patristic theory of atonement dominated theological discussion. Therefore the image of Foy as celestial trickster-physician is here a product of
elite theological *topoi* more than it is one of folk understanding.

Having "sung a few things in epic verses about the holy martyr's exceptional stature in heaven and great glory on earth," the narrator switches
abruptly to prose and to the low style to tell about the fortunes of a warrior
whose intestine had left its "proper place and ruptured into his scrotum
with a great roaring of his bowels." The miracle is told as straightforward
narrative with an emphasis on gross physiological detail, a rather shocking
contrast to the rhetorical elaboration and hyperbole of the poem. Within
this rhetorical performance, the narrative in low style plays with actual
medical therapies for the treatment of hernia and parodies the folklore figure of the blacksmith.[39]

We have already remarked that the introductory poem carefully positions Foy as a medical expert in general terms: she is superior to ancient
traditions of Greek medicine, to contemporary treatment by the rough and
ready surgeons who wield knives to cut away dead flesh, and to the wise
women of folk tradition, with their bubbling cauldrons and magic spells.
What may not be so evident is that the prose narrative demonstrates Foy's
superiority to the medical profession as well. Through what appears to be
an especially tasteless and cruel practical joke, Foy effects a cure, but the
author suppresses the information that the cure represents a creative adaptation of a classical treatment for hernia, which involved an inverted position of the body for hernia operations.[40] It seems that our monk-narrator
incorporates this medical treatment into Foy's practical joke.

When the warrior suffering from scrotal hernia prays exhaustingly at
Foy's shrine she appears to him in a dream saying:

"You should know that although I have cured serious ailments caused by many
different diseases I've never been called upon at all to treat the kind of problem you
bring to me. But you shouldn't leave here without some advice. Pay attention and
I'll explain to you how you will be healed. Do you know the blacksmith who lives
near you?"

He replied that he knew the man well, both his name and his appearance, and she went on: "Go to him straightaway and ask him to take up the hammer he would use to pound a mass of iron heated in the furnace till it is glowing white. Then put on his anvil the part of you that is suffering and tell him to strike his most powerful blow. This will quickly give you the recovery you desire."

At these words the man woke up. Stupefied and incredulous, he thought she was surely mocking him. He debated for a long time in his noble heart about what such a vision could mean. Finally he returned home, having made up his mind to die. Without telling anyone he went to the blacksmith and secretly told him what Sainte Foy had instructed him to do. And when he had heard it, the blacksmith's heart sank. He swore that he would not perform this fantastic practical joke:

"Believe me, my lord, these weren't the words of a healer but of some joker. If you are naive enough to follow this advice, you could be accused of your own murder. And I will never enact such an evil crime, for I am completely convinced that you will meet an instant death with this."

The suffering warrior finally convinced the blacksmith to administer this unconventional treatment.

His swollen scrotum was stretched out over the anvil and his diseased genitals were prepared for the blow. Soon the blacksmith flexed his muscular arms and swung the enormously heavy hammer high into the air. When the warrior saw what awaited him he was struck with incredible terror, slipped backwards, and lay prostrate, as if all his bones had been broken in a fall to his death. And in this headlong fall, wondrous to report! all at once his herniated intestines were sucked back inside so completely that they never ruptured again for the rest of his life. So he came out of it in good shape, for he was cured without being cauterized with a hot iron or taking any potion as a remedy. And Sainte Foy's joke, if I may call it that, was quickly going to become a miracle that people would marvel at ever after.[41]

The course of treatment Foy prescribes comes equally from her roles as trickster and as physician. That is, the saint's medical knowledge of the efficaciousness of the operating position intersects perfectly with the trick required to get the patient into a position where his herniated intestines would be sucked back inside.[42] This divine trickster-physician saint is a far cry from the businesslike healer of book 3 and might even be read as a parody of that representation. The monk-author of this chapter may also be intertextual with Bernard in this joking episode, a construction of Foy in both low and celestial modes of trickery.

Style and Language

As might be expected, all of the books in the *Liber miraculorum* make comparisons between Foy's miracles and biblical precedents. There are only subtle differences among authors in their use of the Bible. Bernard of Angers uses biblical analogies to encourage belief in the miracle stories and to justify his mission of writing them. Thus he writes in 1.1: "Don't be amazed that God entrusted the rescue of Guibert's eyes in the wilderness to a winged magpie, for in time past He used ravens to send food to Elijah in the desert." He resorts repeatedly to the Scriptures to justify the anomalous behavior of the warrior-monk Gimon. For example, to reconcile Gimon's angry outbursts with Bernard's very positive opinion of him, Bernard invokes the biblical distinction between words and actions (1.26). He rarely cites biblical sources explicitly and tends not to use typological explanation in any explicit way. By contrast, an integral part of the monk-continuators' rhetorical style is to make comparisons between their narratives and biblical scenes. Arnold, a "savage usurper" who attempted to reclaim lands his daughter-in-law had given to Sainte Foy, was chased into the "very church of Sainte Foy that he had ravaged" where he was killed. The monk draws the moral using a biblical type: "This is like the fate of wretched Jezebel whose body was thrown to dogs as plunder. For she stained Naboth's vineyard with her warm blood, the very vineyard that this most wicked of women had dared to seize after Naboth had been slain through her deception" (4.22 [4.24]). Similarly in C.4 (4.26), Foy delivered some men from Albi who had come to plunder her lands "into [the] hands" of their enemies "in the same way that once the king of Samaria received thieves through the hand of Elijah." In particular, the monks compare Foy's miracles to biblical miracles, whether those of Elisha (3.8) or of Peter (C.1 [4.12]), a standard device of hagiographers. For them the Scriptures provide a set of analogous stories.

A comparison of the classical texts cited in Bernard's books and those cited by the authors of books 3 and 4 reveals that with respect to education their backgrounds were similar. The monk-continuators also share a basic quality of prose style with Bernard; that is, composition through a pastiche of phrases lifted without attribution from classical authors. An example of how the monks used their classical education—weaving in short phrases from classical texts—can be found in 3.20: "A Little Boy Called back from Death at Millau." The mother's words, "what great crime could my little boy have committed against you . . ." ("quid tantum in te potuit hic meus committere parvulus") echo the *Aeneid* 1.231–32: "quid meus Aeneus in te committere tantum." Another line of her speech—"Either return him to me or take him to yourself" ("Eum vel redde mihi, vel redde sibi")— comes from Sedulius (*Paschale carmen* III, 302–03: "Hunc, precor, . . . / redde mihi vel redde sibi"). Here a first-person, emotion-filled speech *(pathos),* seemingly taken straight from life, is actually a pastiche of quotations.

This was the prose style that resulted from the techniques of traditional liberal arts education in the early and high Middle Ages.

Despite the similarity of their classical education, Bernard and the monk-continuators exhibit striking stylistic differences in their narratives. In his prose style, Bernard underplays or even obscures his classical learning, whereas the monks seem eager to parade theirs. As we have suggested above in chapter 1, Bernard exemplifies the aesthetics of obscure reference, where only the elite reader will understand an allusion or get the joke. As his letter to the abbot and monks of Conques (1.34) makes clear, Bernard does flaunt his Latinity relative to the monks, but he has another, more Augustinian, model for demonstrating his erudition in the miracle narratives.

The continuators, however, believe that their learning should be displayed. The monk-authors delight in overt classical allusions; they employ biblical typologies; they import Greekisms as signs of their knowledge, deliberately substituting them for expected common words. A form of stylistic display the monks enjoy is the use of obscure or exotic words deriving from Greek: "melotem" (3.4); "malagmata" (4.1); "horoma" (4.8); "sintheses" (4.14 [4.15]); "Bistonidum," "Lieo" (4.15 [4.16]); "cosmeta," "periscelides" (4.20 [4.21]); "Potniadarum" (C.5 [4.27]). Book 3 repeats one of the extremely few classical allusions in the Bernardian books: the soul sent down to Orcus ("demittitur Orco," 1.5; "Orco demisit," 3.16) and introduces several others: a resurrected boy is "Virbius" (3.8); a wicked warrior is a "cyclops" (3.17). Rather than announce the dawn, the author of 3.16 reaches for a high style simile: "Aurora, rising, left the bed of Tithonus." Book 3 also contains a rare reference to Roman history (3.23).

Book 4 is even more liberally sprinkled with classical allusions, and in a number of cases they are much more fully developed than in the earlier books. For example, rather than simply send a soul to Orcus, the monk-author of 4.1 paints a vivid picture of this monster: "Indeed in a singular fashion ravenous Orcus is forced to give back uninjured from his bloodstained mouth the bites of souls he has swallowed, bites for which his mouth always gapes so he can stuff his harpy's belly, for he ever craves to satisfy his insatiable hunger." Classical allusions heighten the descriptions of wicked characters: a Saracen "was roused by a fury worthy of Tisiphone" (4.6); Adalhelm, the evil lord of the castle of Roche d'Agoux, was "as harsh as the cruelest Achaemenid," and "grew as savage as that tyrant who shut living men inside a bronze bull and burned them to death" (4.7; the reference is to a Greek tyrant, Phalaris). We also hear of Orestes (4.3); "a Gaetulian lion" (4.7); "the portals of Leucata" (4.10); "a Bistonian woman" (4.15 [4.16]); "the Emathian fields" and "the pit of Tartarus" (C.4 [4.26]). Perhaps most telling is the way the monk-author of 4.16 (4.17) implies that it is natural for a monk to think in such terms even in the midst of a riot: "It occurred to one of the monks that they ought to carry the majesty of the holy virgin out of the sanctuary to subdue these savage evil-doings and bring down her heavy fist on Erinys, the greatest of the furies, who was venting her rage there." The monks' display of classical learning reaches a climax in book 4 as they elevate their saint into the high style and intensify the portrait of the forces arrayed against her.

One marker of elevation in late classical and medieval writing was the use of *prosimetrum,* the interweaving of prose and verse.[43] Important models for medieval writers were Boethius's *Consolation of Philosophy* and Martianus Capella's *Marriage of Philology and Mercury.* The alternation between prose and verse was thought to be pleasing, with the verse a technique for heightening the effect of the content.[44] Bernard of Angers uses verse sparingly; in 1.6 he describes the punishment of a man making a meal out of food and wine stolen from the saint in vivid if not sensational detail. Uniquely for Bernard, the verse continues until the very end of the chapter. The anomaly is acknowledged in the first line of 1.7, which is his self-reflexive commentary on what he has just done: "The second half of the preceding miracle is composed in verse, contrary to my usual practice of writing in prose. A monk named Arseus persuaded me to write them with his insistent pleas. But lest the second half should seem to be out of harmony with the first, I have chosen to set those verses on the page like prose."[45]

After making his reservations about the use of *prosimetrum* clear, Bernard employs it again in one other chapter only (1.12). The first passage again imparts a sensational heightening effect *(enargia);* having been struck by lightning, a warrior is completely burned up, "reduced to a piece of charcoal," which Bernard likens to the trunk of an oak that a farmer attempts to remove from his field by burning it: "And in the end he leaves a blackened tree trunk in the middle of his fields. Just so, the wretched corpse looked horrible, its limbs burned off on both sides." The first passage in verse is followed by a florid series of prose questions in the *ubi sunt* mode:

Oh, bold fighter, oh fearless warrior, oh most outstanding of men, you who exalted yourself up to the heavens, you who considered the very saints of God as if they were nothing, where is your power now? Where your strength? Where your vigor? Where the violent storms of your threats? Where your unconquerable force?

The taunting questions addressed to this dead warrior are then continued in a second verse passage, after which Bernard switches back to prose to complete his excoriation of the dead man. The whole chapter is written in a rhetorically exaggerated style, very foreign to Bernard's usual philosophical mode. He ends his diatribe by pulling back almost in embarassment at his stylistic excesses: "But now I have ridiculed this most wretched man enough. Since he was a human being, it would have been more fitting to lament. I'll hurry to end this overly long text." Bernard seems here to recognize that the very use of verse has caused him to lose control over the moral content of the miracle story.

The monk-authors of book 3 share Bernard's reluctance to use metered verse; one line from Horace is explicitly signaled—"Just as the Poet says" (3.15)—and another single line (3.23) is adapted from Virgil; no extended passages of verse occur in any of its twenty-four miracle stories. However, the monk-authors of book 4 have none of those reservations; rather they enthusiastically embrace this classical technique. As we have seen, the significantly placed first miracle not only describes a celestial virgin saint but contains a child's death and resurrection. The tear-filled prayers of the father to virgin Foy and the physical description of bodily resurrection are both put into verse heavily borrowed from the *Aeneid,* Boethius, Venantius Fortunatus, and Ovid. In *Prosimetrum,* commenting on this narrative, Bernhard Pabst observes: "The metric form not only serves to emphasize the miracle; the abrupt change from prose to verse also points to the turn of fate, the sudden introduction of incomprehensible events; the swift beat of the hexameters symbolizes at the same time the heightened tempo of the action of the events following in rapid succession." [46]

Pabst points out that Bernard's few examples of verse are employed for grotesque scenes, whereas the verse in book 4 is used for praise and prayers to Foy and other saints. For example, in book 4 verse in apostrophes to Bishop Front of Périgueux frames a miracle narrative in which a citizen of Périgueux came to Conques to ask Foy for help:

Great bishop Front, you rightly deserve to be called
The splendor and leading light of all Aquitaine.
Apostle, follower of Peter, the first known
To carry your teacher's lessons to western soil,
When you spoke, doctrines of holy law radiated from you,
Doctrines that emptied pagan temples and illumined holy churches.
In this little book that spreads the holy virgin's glory to the whole world,
It is proper that your distinguished name be included.
For you, potent with miracles and visible through signs,
Deigned to ennoble it with your own gift.
You demonstrate that your home is known to be
A place that the holy virgin illumines with her goodness (4.15 [4.16]).

As in the miracle-trick cure of the herniated warrior, this chapter opens with a poem of praise in the high style. First Bishop Front is celebrated for his learning and his role in the conversion of Aquitaine through "doctrines of holy law." But Front is then deftly subordinated to the fame of the holy virgin Foy.

After this poem in elevated diction, the prose miracle narrative about a blind widow employs the lower grotesque register. The widow's blindness was cured when

a boy led her by the hand to the holy virgin's abbey church, and there she soaked the dust with streams of tears. But, wondrous to see! and contrary to nature, her tears turned to blood, which flowed down in waves and lay in red clots on the ground. After this gush of blood stopped, a tiny spark of light gradually began to light her eyes and she distinguished the shapes of things inside the church.

The references to dust as well as blood clots signal the grotesque mode. However, the prose narrative in the low Virgilian mode concludes with another poem celebrating God and Sainte Foy.

The literary display of this brief miracle entry seems excessive. It is also highly reflexive of hagiographic composition, since both the first poem and the second poem mention the book. The first poem describes "this little book that spreads the holy virgin's glory to the whole world," and the second poem celebrates bishop Front:

as topaz is well set in reddish-yellow gold,
so mention of you gleams in this *Panaretos*.

The effect of this celebratory sandwich is that the miraculous events seem less important than the project of writing florid poetry to be recorded in Foy's *Panaretos*. The chapter becomes a demonstration of stylistic variation. Chapters like this in book 4 exhibit mannerist style, taking the writing of hagiography to an artificial extreme of experimentation with the genre.[47]

The monk-continuators of books 3 and 4 claim to continue Bernard's work but actually enact a reappropriation and a revisioning of what the *Liber* means. The resulting collection of miracles is now more firmly tied to monastic ideologies and centered on Conques as the magnet toward which cult activities are properly and ultimately directed. Monastic themes found in these narratives include descriptions of ritual actions, the bringing of artifacts as testimonials, fulfilling vows, as well as acts that express acknowledgment of Foy's ownership of property. All cult activities flow toward or from the ritual center, Conques monastery. Perhaps most significantly, the literary flourishes these monk-authors proudly exhibit in their accounts of Foy's miracles serve the corporate task of celebrating the fame of their patron saint and thus elevate the status of the cult at Conques.

4 LATE MIRACLE NARRATIVES

 The last chapter of book 4 of the *Liber miraculorum sancte Fidis* ends with a statement whose tensions condition the entire project of redacting Sainte Foy's miracles:

Thanks to divine grace, a very splendid accumulation of so many miracles has been spread over the whole world through the outstanding merits of Christ's most glorious virgin and martyr, the wondrous Sainte Foy. Now their very number warns against continuing this book. It is not that there is a dearth of miracles, for immense heaps of them are always piling up. Rather it is so that those that are not included in this volume might be prepared more fully in a third, if by chance our tender age should provide enough time to relate them.

The central assertion that Sainte Foy continues to work miracles is a leitmotif of the monk-continuators. For example, in 4.7 an account of a warrior freed from his fetters opens with the statement: "There are so many miracles springing up everywhere through the whole world that writing them could have kept even the learned Jerome occupied. We have no choice but to skip over many thousands and attend to rendering in writing only those whose witnesses experienced them either by sense or by sight." The monks understand that if Foy is to function as a universal saint, it is crucial that her powers be unlimited. Since miracles continue to occur, narratives will continue to be written. For the monks, the *Liber miraculorum* of necessity could not reach closure. Further, the need to select some miracles to be rendered in polished prose indicates that there was no conception of a fixed body of narratives that constituted *the* miracles of Sainte Foy. What was written was only a subset of what Foy had done or might do.

On the other hand, the monks' project demands that they gain some kind of control over their material, as they repeatedly emphasize in their writing. They worry about sequence; they defend the decision to write succinctly rather than at length; they justify their choices among the miracles; and they work toward the unattainable goal of closure. This is especially clear in the lengthy introduction to 4.24 (4.29), which defends the narrative as the closing chapter of book 4:

> Putting it here seems to be the right way to complete the sequence of the preceding miracles. Just as a boundary stone establishes the limits of a field, this miracle completes the second book [of the monk-continuators], which is already long and must now be brought to an end. And even though this miracle occupies the last place in this book it deserves no less praise than the rest, because after heavy sorrow it gave us the joy of an unexpected cure.

In spite of the narrator's marked insistence on closure, only when a manuscript containing narratives of Foy's miracles was made in the scriptorium did the Conques monks actually produce a completed book. They apparently did so not by gathering all the miracle narratives that had been redacted, but by selecting among them. In the strict sense of the words there is no *one* book of Sainte Foy's miracles.

In this chapter we emphasize the openness of the *Liber miraculorum* by discussing miracle narratives written during the second half of the eleventh century. We focus on ways that these later authors changed the patterns and emphases they found in the earlier narratives, and we explore the closure the monks created in specific manuscripts. Governing both tasks was the monastery's goal of disseminating the cult of Sainte Foy.

Although the monastic continuators did not create the third book to which 4.24 (4.29) refers, they did continue to produce miracle narratives. Usually identified by the individual manuscripts in which they survive, these narratives are known as the A group (in the Chartres MS), the V–L group (in manuscripts in the Vatican and in London), and R (in a fragment in Rodez). Composed during the second half of the eleventh century, these narratives (which we call collectively the "late miracle narratives") stand in a very different relation to the cult of Sainte Foy than either Bernard's books 1 and 2 or the monks' books 3 and 4.

Location in the Late Miracles

The narrative voice of the late miracle narratives is once again that of the Conques monastery. Located there, authors enjoy the privilege of observing rituals of thanksgiving at the saint's shrine. The continuator-voice emphasizes this by, for example, concluding A.1 with an eyewitness addendum: "and I also saw afterwards that Raymond came to Conques and offered at the altar of the most blessed Foy the gold coins that his mother had promised for his recovery." A.2 ends with a similar comment: "In the presence of us all and in witness of this miracle, he hung in front of the martyr's tomb the hair shirt he had worn." In A.3, Foy frees some Catalan Christians from their Saracen captors, and the liberated men make their way to Conques to offer the saint the chain that had bound them. A.4 similarly ends at Conques, and with an offering to Foy. Like the monk-continuators of books 3 and 4, the narrating voice of the late miracles clearly writes from Conques, where the monks witness grateful pilgrims coming to the shrine to enact rituals of thanksgiving. In the consistency with which they conclude their narratives with pilgrim rituals at Conques, the monks set out a model of ideal behavior.

During the second half of the eleventh century, the major sources of the Conques monastery's funding shifted from local to international donors, and from peasants and small landholders toward those of high status. As the monastery's holdings became more far-flung and cult sites were founded in the Alsace, England, and Spain, the monks chose to emphasize miracle narratives set in distant locales. Of the fifteen late miracle narratives, only two exorcisms and one healing take place in Conques itself. These on-site miracles resulted from pilgrimages specifically in search of miracles, or quest pilgrimages, and in two of the three cases the petitioner had unsuccessfully visited the shrines of other saints before receiving a miracle at Conques.

This *topos* of international quest reaches its ultimate development in L.5, the case of William of Reims, who was seeking a miraculous cure for partial paralysis: "William made himself a continual exile, and he wandered all through not only Frankish and Germanic, but also Celtic and Belgic and even Ligurian regions. He went on to Italy, turned around, and planned next to see Ireland and all of Spain." On his return trip from Santiago de Compostela, William went to Toulouse, and then to the shrine of Saint Martial in Limoges. There he dreamt of Conques and sought guidance from the townspeople, who strongly advised him to go there. As the narrator puts it, "The celebrated honor of this miracle awaited Sainte Foy, the glorious virgin who was adorned with a singularly privileged martyrdom— *pace* all the other saints." Foy's status relative to other saints is measured by her pan-European reach.

The other late miracle narratives unfold in places like the Middle East (in A.2, the fetters of the freed prisoner were sent "to a church that a brother named Robert had built in honor of Sainte Foy on the bank of the Euphrates River"), Spain, Normandy, and castles and towns in southern

France. All but one of these other late narratives that are complete (the two R miracles are fragmentary) culminate in pilgrimages of thanksgiving to Conques, where the appropriate offerings are made—gold coins, a hair shirt, an immense chain, a golden collar, weighty fetters—and where, as we have noted above, the monastic community functions as witness.

The pattern of a shift in predominance from quest pilgrimages culminating in on-site miracles to distance miracles complemented by pilgrimages of thanksgiving replicates a pattern identified by scholars of other medieval cults. Christian Krötzl finds this shift (which he calls a pan-European phenomenon) in Scandinavian miracle collections and dates its beginning to the thirteenth century, with a great preponderance of distance miracles by the fifteenth.[1] Scholars such as André Vauchez and Pierre-André Sigal associate the shift with the rise of devotional images, arguing that, since they substitute for relics, devotional images in local churches distant from the saint's primary shrine are thought to have miracle-working power; thus they obviate the need for travel to the shrine, and the number of quest pilgrimages drops accordingly. Krötzl, who finds no connection in Scandinavia between distance miracles and devotional images, suggests that the rise of the two phenomena may be parallel rather than interrelated. In the cult of Sainte Foy, we note that the rise in distance miracles takes place in the second half of the eleventh century, well before the general increase in devotional images of saints, so the correlation suggested by Vauchez and Sigal does not hold for Conques. Krötzl attributes the rise in distance miracles to increasing competition among shrines, the need for more impressive miracles to support claims for canonization, increased decorum at shrines, and decreased need to care for the sick at shrines (both of the latter, he thinks, were surely desirable). Assessing the evidence from the Conques miracle collection, we suggest that the pattern may be correlated with the life cycle of a shrine; a rise in distance miracles may have more to do with the maturity of a cult than anything else.

In our view, it is likely that the pattern in which the number of distance miracles increases over the life span of a shrine was created by those who were recording the later miracles and was part of a deliberate strategy to enhance the saint's reputation. Quest pilgrimages resulting in on-site miracles, such as the two exorcism miracles in the V-L group, may have continued to occur but not to be recorded in proportion to their occurrence. In fact exorcism may have been selected for inclusion because it was a relatively new kind of miracle for Sainte Foy, there being only one example of it among all the other miracle narratives. We would argue that the selectivity of the monk-recorders of miracles offers the most likely explanation for the existence of this and other patterns.

Another striking difference between the late miracle narratives and those of books 1 through 4 is in the construction of what is Other or hostile to the monastery and the cult. For Bernard of Angers, as we have seen, Conques itself is ambivalently Other, while the monastery's enemies are within local human society—the skeptics and lawless castellans. Although the monk-continuators also battle local castellans, as part of their work to construct a universal saint they portray a struggle of good and evil between Foy and the cosmic powers of darkness. However, in the later miracle narratives, the monastery has no effective enemies; neither its property nor its monks suffer attack. Castellans attack one another, and Foy heals their wounded or resurrects their dead. These late miracles function as confirmation of the saint's already established reputation. As the author of A.4 reports, "They believed that what they had heard about the holy virgin Foy was true beyond any doubt, and they proclaimed that her miracles completely deserved their renown." What is both Other and hostile to this Christian world is a specific kind of non-Christian, the Saracen.

Saracens are not new occurrences in the late miracles; they make an exceptional appearance in 2.2, a fantastic narrative composed by Bernard of Angers. Many features of this story of Raymond's adventures after being shipwrecked are strongly reminiscent of the *Odyssey*, as are the delays in Raymond's regaining of his position after he returns home. His faithless wife seems to be the literary antitype to Penelope. Robertini points to a number of other parallels, though he does not believe that Bernard invented the story out of whole cloth.[2] What is clear is that Bernard in no way alludes to his source directly; this self-consciously literary writing is for the delectation of the elite reader who has the ability to recognize Bernard's tale as a clever adaptation.

Significantly, some of Bernard's place references in this story lack precision.[3] The pirates who rescue Raymond come from an otherwise unknown "Turlanda." Recognized as a warrior, Raymond fights alongside the pirates until they lose to Berbers, then along with the Berbers until their defeat by Saracens at Cordoba, then with the Saracens until they lose to "Alabites," followers of a pretender to the caliphate. As a captive of the Alabites, Raymond is with them in a battle against Sancho García, count of Castile in 1009, a battle in which Sancho had been paid to fight on the side of Imam Sulayman al-Hakam. Bernard does not refer to this alliance, but only to Sancho's defeat of the Alabites "with the help of Christ omnipotent" and to the number of Christian captives that Sancho freed. Bernard may regret that Christians had been "overrun by barbarians," but his knowledge of the factions within Islamic Spain and of strategic alliances between Muslims and Christians preclude his creation of an Other in the present tense. Far from demonizing Muslims, in 1.12, Bernard actually speaks with admiration of

"Saracen engraving, which is so subtle and ingenious that among our gold-smiths no one tries to imitate it and there isn't even one who has the discernment to appreciate it." For Bernard, the Saracen is simply an exotic, a distant analogue to the Conques region and cult he also portrays as benign "Other."

By contrast, the monk-continuator of book 3 tells of a man captured by "Saracen shepherds" on a return journey from the Holy Land (3.19). They beat and tortured their captive, and attempted to burn his clothing in the hope of finding hidden gold. By diverting the flames, Foy saved the pilgrim's garment: "When the uncouth peasant shepherds saw this, they clapped their hands and burst into gales of laughter. Hoping that the deed had come about by chance rather than through the power of God, they left him there and betook themselves to their sheep pens in the mountains." The shepherds' response suggests that the narrator attributes to them an intuitive appreciation of Sainte Foy's trickery, but his characterization also sharply distinguishes their naiveté from his own sophisticated point of view.

For the monk-continuator who wrote 4.6, spoils taken from the Saracens have become a significant source of monastic wealth. A Saracen, overcome by greed, invades the house of an innocent Christian and subjects him to hideous torture to gain a ransom. The captor is, however, one individual, not all Muslims. By contrast, the authors of the late miracle narratives reduce Muslims to two starkly drawn types—either they are converts to Christianity or they are entirely vicious and evil—and these authors portray Foy as an agent of conversion. Thus in A.2, which is set near Jerusalem, an imprisoned Saracen warrior known as "Iron Man" hears of Foy from a fellow captive and invokes her aid. In return, he promises:

I shall find a church, I shall receive the water of baptism,
And I vow that I shall abandon the world and become a monk,
And that I shall go visit your church clothed in goatskin,
If you deliver me safe and free.

In a different version of the same narrative, the fragmentary R.2, Iron Man had "persecuted Christians by waging war against them," and practiced "pagan superstitions" before his conversion. As further evidence of their evil, in A.3 Saracens capture Christians in order to sell them as slaves: "First the pagans robbed them of their money, and then they began to divide up their prisoners so as to sell them in a distant region." When Foy enables their escape, the narrator explicitly describes the violence enacted against one of their captors: with a lance, one of them "tore the man's face open with a fierce slashing motion. As he was falling to the ground another of the prisoners named Goodson kicked him so hard in the chest that he had no breath to call out. Then the other two fell on him and wrenched away his soul."

The clear distinction between right and wrong signaled by assigning one of the Christian prisoners the name Goodson (Bonus Filius) belies the morally ambiguous situation with regard to slavery at this time. As Olivia Remie Constable notes, "By the eleventh century, the Iberian slave trade had grown more complex, and its commercial aspects became less clear-cut in the face of war. With the new military reality of the reconquest, an increasing number of Christian Spaniards were taken as prisoners of war by Muslims, destined either for ransom or for enslavement. At the same time, we find exactly parallel developments in the Christian slave trade, whereby large numbers of Muslim captives began to appear as slaves in Christian cities." [4] The late miracle narratives give no hint that the outrage of taking Christians as slaves was actually a reciprocal practice.

The latest of the late miracle narratives, those of the V-L group, treat Saracens as the undifferentiated Other. L.1 is the story of two hapless workers in vineyards, Gumfred, "native to the region of Girona," and his friend Raymond, who were captured by Saracens and taken to Tortosa, where they were forced to work at hard labor and imprisoned in inhuman conditions. During one of their "detestable festivals" the Saracens were enjoying "the buffooneries of some actors" and the "guard consoled himself with wine," enabling the prisoners' escape. This narrator has a clearer and more detailed knowledge of interactions between Christians and Muslims in Spain than earlier miracle writers, and he uses that knowledge to create a vicious parody of Islam.

The narrator invokes another stereotypical quality of the Muslim Other in the introduction of L.1: "It is well known that the Spanish Arabs are characterized by such treachery that people everywhere speak of them as bringers of misfortune. By this, people refer not only to the way these Arabs commit every kind of disgraceful act but also to their inclination toward perversity. This is what Horace said about similar people in his day: 'It is bad to let a dog taste the spoils.' In their base nature these Saracens are just like brute animals and they will commit any disgraceful act for filthy profit." Here the author uses a classical tag to legitimate his association of Muslims with perversion. Vilification of Muslims for unrestrained sexuality and male homosexuality, especially pederasty, became an important part of Reconquista rhetoric.[5] As R. I. Moore has shown, during this same period western Christendom was forming itself into a persecuting society, and one of the groups it would single out for persecution was homosexuals.[6] In the semiotic system of the late miracle narratives (which sees Christendom locked in struggle against its enemies) the traits attributed to those enemies slip easily from one group to another. As the cult of Sainte Foy expanded outside of its regional base around Conques, eventually coming into contact with the Muslim world, authors of the miracles exploited this new Other to construct a monolithic Christian identity.

A.1–A.4

The most striking characteristic of the A group of late miracles is a very specific use of *prosimetrum*. As Bernhard Pabst has commented, the prosimetric forms in the A miracles show great unity and consistency; each chapter includes in the midst of its prose narrative a petitioning prayer to the saint that is entirely in metric form.[7] The surrounding prose emphasizes the affective character of these prayers, explicitly noting the anguished and beseeching pleas, cries, tears, and deep sighs that accompany the petitions. Those prayers with a lamenting theme are in elegiac distichs, whereas the Saracen's prayer for conversion (A.2) is in hexameters. One additional metric passage is reminiscent of the way the author of book 4 uses *prosimetrum* for grotesque scenes. It opens with a description of the mother in A.1 whose son has died:

She ripped her clothing and tore her hair,
So wracked with pain that she was speechless, she threw herself to the ground.

In the last four lines of this eight-line passage, the mother voices her anguish that she has outlived her son, and the second use of *prosimetrum* in A.1 is devoted to her prayer, asking Sainte Foy either for her son's resurrection or for her own death. One way to read these prayer poems is to see them as signs of an established and stable cult that is generating ritual behaviors or practices. The prayers inscribed into the A-group miracle narratives can be subdivided into generic and specific parts. For example, A.4 treats the resurrection from the dead of a beloved son. The prayer placed in the mouths of mourners gathered at the funeral, including the grieving parents, begins with an emotionally intense but generic appeal to the saint:

As you shine brightest among the saints in high heaven,
Look upon us crying out to you, virgin Foy.
We believe that you are radiant with virtues and potent with power,
And so we beg your help.

Such a model prayer could have been easily adapted by other petitioners. The metric passage continues, however, in lines that link the prayer to the specific miracle:

We beg you: do what you can, return him for whom we weep, we implore you.
Here are his mother and his mourning father themselves, asking this of you.
Raise him up, alive, whom we know lies dead.

Although the use of prosimetric prayer in the A group suggests a different author than those of books 1 through 4, identifying individual authors
is not our major goal. The composer of these four miracles, whoever he
was, writes within a hagiographic tradition well established at Conques by
the mid eleventh century. What is striking to us are the continuities in the
collection of miracles, as well as the expectation that miracles would continue to be produced. For the collectors of these late miracles, Foy is pre-
eminently a miracle-working saint. As A.4 puts it, the relatives and neighbors of the grieving parents try to persuade them to beg for a miracle of
Sainte Foy, "for they knew that in the wondrousness of her miracles she
excelled all the saints."

Here the author enunciates a conviction he shares with the other authors
of Foy miracle stories and one that justifies his task: "Among the countless
throngs of saints we know that some are of higher merit than others, and
we believe that the most blessed Foy easily stands out as even more remarkable among them all. Our faith affirms this, but not as a personal opinion
based on favoritism; rather it is the great multitude of her miracles that
commends her excellence to us" (A.3). In portraying Foy as the incompa-
rable miracle-working saint these hagiographers authorize their own task.
Though Bernard of Angers's philosophical intellect and clerical training
lead him to use different means than the monk-authors of books 3 and 4 or
the writer of the A group, all of these miracle writers participate in the
ongoing hagiographic project of constructing the cult of Sainte Foy.

The V–L Group

Another distinctive group of miracles that were written at Conques, probably between 1060 and 1080, exhibits the same attention to the hagiographic task. However, their unique style and mode of narration justify
treating them separately; they are called the V–L group. As we noted in the
Introduction, the Bollandists omitted three of them from their grand synthesis of hagiography, the *Acta sanctorum,* due to "particulars and details that
seemed to them strange and inexplicable."[8]

Something of this uniqueness may be seen in the tone with which the
author of L.6 begins one of his resurrection miracles: "Although I follow
the path of our predecessors according to custom, even if my stride is not
equal to theirs, and I rely on the kindness of the illustrious Foy, not only

have I been afflicted by the hypocrisies of my enemies' hatred but because of the slanders they have launched against me I have been hampered in my writing. I hadn't been torn to pieces by the attacks of abusive people until I began to be involved in pursuits like this." This admittedly histrionic tone (also found in L.3, L.4, and L.5) is an indicator of the florid style that this writer (or writers) has adopted for his miracle narratives. A self-consciousness and reflexivity about the hagiographic task are clear from comments such as that in L.4: "Since we are striving to write the outstanding deeds of the outstanding virgin, we must still set about to put the remainder into an appropriate style so that the result may become an example to future generations, an exhortation to those who are well-disposed, a punishment to the spiteful, and for us may it result in a reward."

The "appropriate style" this writer alludes to is one in which a variety of heightening techniques forms a heady brew. Fond of *prosimetrum,* the author or authors of this group of miracles insert verse prayers and petitions to Foy into their prose narratives. They also include a kind of invective, as we have seen, often directed at general groups rather than at specific erring individuals. This unrestrained invective is laced with references to classical authorities, as in L.4 where, railing at "the maliciousness of envious mortals and their minions," the author cites the opinions of Cicero, Augustine, and Solomon.

This love of authoritative quotation is allied to a similar love for aphoristic statement: in L.5, for example, a certain Guy of Reims selected one of his sons to educate for the clergy, but sent him to be a warrior instead. The narrator comments, "The minds of worldly people are always changeable and mutable; Horace spoke truly when he said:

You may drive nature out with might and main,
Nevertheless she will return again.

But more pungent than any of the preceding stylistic traits is the author's use of a source entirely new to Foy's *Liber miraculorum,* the writings of Sidonius Apollinaris, "an antiquarian rhetorician" who displays "a perpetual striving after stylistic effects." [9] In spite of their habit of citing classical, biblical, and early Christian writers by name, the authors of this group of miracles never acknowledge Sidonius's pervasive influence on their language and style. [10] Robertini notes that "the monk seems to have had at his disposal Sidonius's entire epistolary and poetic production," [11] and it seems that we can attribute a large part of the baroque style in the V-L miracles to the influence of Sidonius.

One characteristic of Sidonius's style that the author or authors of V-L

imitated is what C. E. Stevens calls Sidonius's "laboured verbal antithe-
ses."[12] Stevens comments dryly, "As a writer he pursued the cult of antithesis and paronomasia farther than one would have believed it possible."[13]
Although the V-L group of miracles draws on the same repertoire of
classical authors as many of the preceding miracle writers, it is clearly the
Sidonian influence that sets the style of L and V apart.

Like many of the miracle writers, the author of V.1 is reflexive about his
hagiographic task: "We have almost fulfilled our purpose in writing this
work and we intend to bring it to a conclusion right away." However, he
picks up Sidonian vocabulary, which gives his description an unexpected
twist: "Therefore we must disregard the ill-will of this decadent age *(nostri
seronati)* we live in, because our heart clings fervently *(heret cordicitus)* to these
words from Holy Scripture: 'Vengeance belongs to Me, and I will repay.'"[14]

As in previous monk-authors, the voice here is that of the Conques
monastery, for whose perpetuation and glory this author produces his miracle stories. The narrator voice in this group, in common with most other
monk-authors of Foy's miracles, posits Conques itself as the symbolic center
of the cult and models a pilgrimage to Conques for healing by the saint or
thanksgiving to her. At the end of V.2 the narrator concludes in the monastic voice: "As for us, we happily praised the King of Glory, Who never
stops glorifying His own handmaiden with so many miracles that even
while I write I am sure that she lingers in our village." A brief miracle
narrative in which a girl possessed by a demon is brought to Conques
for her cure exploits the Sidonian style of punning and other wordplay
throughout. For example, the girl's parents were "secure in their faith,"
a pun on the saint's name. The celestial doctor we have already seen in
books 3 and 4 is the subject of wordplay: "Celesti medicine medicamen-
tum relinquunt."[15] In V.3, Foy is ostensibly the holy virgin-martyr, bride
of Christ, and celestial doctor that previous monk-authors have also described. The V-L group author, however, elaborates his description of Foy
in new directions; for him she is "Lady" *(Domina)* of the town of Conques
and he doesn't hesitate to pun wildly on her name: "donec fida fides fiat
Fidei" ("until there should be confident faith in Faith").[16]

Of all the post-Bernardian miracles discussed, the narrative voice of the
V-L group most resembles that of Bernard of Angers. Like Bernard, the
narrator appears at times to stand both inside and outside the Conques monastic point of view. So, although the conclusions to the narratives almost
always reinforce the author's ideological location at the Conques monastery, other, often introductory, passages give us a sense of an author writing
to readers who do not know very much about the cult or who may be
puzzled by or even unsympathetic to his efforts. In V.1, for example, a lu-

natic peasant, his arms tightly bound, is taken to Conques. In the middle of his narrative the author inserts a small disquisition: "It is necessary to note that here the faithful revere Foy not out of a general esteem for religion; rather, this holy virgin of Christ is a focus of popular devotion due to her miracles." This explanation sounds very much like Bernard of Angers addressing his elite readers back in northern France who do not fully understand the strange southern cult. At the same time, the narrator of this miracle seems totally familiar with the steep gorges of the valley of the Dourdou River where Conques is located, but like Bernard seems to be recounting the local landscape color for outsiders. Unlike most of the other monk-continuators, this author does not always seem to be writing to readers who are part of the same interpretive community.

Furthermore, the position of this narrative voice within hagiographic discourse about Foy resembles Bernard's more than that of his fellow monk-authors. Like Bernard, the author or authors of the V-L group remains somewhat detached from his miraculous materials, a detachment that leads to the insertion of many explanations and moralizations. For example, the narrator first reports that the lunatic peasant was "raving wildly and running all over the place, endangering his life by the way he dashed along steep mountain ridges." He then interjects the comment: "How sad it is that the Enemy of humankind has dominion over us again and again! And while this Enemy befriends the faithless, he lures the minds of the good into danger of eternal death." The solution to this poor peasant's plight is that his mother offers the gift of a donkey to Foy, as a result of which "the invading demon was put to flight and the man was completely cured."

The narrative does not conclude, as early monk-continuators had, with closure at the shrine at Conques and communal celebration of Foy's power. Rather our narrator ends with a question to his readers: "How strange! What happened to him?" With a kind of analogical pun he concludes, "She was not in doubt about giving a stupid animal, by means of which a more stupid one would be freed from the most stupid of all." This narrative move has clear affinities with Bernard's subversive questions about the ontological status of the little hammer back in 1.32. Like Bernard's philosophical questions—"But what a wondrous thing! Where do you think Sainte Foy got a physical hammer?"—this kind of conclusion puts the focus on the narrator's inquiring mind rather than on the cult shrine at Conques and ritually appropriate behaviors.

Even where the recipient of a miracle performs the ritually appropriate action of returning to Conques to tell the story and render thanks to Foy, this narrator takes up a very Bernardian motif not shared by other monk-continuators—that is, the need to provide signs for belief. In V.3, for example, an arrow lodged in the skull of a warrior named Mathfred is ejected through Sainte Foy's intervention, and Mathfred then enacts the expected pilgrimage to the shrine at Conques, participates in the celebration, and "as a sign of the miracle *[signo fidei]* the arrow was suspended from the paneled ceiling." Typically in other monk-continuators, the fetters of released prisoners or another gift are deposited at the shrine, but these offerings are never explicitly identified as a sign of the miracle. In L.6 as well, the narrator articulates his conclusion as a debate between doubters and believers. A certain resurrected Bernard

took seriously the general opinion that he should go quickly to Conques, give her his verbal thanks, and offer her the linen cloth that had shrouded his dead body and the hand-covers that we call *guantos* in the peasant language. For there may have been ill-will on the part of envious people who were, as so often is the case, endeavoring to disparage this outstanding miracle; why they should denigrate everything I don't understand, for I know of no better way to establish the truth of a miracle for all and to glorify God Who reigns forever.

I avow truly that Bernard came here and that I and others saw him and wondered at the miracle. Who has the ability to give worthy utterance to the praises of this miracle when he sees such great things worked through Sainte Foy? But to dispell any disbelief, the winding-sheet hangs in front of the holy image as a sign of the miracle *[signum fidei]* to this day.

Like Bernard of Angers, this author seizes opportunities to interrogate his own materials and gives reader-responses to them. As a result, his texts have both an autobiographical and a philosophical cast similar to Bernard's.

We also see the narrator voice negotiating interpretations of supernatural events and guiding readers' opinions. In L.1, the story about how Sainte Foy freed Gumfred and Raymond, two peasants, Gumfred knew enough to make the appropriate ritual response; that is, he "decided to bring his praises to Sainte Foy as best he could," and the narrator tells us that "when he came here we saw him ourselves and we rejoiced." But the narrative does not end with this; it goes into a semi-Bernardian mode of explanation: "As for Raymond, with whom he had escaped, Gumfred said that he didn't know what had happened to him. But since Foy can be summoned even by infidels, surely the sacred virgin delivered her devotee once and for all and didn't allow him to become entangled in such a situation." Earlier monk-continuators might have left the plot thread of the absent Raymond dangling, but the narrator of V–L must pull the loose end into his didactic frame.

Since it seems reasonable to assume that the writer or writers of the V–L group were familiar with Bernard's narratives, and this group of miracles is found in manuscript compendia that contain selections of miracles from books 1 through 4, it is possible that the V-L group was constructed to be intertextual with Bernard of Angers. However, another explanation seems to us even more plausible. As we argued in chapter 1, many of the characteristics of Bernard's narrative style might be attributed to his position at the end of the early Middle Ages. Put differently, his early eleventh-century liminality is poised between the old and an emerging medieval paradigm. Such a cultural location produces in Bernard's work an acute reflexivity— an awareness of himself as writer and a playfulness with regard to the hagiographic traditions he employs. Although not as developed and consistent in the V-L miracle texts, a similar self-conscious manipulation of traditional materials (in this case Foy cult materials) seems to be occurring. The narrative persona of the V-L author displays an interesting combination of the Bernardian persona and the communal monastic persona.

We have noted that the subjects of the later miracle stories are entirely conventional: there are prisoners to be liberated, wounded warriors who must be healed, demons to be expelled, and dead to be resurrected by Foy. All of these feats are consistent with the miracle narratives that were produced by the monastery at Conques after the death of Bernard of Angers. Nevertheless, the conventionality of the subject matter does not lead to its conventional treatment. At the beginning of L.4, after a lengthy reflection upon his hagiographic task which we have already discussed, the narrator signals his engagement with a conventional type of Foy miracle, the imprisoned warrior. Like many of the earlier and even Bernardian monastic miracles, this story is set in the Rouergue near the cult site of Foy's shrine, where Bego and Arnold are imprisoned in the castle of Montmurat. Eventually the prisoners begin to pray to Foy "incessantly," appropriately "accompanied by floods of tears." The theme of nonstop emotional petitioning recurs throughout the Foy miracle corpus; "constant prayers and insistent begging" represent the mode in which prisoners were expected to call on the saint for liberation. The anticipated outcome is an appearance of Foy, "the glorious virgin." As in a typical miracle vision, Foy outlines a plan that the petitioner must follow to be freed. With the exception of the self-centered introduction, to this point the miracle narrative follows entirely conventional lines.

Into this traditional liberation-of-prisoners miracle, however, the V-L author inserts, quite surprisingly, an element totally idiosyncratic and unique. It turns out that Foy's plan centers on a decoy operation; the castle dwellers will be distracted by the arrival of some local actors, giving the prisoners an opportunity to escape. When the itinerant actors arrived to spend the night at the castle, they unsheathed their swords and "play-acting, they ran about all around striking wildly here and there and shouting madly, 'Quick, get out of here, degenerates! Flee, lazy bones! Clear off, you miserable creatures! The lord has entrusted your property to us!'" The prisoners recognized an element of Foy's plan; "then they moved quickly to take advantage of the disturbance and busily did as they had been instructed from heaven, with no fear at all of recapture or injury." The rest of the escape goes as divinely planned and would read like a typical prisoner-release miracle were it not for the anomalous actor episode that has been incongruously thrust into it.

The source of the actors' descriptions seems to be four separate sections from the *Epistles* of Sidonius: First, there is their characterization as "mimici sales." [17] The second source is the justification for omitting their names: "If their buffooneries are preserved anywhere, then posterity will not escape from discussing their names." [18] Third, we find the generalization about their tendency to lapse into playacting: "for this is typical of such people, among whom serious business is always on holiday." [19] And, finally, there is the opening line of their act: "Get out of here, degenerates!" [20] Perhaps the inspiration for including this profession was the blind Guibert's activity as *jongleur,* of which Bernard of Angers in book 1 was vocally scornful and disparaging.

This monk-author treatment of the actors as a *topos* is somewhat at odds with the miracle context; although the actors are certainly Foy's agents in distracting the castle dwellers and thus enabling the escape, the narrator's gratuitous statements denigrating actors are unrelated either to the plot or to the moral point. The imported words from Sidonius take the narrator off in a direction that in fact undercuts the conventional account of a miracle, and this narrator, unlike Bernard, does not recognize the conceptual conflicts. For example, why would Foy make use of such reprobates? The set piece from Sidonius that has been adopted as a plot device is not integrated with the conventional miracle structure, but appears to have been added to spice up what perhaps was perceived as too predictable a narrative.

The author of L.6 also takes the by-now-conventional verse prayer to Foy and transforms it by interjecting narrative reflexivity. After acknowledging the "path of my predecessors according to custom"—that is, other Foy hagiographers—he situates himself as a writer and Foy as a miracle worker subjected to slander. This is reminiscent of Bernard's hyper-awareness of critique of his project (1.7). The author of L.6 follows the general structure of four beginning lines that offer generic praise to Foy:

You who are potent with consummate power and gleaming with goodness,
Always our greatest glory, our honor, our aid, our hope,

Our light, our remedy, our salvation, watching over us all our days,
Virgin Foy, remember my humble prayers.

And then, as in other poems to Foy, the petitioner becomes specific to an individual situation. But here the petitioner is not asking for a miraculous cure of liberation; rather he seeks her support in the difficult profession of miracle writer:

Grant me the ability to scorn the spiteful hearts of men who rant at me,
And to perceive truth, so that it may always grow.
Repress the deceitful, curb the habits of the enemy,
Lest he conquer the one who proclaims your praises.
I am often tormented by evils; may your solicitude always be vigorous against them
And help me to ascend to the starry kingdom with you.

That the narrator is fully aware of his unusual approach to the prosimetric form is indicated by his immediately succeeding comments: "But since we take the approach of frequently mixing grievance with praises for such a great virgin, perhaps we may seem to stray from the intended plan. That's why it seems appropriate that the writer appointed to this task should have no regard at all for the nonsensical histrionics of our critics." The authors of the V–L group appear to be using the Sidonian and other borrowings to invigorate a hagiographic tradition that had become boringly predictable.

The V–L group deliberately and very self-consciously exaggerates the celestial virgin of the monastic continuators into the ultimate saint of saints. L.3 offers a progessive intensification in the portrait of Foy. At the beginning of the narrative, Robert, count of Rouergue, decides to "seek out the unparalleled medicine of the unparalleled virgin," and, in exchange for a cure, he promises to Foy the church called Tanavelle in the Auvergne. When his prayer is answered, the monks take their reliquary statue on procession to the church at Tanavelle to mark Foy's and the monastery's possession of the property. The narrator interrupts his account of the procession, which attracted hordes of people in need of cures, with a long panegyric to Foy, claiming that she is the equal of Peter and Paul. "She is extolled with praise fit for angels, she performs miracles in the manner of the apostles, she is adorned with the glory of the martyrs, she participates fully in the great joyfulness of the confessors, and she is among the company of the virgins, with whom she delights in the vision of the Lamb." The narrator also asserts that there is no region on earth where her miracles are unknown.

At this point in the narrative he acknowledges his digression and says he will return to his description of the procession. Before he has narrated much, however, he again digresses to amplify his praise of Foy. Where before he had compared her to Peter and Paul as an equal, now he must extol her as superior to them. He sets the tone with a quotation from Sidonius: "Behold, old ways, oppose this new power if you please" (*Carmina* 2, 299). And continues, "Apostle of great power, I ask you, who is like our virgin in glory, excepting those of your rank? This young girl, our virgin, spreads before us greater works than yours. Great God works miracles for her not by the shadow of the body and, even better, not by a word or the laying on of hands, nor by a belt as Paul is believed to have done. But when she is called on from far away by name only, the presence of her blessing is felt instantly." Here the narrator realizes that he has perhaps gone too far, magnifying Foy over other saints, so he curtails his effusiveness with the comment: "We have an abundance of other examples, but we don't want to criticize these persons with such great powers any further, persons to whom we believe that power over heaven and earth has been granted, lest we be called detractors of the saints, which we are not."

After completing his brief narrative of a miracle worked on the procession—a decrepit old man's mobility is restored so that he is able to "carry the holy virgin's reliquary with his aged hands"—the narrator comments on the emotional response of all witnesses to this miracle and concludes by returning to his celebration of Foy: "And they are eager to glorify God, Who is wondrous in His saints and glorious in His works, Who so magnifies Sainte Foy that her reputation spreads to the four corners of the three-part earth." The rhetoric of this miracle carries to an unprecedented extreme the motif initiated by the first miracle of book 3, that of the expansion of the cult of Foy, from a local to an international phenomenon. This text thus participates in the quality of exaggeration and self-consciousness about writing within an overly familiar tradition that we see as characteristic of the late miracle narratives.

5 THE SOCIAL SEMIOTICS OF THE *LIBER MIRACULORUM*

 The *Liber miraculorum sancte Fidis* creates the impression of a realistic and well-rounded world centering on the cult of Sainte Foy at Conques. As we have argued, however, this carefully constructed portrait omits significant features of the historical eleventh century and can be ideologically deciphered. For example, the world of the *Liber miraculorum* contains virtually no ecclesiastical structures except the monastery of Conques itself. Where are the pope and the rest of the church hierarchy? Or female monastics? Or other monasteries? We might note, in particular, that the rival monastery at Figeac, which was involved in a struggle with Conques for dominance, is curiously absent from the text.[1] When priests are mentioned, they appear as free agents; there is no parish structure in which they have duties to lay people. In this text, virtually all the religious tasks in the region are performed by the Conques monastery.

Furthermore, most of the actual centuries-long history of the Conques monastery has been erased.[2] In the myth-world of the *Liber* there are only two periods in monastic history: before and after the first miracle in which Foy restored Guibert's eyes (1.1). For the purposes of the *Liber miraculorum,* then, Conques has no history before the introduction of the miracle-working saint, as the opening to 1.17 shows: "Long ago the holy martyr's body was secretly carried away from the city of Agen and brought to Conques by two monks. After that Sainte Foy's name prevailed there because of her more numerous miracles. Finally, in our own time, after the renown of the great miracle worked for Guibert . . . flew across the whole of Europe, many of the faithful made over their own manors and many other pious gifts to Sainte Foy by the authority of their wills." Gimon the warrior-monk and favorite of Sainte Foy who lived in the ancient pre-Guibert days is the only developed character from that period. Charlemagne's supposed patronage predates Conques's presumed acquisition of Foy's relics, but the text works to obscure this by claiming that he donated the reliquary containing a piece of Sainte Foy's skull that always accompanied Foy's reliquary-statue when it was carried in procession (2.4). Other historical events, past or present, are simply omitted from the account.

Theological issues of the day are largely absent as well. There is no soteriology, that is, no explicit theory of salvation. There are no heretics (in the usual understanding of the term) and no Jews, although there are "unbelievers," who are mostly represented as crude, bad-tempered ignoramuses. The religious "facts" included in the narratives all have to do with the power and status of the Conques monastery and its patron saint.

Social information is also selected with reference to monastic and cult concerns. The cult agendas at this period have no use for antifeminist rhetoric. Women are never seducers of men in these stories; in fact, the evil characters are usually the men. The text also evinces virtually no interest in the politics of marriage and the family for its own sake. There is no attention to issues of parental conduct, even when in some stories the families are actually abusive to or neglectful of their children. Social institutions other than the monastery are absent.

How, then, can we explain the omissions in the *Liber miraculorum sancte Fidis*? Our fundamental approach to these miracle texts has been to see them as parts of various ideological systems. The insight of theoretical structuralism and semiotics was that any individual part takes its meaning from its relationship to other parts within a structure.[3] The *Liber miraculorum* as a whole may be seen as a system of signs organized by its hagiographic mission, while subsets of the miracles have their own semiotic systems that differ somewhat from each other. What we might see as omissions represent possibilities that do not "fit" within a given structure of meaning.

The entire collection of Sainte Foy's miracles is dedicated to promoting the cult of this saint and, by implication, the fortunes of the Conques monastery. Within the broad framework, however, slightly different semiotic subsystems are employed to this end. The overall hagiographic goal constrains the decisions that are made within any individual miracle narrative, since these narratives celebrate Foy's omnipotence and make every effort to demonstrate the necessity of recognizing the cult center at Conques through concrete economic donations.[4] Aspects of the history of the monastery that do not concern the cult of the miracle-working saint are erased because the overriding function of the collection is the promulgation of this definition of the cult.

The Conques monastery under the patronage of Sainte Foy, who has direct access to God, holds the position of paramount authority in its world. Within this semiotic system no room exists for any other authority; thus, no ecclesiastical institutions that might rival Conques's power can be represented. Bishops appear only occasionally in the miracle narratives. There is the evil bishop Bego (2.5); and there is also Arnald, bishop of Rodez, who called a council to which saints' relics from the diocese were to be brought (1.28; 4.11), but the *Liber* gives no information at all about the council's actions. Rather, the gathering of saints' relics provides an opportunity to demonstrate that Foy's healing powers exceed those of her regional rivals. Abbots of other monasteries appear only to acknowledge Foy's preeminence; for example, visions in which Foy demanded the golden doves belonging to Bernard, abbot of Beaulieu, forced him to yield them: "Finally the reluctant man was compelled to deliver the golden doves, just as though they had only been entrusted to him for safekeeping" (1.16). There is just space for the individual adherent to fall in line with the only hierarchy represented—from the monastery to Foy to God.[5]

Heretics as officially defined presuppose belief in a universal Church, whereas the church of the *Liber* is concretely located in the monastery at Conques or in other places specifically associated with Foy's divine power. The Catholic Church's definition of "heretic" is someone "whose views were 'chosen by human perception, contrary to holy scripture, publicly avowed and obstinately defended.'"[6] In the *Liber miraculorum,* however, a heretic is someone who attacks Foy—that is the primary way the word is used—and the only disbelief dramatized is disbelief in Foy's power. The narrative of 4.21 (4.23) demonstrates that the authors of these miracle texts deliberately chose to avoid using the idea of heretic in its wider theological sense. In the story, a monk builds a crude oratory "filled with heavenly power," but one of the passing peasants "who had been led to take the path of error" denigrates the place, saying "I think you would be as likely to get salvation from a doghouse!"[7] The narrator's comments correctly employ the official view of heresy as deliberately chosen disbelief in theological dogma:

The wretch had not understood that divine glory flourished there because it had been made holy by its dedication and because the holy virgin was invoked there. It seems that he was like those heretics who don't understand the mystery of spiritual grace, so they deny that the water in the baptismal font is able to change its natural properties and assert that it always stays exactly the same. They need to know and understand that there are two aspects to the sacrament of baptism—the water in the baptismal font and sanctification—and it is when they are conjoined that the sacrament is imbued with power. And in the same way, out of a material building and a spiritual sacrament one body is made in the edifice of holy Mother Church.

However, the real heresy of this peasant is to doubt that Foy's power resided in this small church. Foy's punishment takes the form of depriving the "heretic" of his reason, but, after his friends carry him into the church and pray for him, "Sainte Foy's ready kindness" heals him. "And just as she had cast this haughty and proud man down to the depths, so now in turn she raised him, lying humbled before her, back to his erect stature." Lest the reader miss the point that the man's sin was slandering Foy, the concluding line adds, "After they had seen this, all who lived around there began to give the place more reverence, and they believed without a doubt that Sainte Foy's power flourished there."

Our point is not that the writers of this miracle collection *could not* have used the conventional definition of a heretic; obviously, the composer of this story fully understands the usual sense of the term. We argue that the writers knowingly *chose* not to employ the term in that broader theological way since the aim of the collection was to celebrate Sainte Foy. To be heretical in this text means to deny *this* saint's power and preeminence, rather than to doubt church dogma in general.[8]

Within the framework of the whole *Liber miraculorum,* we have delineated several subsystems. Our approach to these texts thus differs from a more traditional literary-historical approach in that, as we have shown through our analyses, the various subsections of the *Liber miraculorum* do not share one uniform set of literary techniques because their rhetorical agendas differed. Even a sophisticated literary scholar like Joaquín Pizarro seeks to establish a new style of narrative that he finds in all early medieval historical genres, a term that for him "covers not only histories and chronicles but also biographies, saints' lives, accounts of miracles and relics, and other ecclesiastical genres."[9] Pizarro argues that "the new style shared by these narrators contrasts clearly with the classical model, and its features, presumably present in the other narrative genres of the period, continue to characterize narrative literature long after 1000."[10] By attending to the ideology of rhetoric we have been able to perceive differences of technique and thematic emphasis in texts written within both the same genre and the same century. In this chapter we analyze the differences in the representation of gender, power, morality, and the body among the compositional clusters in the *Liber miraculorum.*

Gender Systems

It is one of the puzzles of this text that the monastic ideology articulated in the *Liber miraculorum* is not misogynistic. Books 3 and 4, as well as the later miracle narratives, share this surprising lack of hostility to women with Bernard of Angers's books 1 and 2. With very few exceptions, the entire text avoids what has been construed as the pervasive denigration of women in clerical culture.[11] Why might this be so? We would suggest the answer is not that the authors of the text are somehow innocent of the discourses of antifeminism, but rather that the sign of the female has other roles to play in the semiotic systems of the *Liber miraculorum*.

The miracle account entitled "How a Woman Who Wickedly Acted against Sainte Foy Perished through a Miracle" (3.16) shows that the writer is well aware of clerical antifeminism. This chapter describes a noblewoman who "obsessively coveted the holy martyr's lands that adjoined her own fields." The narrator, commenting on her motivation, says she acted as she did "either because womankind is always avaricious—as is written in books—or more likely because she was led on by a demon." We note that the narrator ascribes the misogynistic generalization, "womankind is always avaricious," to books; that is, to the clerical tradition. In this case, however, the monk-author rejects the misogynistic trope in favor of the explanation that the woman was misled by a demon. The absence of antifeminism is a highly significant characteristic of this entire miracle collection, one requiring elucidation.

Although none of the miracle books purveys a misogynist attitude, we see differences in gender as symbolic system between the Bernardian books and subsequent miracle narratives, differences that we connect to the historical ideologies Bernard structures into his text. Bernard's early-eleventh-century miracle stories construct a gender system in which the female stands in a mediating position between positive and negative male possibilities. For Bernard, the monastic vocation is the positive pole, whereas he usually construes the military male negatively.[12]

Recent historians have described the early eleventh century as a formative period in building the institutional power of monasticism over the secular nobility, especially through the Peace of God movement, the name given to the attempts by churchmen to provide ideologies that would contain the violence of the warrior class.[13] The *Liber miraculorum* participates ideologically in building the Conques monastery's political and economic power as against the local castellans,[14] and Bernard's texts portray the life of the monks as the preferred alternative to the violence of lay male existence. Within this dichotomous structure of warriors against the monastery, noble women function as the mediators. These wives are usually portrayed as the allies of the monastery, charged with conveying monastic norms to their husbands, the local castellans.

As Sharon Farmer has argued, these exemplary wives were also being encouraged to persuade their husbands to donate property to the monastery:

Eleventh- and twelfth-century monks who wrote about influential wives wrote from experience. In their dealings with noble patrons, monks encountered women who were favorably inclined towards religious institutions and who developed means of exercising economic influence in behalf of those institutions, despite a system in which men officially controlled and inherited property. Responding to and indeed attempting to encourage and elaborate such forms of behavior on the part of women, monastic authors developed an image of the good matron, the pious wife.

Farmer concludes that, as a result of their need to engage wives as allies, "the monks provided surprisingly positive assessments of characteristics otherwise frequently associated in negative ways with femininity, and with Eve."[15] Farmer thus historicizes a phenomenon that we read as a feature of Bernard's strong ideological structure in which monastic values stand in opposition to the values of the warrior class.[16] Given the semiotic need to present women of the upper class as enablers of monastic ambitions, there is no place in this semiotic system for females as seducers of men or rivals of monks.[17]

The important role of the female in supporting monasticism is illustrated in the story of one of the exemplary figures in Bernard's collection (1.2). In this narrative the famous warrior Gerbert, who receives new eyeballs from Foy in a spectacular healing miracle, enacts the choice between monasticism and the warrior life as well. After his healing and, despite some ambivalence, Gerbert becomes a monk at Conques. However, he soon attempts to return to his former life as a warrior:

At last, he was persuaded by the illustrious Theotberga, wife of Count Pons, that if he ever wished to become well he should neither abandon Sainte Foy nor refuse the yoke of her service. "Because it is evident," she said [to him], "that Sainte Foy did not work such a great miracle for you so that you could return to the turbulence of a fighting man's worldly life where you will also be in danger, but so that you would cling to her as a permanent member of her household and in this way be saved and rise to the gate of perpetual glory." After he had been so strongly rebuked by the wise matron and so beneficially confirmed in his faith, Gerbert completely abandoned his resistance and made no further efforts to thwart divine will. Therefore he serves God and his saint now in that very monastery with the most devoted obedience, content with a monk's daily allowance of food. He is a man of calm character and a simple way of life, measured by our times and our ways of doing things.

In addition to advising the wavering warrior turned monk, a typical upper-class woman of the miracle stories in books 1 and 2 also offers sound advice to her husband when he is bent on hostile or self-destructive acts. Women are far more likely to recognize Foy's power than their husbands are, and they attempt to contain their husbands' excessive violence through monastic rituals associated with the saint. In general, women are authoritative speakers and voices of wisdom. A good example of this female role occurs in the story of the castellan Hugh, lord of Cassagnes near Conques, who is married to a wise woman, Senegund (1.6). A misguided and violent male, Hugh orders his servants to steal wine that the monks have stored two miles from his castle. In this story it is the predatory males who are grotesquely punished, and Hugh's violence is textually contrasted to his wife's wisdom: she "opposed the crime, calling it an outrage, a detestable deed. The good woman urged him not . . . to touch the consecrated wine of the monks, for fear that the condemnation of death would come suddenly, and that he would perish, struck down by the holy virgin's wrath. Far from complying, the savage unleashed his blind greed, and in a fit of wild rage struck her with his fists." Hugh's wife Senegund functions as a spokesperson for the rules and rituals of the cult, through which she saves her husband. Although Hugh lay in a coma for three months, "he recovered through the merits of his good wife." Bernard of Angers remarks, "I believe that this faithful woman brought her unjust husband back to life by urging him to visit the virgin's holy shrine. This time he trusted in her advice. Soon he went to the saint to give his best thanks, and after he returned he was no longer rebellious."

Like church authorities of the early eleventh century, Bernard in his miracle texts is concerned with the problem of secular male violence, and in this ideological context the female represents order, right judgment, and ultimately, of course, the reinforcement of monastic authority. Bernard of Angers's two books of miracles, written between 1010 and 1020, consistently articulate this gender system in which noble women, who function as positive agents on behalf of monastic values, are juxtaposed with lay males who who violently threaten the Church's power. In these years the Peace of God movement, based on a similar ideology, was at its height. The semiotic system of Bernard of Angers's narratives thus seems ideologically related to its historical moment.

One of the most engaging of these gender-ideology miracles (2.6) concerns the sister of the Duke of Normandy, Lady Beatrice, who was at the time married to Lord Ebalus.[18] Pilgrims on the way to Foy's shrine were taken captive by a member of Ebalus's retinue named Gozbert. Bernard the narrator tells us that Gozbert "was a cleric, but only in name; by employment he was a secular fighting man," a description that encapsulates the antagonism between the Church and the warrior class. Lady Beatrice, who was in charge of the castle of Turenne at the time, ordered Gozbert to release the pilgrims, and he did, with the exception of one man named Peter, whom he held and tortured. After Foy's miraculous intervention freed the prisoner, the narrative does not end as the narratives of the continuators usually do—praising Foy's power for a typical miracle of prisoner release. Rather, the author Bernard brings himself into the narrative as well as highlighting the role of Lady Beatrice by mentioning that she gave the pilgrim Peter a protective escort beyond the territories of her castle. Bernard concludes by saying that he encountered Beatrice "almost a year and a half after my second return from Conques" when business affairs took him to the court of William, count of Poitiers. There Bernard questioned her about the miracle and noted the agreement of her version of events with that of the monks at Conques. Bernard, as representative of the clerical class and hagiographer of Foy, thus celebrates Beatrice's role in supporting the pilgrimage cult and stigmatizes the male warrior class for antagonism to the Church.

The monk-continuators of books 3 and 4 maintain a non-stigmatizing view of women, but it is noteworthy that in their narratives there are almost no noble women playing the role of cult patroness in opposition to their misguided husbands. Although Goteline of 3.1 is an aristocratic founder, her husband is not portrayed as antagonistic; he, in fact, enables Goteline's healing through Foy to take place. Some women receive miracles, but in general the monk-continuators operate out of a slightly different structure of gender relations than Bernard. In their narratives, the place of the noble patroness has been taken over by the saint herself, now the "illustrious lady" (*inclita domina,* 4.19). In the monks' narratives, Foy is not the trickster-child but the mature female saint about whom an innkeeper exclaims, "O how fortunate you are to have such a great virgin as your patroness!" (4.18 [4.19]).

Furthermore, the moment of the Peace of God had passed,[19] and the Conques monastery had attained prosperity. Its high point was in the century between 1050 and 1150, during which time the monastery was far less vulnerable than at the beginning of the eleventh century. As a result, our analysis suggests, the enemy is no longer construed as the entire warrior class. In book 4, for example, Foy is referred to as "God's warrior" (4.12 [4.13]), a striking shift in the moral valuation of the term *miles* from the Bernardian section of the miracles, where (with the exception of the anomalous warrior-monk Gimon) to be a warrior is almost always negative.

In the monks' narratives, a considerable number of the miracles center on warriors with some defect or ailment that disables them from professional activity. In 3.3, after a spear strikes a young warrior through the eye, his feudal lord not only comes to console him, but further gives him the good advice to send Sainte Foy a golden ring and an offer of a gold coin in exchange for a healing miracle. In 4.10, the lord of the wounded warrior Rigaud "was utterly consumed with finding a way to help him. He had sponsored Rigaud with his own resources from the time Rigaud first took up arms to his belting as a warrior, and had taken his wounding very hard." The lord traveled to Conques to seek a healing miracle for Rigaud "with vows and prayers." The narrator portrays the lord as wholeheartedly engaged in the ritual acts on behalf of his wounded man.

Chapter 14 of book 4 (4.15) offers another example of a well-behaved warrior. The protagonist, William of Carlat, "a valiant warrior from an excellent family," whom Foy had healed once, was reblinded while he was trying to settle a fight between two of his men. Far from being characterized by unrestrained violence, William is portrayed as eager to be socially responsible and quick to invoke the rituals of Foy's shrine. First he "said that he would not touch any sustenance, neither food nor drink, until he had moistened his eyes with water blessed and consecrated by the majesty of Sainte Foy." And when that remedy did not completely heal him, William went to Conques on the vigil of Foy's feast day and spent seven nights "at the foot of her tomb, praising God." After the mass on October 6, William "fell prostrate at the feet of the sacred majesty," and his sight was restored. William, then, is represented as the exemplary pilgrim in need of healing; his warrior status is not held against him.

One of the most amusing of these later stories is about a "brave warrior named Bernard" who, as a result of a serious illness, became bald (3.7). "He was so ashamed of his baldness, which seemed ugly to him, that he abandoned all his martial activities and stopped going to the places frequented by the noblemen who were his peers. He wanted only his mother to take care of him, just as if he were a little boy." Although menacing neighbors were trying to seize Bernard's lands, he fell into a deep depression and was unable to act. The warrior's crisis of masculinity is treated sympathetically, if comically, and he is eventually rewarded for his faith in Foy by "recovering the lost glory of his hair."

In spite of this new tolerance for warriors, the occasional member of the warrior class still opposes Foy. The warrior Siger in the castle of Conques, discussed above, "was characterized both by excellence of lineage and by prowess in the martial arts." But he was arrogant and hostile to Foy and, "enflamed by the fires of avarice, he stole everything he could from the martyr's property," harassing her monks and "mutilating the men who worked on her lands." The subsequent punishment of Siger and his entire family culminates in the literal leveling of their castle. The narrator moralizes this as Foy's punishment of pride and the delivery of "the holy monastery from the assault of the impious." Siger represents the errant individual who entirely deserves his punishment; the warrior class as a whole is not the subject of reprobation.

The late miracle narratives generally follow the pattern of books 3 and 4 in avoiding misogyny and in replacing the female mediator with Foy herself. However, in a heightening maneuver typical of these late compositions, the author of V.3 provides not one but two wise women. After a warrior named Mathfred suffered a graphically described head wound in a siege and lay near death, the wife of Mathfred's lord perceived that the wounded man's wife "was overcome by sorrow and was suffering the pain of great anguish, and she felt deep compassion for her." She spoke to the anxious wife: "I see that you are deeply devoted to your husband. If your actions carry out my words, he will regain the health you despair of, and the joy you wish for will fill your heart." The lady extracted a promise that her instructions would be followed, and continued: "We all know that the holy virgin Foy, the lady of the town of Conques, heals unfortunate victims like this. When those who invoke her have faith there is not doubt that she effects a cure. If you plead with her devotedly and from the bottom of your heart to help you in your misfortune, and if you are completely firm in your conviction, I am sure you will rejoice because you will have won what you sought." Foy responded immediately to the prayers of the obedient wife; thus a chain of female actions resulted in a miraculous healing. It is tempting to view these women as intertextual with Bernard's wise women and as another attempt by the late authors to overcome the predictabilities of their genre.

From Power to Morality

In the Bernardian books, almost without exception, Sainte Foy renders punishment for overt acts of hostility toward the cult and lack of recognition of either her own or the monastery's power. Bernard explicitly states that Foy releases prisoners who call for her aid, whether they are guilty or innocent (1.31). Rather than a moral system, this is a system of power and patronage in which might makes right; what counts is being on the side of the monastery and its saint. Whereas the disorderly male tends to be the stigmatized character, there are virtually no disorderly females.

A shift in this power system takes place by the time of the monk-continuators, when it begins to yield to the penitential system as we know it from the later Middle Ages.[20] Certainly in book 4 and the later miracle narratives there is a moral economy of punishment for evil deeds defined as sin, whether avarice, pride, or lechery. In Bernard's books, a character like Guibert, though lecherous, is still a perfectly acceptable recipient of a heal-ing miracle from Foy. That would not be the case in book 4, since there are different moral economies at the beginning and at the end of the *Liber mi-raculorum*. In the Epilogue to book 4 (4.24 [4.29]), after a litany of Foy's praises, the monk-author can claim that Foy "not only gives strength to feeble limbs, but what is more she wipes away the filth of sin." This fore-shadows an entire penitential system and a very different sense of morality than the feudal power politics in Bernard's miracle narratives.

The monk-author of book 3 introduces a correlation between the sin of lechery and punishment in his chapter on Foy's resurrection of a young man from death (3.8). After he recounts the miracle, the author intro-duces an excursus on the age of responsibility by saying that some people may not believe the story he has just told because the boy was not old enough to sin:

But because I reported above that the young man about whom I am writing had been led down to dark places, perhaps some people may hesitate to believe this narrative. They may ask this: since he had scarcely reached puberty and, according to the testimony of his neighbors, was not implicated in murder or any other seri-ous crime, why was he condemned to bear such harsh punishment?

The narrator explains that, of the ages of man, youth is most likely to "become more lascivious and more prone to every kind of fleeting plea-sure. . . . If so, [the young man] needed to expiate his sin after his death before he could go to his heavenly home. . . . Sainte Foy wanted him to repent so that he would not again be given over to the peril of God's judg-ments." The narrative clearly promotes the penitential system.

By contrast, in Bernard's miracle stories lechery is a sin, and lust may occasionally motivate behaviors, but they don't provoke ethical instruction or require penance. Books 1 and 2 appear to take place before the new penitential system was put into place. For Bernard, lechery is stupid behav-ior because Foy inevitably responds with punishment. Similarly, having sex before going into the sanctuary should be avoided because Foy doesn't like it; as we discover in 1.27, Foy "loves the chaste and spurns the unchaste." This taboo, however, is one against impurely entering her sacred space,[21] which violates the norms of her territory and her power to determine those norms.

Bernard cares about behavior; infractions may bring punishment, but he is mostly interested in the actions surrounding those infractions. In 1.5, a castellan named Rainon "was dazzled by wretched greed and carried away by contemptible pride," Bernard tells his reader. The effect of these sins, however, was to drive Rainon to rant and rave "irrationally with furious passion, showing respect neither for God nor for His saint." As a result, this arrogant man was thrown from his horse and died from a twisted neck and fractured skull. Bernard then exclaims that

You should rejoice, scholar, that now Pride, not in imagination as you have read in Prudentius's *Psychomachia* but actually and in human form, was overpowered by the whirlwind of her own speed and lay there dead. Thrown down headlong from the lofty height of her vainglory into the bottomless pit of the abyss that the deception of sin had secretly prepared, Pride was irrevocably cast down.

The prideful death becomes an occasion for Bernard the writer to parade his literary prowess ironically for a scholarly reader (Prudentius's allegory of the vices and virtues is subordinated to human actuality). At the end of the account, Bernard tells those who have proud hearts to come to their senses and "learn to do right," but even in calling for an act of repentance he typically uses the language of power: "For injustice does not always have the upper hand and divine judgment is not a trifling matter."

For the monk-continuators, however, sin is an ethical category that provokes abstract issues of guilt and responsibility. Chapter 11 of book 4 is designed as a demonstration that "Sainte Foy wanted to show that the worst thing, for both the body and the soul, is greedy desire for money." In 4.16 (4.17), too, although Foy seems to be taking revenge against a castellan named Hector, the author demonstrates that the saint is just and Hector deserves his punishment. Hector had come to Conques on the saint's feast day solely out of lust for a woman. In the course of the day, Hector got into violent fights with other warriors, and the reliquary-statue of Foy (which had been brought out to quell the melée) was damaged. Hector is one character who never repents but is permanently ostracized. After his wife and children threw him out of the house, "he lived like Cain as a wanderer and fugitive." Yet the monk-author wants the saint to be seen as acting with justice, not blatant power; therefore he emphasizes that she normally gives people a chance. Hector has simply gone too far in desecrating Foy's relics, so "Sainte Foy gave him over to the punishment he deserved for his wickedness, for he had always acted wrongfully against her, not only in this one offense against heaven but in many other misdeeds as well." In this new moral economy, the lust, greed, and sacrilege of an unrepentant sinner receive eternal punishment.

Images of Innocence

The functional presence of an ideology of repentance changes the semiotic system of the monk-continuators' miracle stories, we argue, and as a result their narratives differ from those of the Bernardian books. One of those differences is the role of warriors and their wives. Another is the role of children. In the two books of miracles attributed to Bernard of Angers we find no sentimentality about children, who are not treated as innocent victims. However, in the different semiotic system of the monk-continuators' narratives, children represent innocence as opposed to adult guilt. In the post-Bernardian stories, children have a positive moral role that they do not have in Bernard's narratives, and parents typically dote upon their children. These features, however, do not result in a positive ideology of the family; rather they heighten the portrait of the monastery and its saint as powerful rescuers.

These later miracles often feature sentimental parents, such as Hunald, the father in 4.1. When his son died, "his father, who was unable to endure the loss because of his deep love for his son, embraced the ice-cold body. Hunald's eyes were wet and his entire face was streaked with flowing tears; he filled the whole place with bitter cries" as he pled with Foy to raise his son from death. Chapter 3.8 adopts the sentimental tone of the post-Bernardian narratives and also shows the connection of emotion to penitential ideologies—hence the need (discussed above) to determine the teenager's status with regard to guilt and innocence. This chapter first recounts the birth of a son to a childless couple after they had prayed at Foy's shrine. When the son died at age fifteen, further parental prayer to the saint in an emotionally efficacious (if somewhat harassing) mode persuaded Foy to resurrect the youth. The second half of the narrative takes up the issue of how such a young man could be sinful enough to have gone to "dark places" instead of heaven when he died. In other words, since the facts of the story appear to violate the penitential system they require explication. Although this begins as a resurrection miracle, it turns into a meditation on the penitential system.

A child's innocence is also at issue in 3.20, which raises the question of just punishment for sin and the necessity for repentance. Watching a procession, the child's father, Lambert, had jeered at the reliquary-statue of Sainte Foy, "for he had been ensnared by pagan error." In retribution, Foy reduced him to "a fool, empty-headed and irrational; he was scarcely able to find the way to his own house." The saint's "righteous anger" then reached to Lambert's "small son, resting on his nurse's breast." The child's eye and head swelled up until he lay close to death. Seeing her child in pain, the mother rushed to the reliquary-statue and "shouted in her loudest voice," begging the saint to heal her son. "O glorious virgin, what great crime could my little boy have committed against you, he who has not spoken a single word, who can't even talk yet? How can it be that he deserves punishment when he has not committed a single sin?" Eloquently, the mother pleads with the saint not to take out her rage by crushing "this innocent child whose purity of life makes him a stranger to every fault of human depravity." Foy rewards the mother's emotional reasoning by resurrecting her son, and the father Lambert goes through a penitential process: "His father confessed his own guilt and appealed for the holy virgin's pardon in an attitude of humble entreaty. And so he too was cured by divine medicine." Had Bernard written this story, he would most probably have concluded with the child's cure and the parents' acknowledgment of Foy's power.

Another story of parental love shows that such sentiment toward children is not connected with ideologies of family *per se* (3.9). Again, a childless couple prayed at Foy's shrine; they received twin boys. "Elias (the father) cherished his boys with such intense love that he even used to call them not his sons but Sainte Foy's." In order to prove that the boys were really under the protection of the saint, the father forced the children to walk through a huge fire with bare legs and feet. The narrator concludes that their emergence unharmed demonstrated Foy's particular guardianship. At another time, Elias decides to "take his boys to the holy martyr, since she was their spiritual mother. Terrible winter had caused all the rivers to flood, and it was venting its rage with huge storms everywhere. Elias's wife and the rest of the household were persuaded that the pilgrimage ought to be postponed to another time." Elias, however, insists on taking the "holy martyr's boys" on this dangerous trip, which turns out safely and concludes with the children pledged to the monastery. In spite of its family setting, issues of marital fertility or family relationship do not stand at the center of this narrative. The human mother's role is to represent human ineffectuality against the "spiritual mother," while the narrative uses the children as extensions of the saint's power.

One particularly gory story (4.3) illustrates a child's vulnerability and total innocence. It involves a five-year-old boy whose eyes were put out when both his parents fled Conques after killing an arrogant townsperson named Hugh:

They left behind at home a son almost five years old whom the fugitive parents could not carry with them. When the dead man's kindred saw the little boy and understood that his father, the murderer, had fled—alas! cruel and horrible deed! They were impelled by the same Furies who drove Orestes to slay his mother! They seized the little boy and, disdaining to kill such an insignificant person, they pierced the pupils of his eyes with sharp, pointed sticks and left him half dead.

Despite the dramatic emphasis on the child's suffering, the story never makes an issue of the parents' culpability in leaving their child behind. The community's solution to child abandonment was to deposit the five-year-old near the monastery church, where he could use his disability to beg alms from pilgrims. After several months of begging at the church door, the child's eyesight was miraculously restored by the saint before her altar.

The end of the story articulates the monastic agenda; the boy—as a living example of a miracle worked by Foy—was celebrated and supported by the monks from that time on.

The people gathered and no one of any sex or age stopped praising the holy virgin. . . . The boy was reciting the Psalmist's words, "My father and my mother have left me, but the Lord has taken me up," as the brothers carried him to the blessed virgin's holiest place. They nourished him with monastic support for the rest of his life, until death claimed what was owed and his soul flew up to the heavenly kingdoms.[22]

The narrative has no interest in family roles and responsibilities. Husband-wife relationships are pertinent only as they relate to cult functions. The story focuses on miraculous healing, with the vulnerable child as exhibit for the saint's power and the monastery's role.

The extreme of narrative exploitation of the trope of the youthful victim is reached in 4.12 (4.13), which features a girl who was not only young, but also "had lost the use of all her limbs." On her journey to Conques in search of a healing miracle, the paralyzed girl was abandoned on the riverbank opposite the monastery. "She lay there without shelter, her face and body were touched every night by wild animals as she herself later testified . . . since no one took pity on her and carried her to the monastery, she remained for many days in this wretched state." Finally, the monks, "moved to mercy," took the girl to lie at the main entrance of the monastery, where she was healed on Foy's feast day. The reported response of witnesses serves to celebrate the monastic and miracle-working saint: "The people standing there were filled with great joy on account of this marvelous deed and with one voice they praised almighty God, Who deigned to invest His own warrior Foy with so much power through all the splendor of her miracles." This concluding line makes clear the function of the healing miracle as well as the need for a vulnerable recipient to highlight the saint's omnipotence.

The Body

To an unusual degree, the *Liber miraculorum* narratives depict human suffering and the saint's miracles as things that happen to *bodies*—these eleventh-century miracle stories reveal fascination with embodiment.[23] For this reason we could say that, ideologically, the collection is deeply antithetical to any of the heresies like the Manichean or Albigensian that regarded the body as evil. Within these narratives, the body itself witnesses to miraculous events. Guibert, Gerbert, even donkeys' bodies, provide evidence that a miracle has taken place. The body functions as an important vehicle for and valid sign of healing. After a miracle has taken place, practice dictates that a physical token representing the miracle should be brought to the shrine, especially objects that have been in contact with the body, such as shrouds or fetters.

Rhetoric accounts for some of the interest in the grotesque body, since the low style on the Virgilian wheel exploits physical violence, bodily pain, and sensational gore.[24] In the Bernardian materials of books 1 and 2, this grotesque mode creates a distinction between high and low cultures. Needing to distinguish himself from Conques and its popular cult, Bernard employs the low style to represent his Other. Ironically, however, in the plot of his spiritual autobiography, he represents himself as deposed from his elite rationalism to join the low Other. The movement of his text requires that he violate his own elite-popular binary by believing in Foy. When Foy finally worked a healing miracle for Bernard's brother (2.13), she relieved "grievous and horrible physical pain." The saint's intercession was immediate and physical: "Sleep suddenly came over him, and a health-giving sweat flowed from his open pores." Bernard thus assimilated his own family to the low culture he had originally disdained.

In Bernard's system, Foy is at the level of the cult in Conques, often as the low Other. She is very physical—literally a body-shaped reliquary—and often touches people or even beats them to enforce her will. When she appeared to Guibert, she "slowly and sweetly reached out her hand toward the sleeping man's right cheek." To motivate a thief to return a small ball of her gold, she "thrust toward his sore eye a hazel wand that she seemed to carry in her right hand" (1.25). In a dream she "seemed to thrust her fingers into the rotted mouth [of a wounded warrior] and to implant and reshape one by one the teeth that were already loosened and gave off the stench of putrefaction. Then she placed the palm of her hand underneath his chin and, lifting it, she healed the gaping fissure" (2.7). The physicality of Foy's representation in Bernard's texts contrasts sharply to the image of Foy in most of the monk-continuator texts, where she is the ethereal and splendid celestial virgin.

For Bernard, hostile males are the chief characters portrayed as negative grotesques. Entrepreneurial or poor females are also described in this bodily grotesque mode, while upper-class female bodies never receive this treatment. In fact, Bernard offers almost no description of upper-class female bodies, and female sexuality—except for the reproductive function—is largely absent. Countess Arsinde, for example, owned some golden bracelets or armlets that Sainte Foy coveted for her new altar frontal (1.19). When the saint appeared in a dream to demand a donation of the bracelets, Arsinde cleverly bargained to conceive a male child in return for her gift. Although Bernard tells us that she bore not one but two male children, he avoids any representation of the body. The narrative focuses instead on the character of Foy and the self-possession of Arsinde—portrayed as well-matched tricksters.

As we have suggested, the monk-continuators move to a somewhat different conception of the body. Their narratives employ the moral system of sin and portray the body as the innocent victim of evil, disorder, or disease. Foy, who is high, celestial, omnipotent, and pure, does not appear as a corporeal body in these texts; rather, her body is described in metaphors: "the alabaster perfume jar that was her body [*corporis alabastro*]" (4.1). She can also be metaphorically hurt by slander that attacks the body of the saint and the Church. She manifests herself through the revealed signs of her miracles. The monastery is also powerful, good, serene; it is, in a sense, disembodied.

Conversely, the vulnerable points in the system—the body and children—both need protection. The blinded boy who is saved by the monastery in 4.3 is the typical victim for the semiotic system of books 3 and 4. One of the clearest examples of the body as vulnerable sign in these two books may be found in the story discussed above of Hector, who exemplifies how the semiotic structures of the monastic text function. He violated the purity of the monastery, misbehaving in the precinct and in the church itself. When he caused a brawl, the "holy virgin's golden effigy" was brought out to calm the clash. During the chaos an ivory and gold crucifix that hung around the neck of the statue was torn off and broken. The monks gathered up the pieces and "before they went to the refectory to eat, they came back again to see the broken body of the image. . . . Still distressed, they took the pieces of the shattered *corpus* and laid them reverently on the cross." We note the emphasis on the word "corpus"; the body of Christ here is vulnerable, fractured through Hector's violations. However, "with His power, the Supreme Maker, through the intercession of His own warrior, Foy, joined together the broken limbs of the *corpus* in such a way that even under close examination no trace of a scar could be found." When the crucifix was miraculously made whole, the monks responded ecstatically to the "restored *corpus.*" In response to his violation of Christ's, Foy's, and the monastic body, Hector was purged from society.[25] The function of body as sign of vulnerability in the semiotic system of books 3 and 4 explains the hypersensitivity to slander in these texts. Swearing and denigrating the saint damages the body of the monastery in the way that sacrilege damages Christ's body; slander is unacceptable because it damages this body.

The positive role played by vulnerable bodies in books 3 and 4 also accounts for the presence of suffering upper-class female bodies that are treated as grotesques. In the monastic structures of meaning, the grotesque body has no association with evil, the rustic, or the popular. A character treated as a grotesque may, in these miracle stories, be upper class. In 4.20 (4.21), Avigerne—"an adolescent girl of a wealthy and high-ranking family"—was disfigured by ugly clusters of warts on her right hand, which Foy heals at the time of her marriage. Both the new husband and the rest of her relatives rejoiced at the cure, but Foy had transferred the "mountainous crop of warts" to the girl's foot! Avigerne's appropriate response is to be "grateful that her own body offered proof that she could claim for the rest of her life to proclaim the powers of Sainte Foy." Physical grotesqueness is no longer a sign of the popular in the monk-continuator narratives.

The Laity

In the very late miracle narratives we glimpse the beginnings of an emerging paradigm, one which sets the monastic life against lay life. For the first time, the authors centrally take up issues of secular life for their own sake, although their paradigm casts the laity as the lower status term. Typically these miracles concern wealthy urban laymen. Whereas in the early eleventh century Bernard and the monastery had seen the powerful castellan as the chief enemy of monastic agendas, by mid century the writers of miracles perceived the emerging bourgeoisie as a potential problem.

Lay existence is increasingly marked as problematic in the late miracles. The resurrection story A.4 begins not with Foy's gift of a child to a barren couple, as earlier narratives had done, but with a father's attentive care of his sons: "He devoted himself to supervising their care and expended great effort in bringing them up, because he deemed that the greatest part of his own happiness rested in this, which was the natural purpose of human-kind." However, as the monk-author reports next, the father's investment was misplaced; one by one his sons died until only a single child remained. Next this author, who characteristically moves to the level of aphorism, reminds the reader of the limitations of worldly existence: "But none of the frail things of this life stays the same for long, for many misfortunes persis-tently intrude themselves." This moralizing narrative voice places blame for this tragedy on the vissicitudes of life to which the lay person is far more subject than the monk, as monastic propaganda was always emphasizing.[26]

But the narrator does not always display sympathy for the suffering in-herent in lay existence. Other later miracles adopt an openly critical view of lay life. In L.5, Guy of Reims, "who put great trust in the things of this world," nonetheless decided to educate one of his many children for the religious life. "But [the narrator interjects] the minds of worldly people are always changeable and mutable"—Guy sent his son William to the military instead. Here William became "entangled in the false values of the world," giving the author opportunity to unleash a diatribe: "It is well known that young men devote themselves to entertainments and spectacles. They live in the present, scorn the past, and give no thought to the future. Like an unbridled horse, William involved himself in the pursuits of his fellows and feverishly chased after the delights of this world." The object of condem-nation here is not (as in the Bernardian miracles) the warrior life, but the worldly temptations to which secular youth are inevitably exposed.

The semiotic system of the *Liber miraculorum* makes sense once we rec-ognize its overriding goals of winning adherents to the cult of Foy and bolstering the fortunes of the monastery at Conques.[27] Since it is not a pastoral text, it does not concern itself with religious instruction of the laity.[28] Essentially, the texts evince no interest in secular life; they are de-signed for a kind of institution that has almost no role in serving lay society with religious counsel. Rather, these texts aim to help the monastery domi-nate and govern the laity. Moral teaching is thus subordinated to demon-strations of the power of the monastery's patron saint, and the miracle nar-ratives promote the ideologies of a male monastic institution. In order to be usable in later contexts, the *Liber miraculorum* therefore would have to be adapted—and in the process rewritten and reinterpreted—in a variety of ways for a variety of audiences, and its child saint would have to be remade in the mold of later medieval sanctity.

CONCLUSION:
THE CULTURAL WORK
OF MIRACLE COLLECTIONS

 As we have shown, the narratives known collectively as the *Liber miraculorum sancte Fidis* are deliberate constructions. Close literary analysis reveals the care with which the miracle stories have been written, and the selection of narrative materials can furthermore be connected to the *Liber*'s ideological project. The world represented in the texts has been created out of the larger set of possibilities available to its authors and redactors at specific historical moments. Another miracle collection constructed at roughly the same moment might well make a different selection because it intends to perform different cultural work, as a comparison of the miracles of Sainte Foy with the posthumous miracles of Saint Benedict of Nursia written at Fleury demonstrates.[1]

Although in our analysis of the miracles of Sainte Foy we have emphasized the variety of authorial stances and ideological projects that characterize the subsections of the collection, nevertheless the whole represents the cult center at Conques as a powerful institution that almost stands outside of history. The first author, Bernard of Angers, wants to use the miracle collection to exhibit his talents and relate his spiritual journey for a northern French textual community. In describing his discovery of the cult and production of the narratives, Bernard deliberately represents Conques as isolated and backward. For their part, the monk-continuators, who are single-mindedly trying to popularize the cult and spread its fame, also represent the monastery as isolated, but for them its isolation results from its regional dominance—they write as if there is no rival institution in the Rouergue. Bernard needs to show Conques as the Other, and the monks need to show it as the numinous center, but both ideological projects result in a picture of the monastery as occupying a liminal zone. Time appears to be suspended; chronology is only sporadically noted, and even the history of the monastery is reduced to moral essences. Thus the various writers of the Foy miracle stories, although impelled by different ideological objectives, ultimately use the stories to do the same cultural work.

The distinctiveness of the *Liber miraculorum sancte Fidis* can be perceived through a comparison with miracles of Saint Benedict written at Fleury or Saint-Benoît-sur-Loire during approximately the same historical period.[2] Like the Foy collection, the Benedict miracles were redacted at various times—the ninth century, the beginning of the eleventh century, and the middle of the eleventh century. All of its authors were monks of the monastery, whose names are recorded: Adrevald, who wrote from 865–77; Aimo, who began writing in 1005; and Andrew, who started adding chapters in 1043.[3] There are differences among the sections each of these men wrote, deriving both from their roles as narrators and from the historical situations, but despite those differences the Benedict miracles as a whole appear to perform a distinct cultural task. A major project of the entire collection is to connect the cult institution with outside political institutions. The miracles function to demonstrate that through Benedict the monastery has consolidated its power and therefore deserves to be taken seriously within the political structures of northern Francia. The cultural work at every stage of the miracle production seems to be centered on insuring patronage.[4]

A concern with royal patronage is especially strong in the chapters written by Adrevald. In the early eleventh century, Fleury's anxiety about patronage manifests itself as a representation of the dire effects of weak royal power and consequent lawlessness,[5] though Aimo offers an example of desirable royal behavior when he reports the story in which King Ralph hunted down a warrior who had taken possession of Fleury's property at Dié (2.3). Andrew motivates noble patronage by telling a story in which the nobles who invoke "Father Benedict, chief of battle" win the day (5.15). We know from sources other than the Foy miracle collection that Conques had significant Carolingian patronage, but the cultural work of that collection is not primarily concerned with sustaining royal patronage or garnering aristocratic patronage from outside; therefore its cultural work is articulated very differently from that of the Benedict collection.[6]

The major mechanism by which the Benedict miracles carry on their cultural work is delineating the links between monastic events and chronological history. The Benedict miracles show that the Fleury monastery wanted to be a player within a very large political framework through its insistence on the connections between monastic and political histories. Within the Benedict collection many miracle stories begin by positioning the narrative event relative to chronology, both external and internal to the monastery. These chronological events include natural disasters such as the outbreak of ergotism in the Limousin in 994 (4.1) and a great flood of the Loire in 1003 (3.9).

The historical specificity extends to including transcriptions of legal documents; for example, the peace oath taken in the diocese of Bourges by all male inhabitants over the age of fifteen (5.2).[7] The Benedict collection puts a much higher value on the project of documentation than does the Foy miracle collection. Where Andrew, one of the narrators of the Benedict miracles, devotes his full attention to the political issues of the Peace of God and their implications for the monastery, Bernard of Angers uses the reference to a synod convened by the bishop of Rodez (which, historians have deduced, was a Peace of God council) to stage a competition among the saints' relics of the region (1.28). Not only does Sainte Foy win the competition, but the miracle is called one of her jokes. The political context is essentially irrelevant here except as a setting for the display of Sainte Foy's personality and power.

As we have noted, the Foy collection explicitly rejects chronological organization. Bernard of Angers had instituted a topical arrangement, and the monk-continuators acknowledge that they are following his model, with the result that the *Liber miraculorum sancte Fidis* is structurally detached from chronology. The unimportance of chronology for the Foy materials is clear in comparison with its overriding centrality in the Benedict collection.

The collection of Saint Benedict's miracles opens with an account that traces the history of Benedict from his life on earth through the translation of his relics from Monte Cassino to Fleury. Here Adrevald incorporates material from an Italian author to authorize Fleury's possession of the relics and appropriation of Benedict's powers (1.1–1.11). From the very first chapter this author interweaves political history, situating the events he relates within the reigns of emperors and kings. His account of a papally supported but unsuccessful attempt to effect the removal of Saint Benedict's relics from Fleury in order to return them to Italy makes it clear that Fleury participated in the international political arena along with the pope, the king, and divine will (1.15–17). As Louis succeeded Charlemagne, monastic politics were involved in imperial politics and in wars between Odo, count of Orléans, and other lords (1.20 and 1.21). In the aftermath of the division of the empire among the sons of Louis, Norman invaders pillaged and burned the abbey (1.33–35). The reign of Charles the Bald also produced calamities for the monastery, although the emperor donated gifts and therefore exemplified the good patron (1.41). Aimo's initial chapters retrospectively recapitulate the events of the preceding century, including the ravages of the Normans as well as the reigns of various kings and private war among the nobility in Aquitaine. Book 3 opens with the accession of Hugh Capet, to which the naming of Abbo as abbot of Fleury is connected. Andrew dedicated his prologue to book 4 to King Henry I in the twelfth year of his reign, and, finally, book 7, Andrew's last, reports Henry's actions in defense of royal dependencies (7.1–2). Throughout the collection, monastic events are consistently related to imperial and royal history.

The writers of Benedict's miracles are also keenly aware of the power of other religious institutions. They portray power struggles in which Benedict protects the rights of the monastery from the bishop of Orléans and from other monasteries. During the abbacy of Boso, Fleury clashed with another monastery over the possession of serfs (1.23) and contested the ownership of a piece of land with the abbey of Saint-Denis (1.25). In book 2, Aimo describes the hostility of Arnulf, bishop of Orléans, toward the abbey, exemplified by his attempt to prevent the monks from harvesting grapes at a vineyard they owned near Orléans (2.19). The monastery's self-presentation as a religious institution is symbolized by Benedict's abbatial attribute, his crozier, which he wields to punish malefactors when he appears in dreams and visions. In a miracle crucial to the abbey's assertion of its rights he used this staff to strike the count of Orléans, who subsequently died (1.18).

In addition to this continuing attempt to connect to external chronologies, there is also an ongoing construction of the Fleury monastery's internal history. Elections and deaths of abbots are reported, and some of these same miracle writers wrote lives of abbots: Aimo wrote the life of Abbot Abbo, and Andrew composed a life of Abbot Gauzlin.

Just as the chronicle of the Fleury monastery is at the same time a chronicle of contemporary events in Francia,[8] so their saint, Benedict, is presented as a historical agent, unlike Sainte Foy, who is represented in her miracle collection as a liminal or ahistorical figure. For Bernard of Angers she is the trickster-child and for the monk-continuators a celestial virgin; in either case, her relationship to chronological political history is undeveloped.

It is tempting to think of this difference as the gendered representation of the two saints, in that males act in history and females do not. Certainly the world represented in the Benedict collection is an overwhelmingly male world. The few females mentioned in the ninth-century chapters are literally kept at the margins: "Women . . . were prevented by what Adrevald variously termed *antiqua auctoritas* and *religio monastica* from going past the exterior gates of the monastery."[9] By the eleventh century women were allowed into the church, but writers of miracles from this period make women marginal to monastic social order by portraying them as victims of disease, demonic possession, or violence, such as the woman named Rojantric whom a warrior stalked "day and night, with threats and pleas, with torments and presents," before breaking into her home (7.7). In general the narratives represent male political concerns, and this may be a significant point of historical connection with political realities of the ninth through eleventh centuries in the north, a period during which female aristocrats were no longer the influential players they had been during earlier centuries. If we accept this reading, then to participate in this world the Fleury monastery must present itself as gendered male.

Historians have argued that noble women retained their independence and power longer in the south of France than in the north, but in any case, the Foy miracle stories represent numerous wise and powerful women of the nobility, women shown to be allies of the monastery in most cases. But perhaps the most potent reason for the positive presentation of females in the Foy collection is the need to present the monastery as a unique force separated from political power structures. Foy's gender reinforces her portrayal as a liminal being whose power transcends political structures.

Varied as it is, the representation of the saint in the Benedict collection is far more consistent and coherent than the representation of Sainte Foy in her *Liber miraculorum,* which we might explain again by the differences in cultural work done by each set of narratives. The iconography of Saint Benedict is much more stable; he appears in dreams and visions as an old man with shining white hair, wearing a monk's habit. Benedict, of course, had been brought to Fleury well after his place in the heavenly hierarchy was secure; not only had his life and miracles been written, but their author was a very highly regarded figure, Pope Gregory the Great, who gave Benedict pride of place in his widely read *Dialogues.* Thus Fleury had acquired a fully delineated and documented saint. Foy, by contrast, was fairly unknown when Conques supposedly acquired her relics. In order to claim a place for the saint, the monastery had to insist on her uncontested power, but the lack of pre-existing conditions meant that she could be redefined more easily.

Throughout the miracle collection, Benedict is consistently referred to as "Father Benedict," and there are repeated references to his *familia,* which includes all those under the authority of the monastery. As *paterfamilias,* Benedict can tap into the ideology of the family with himself as head, authority, protector, and enforcer. The later role has chilling resonance in the story of the serf Stabilis who had run away from Benedict's *familia* and made a new and prosperous life for himself, but, as monastic property, was compelled to return (6.2), or "another serf, Alberic, who merely contemplated seeking his freedom and had his hand crippled for this presumption" (5.8).[10] Thomas Head follows Patrick Geary in considering the period between the Carolingians and the late eleventh century to be "a coherent epoch in the piety of relics within western Christendom," an epoch focused on the patronage of long-dead holy men. The Orléanais in this period venerated the "fathers" of the diocese and sought their pious local patronage through cults of saintly fathers.[11] Such a patriarchal ideology was not appropriate for the monks at Conques, whose saint was a female child; therefore they were forced to construct a different constellation of power and gender.

As the comparison of the Benedict miracles with the miracles of Saint Foy reveals, even within the same historical period or the same type of religious institution we cannot generalize. The cultural work to be performed by the saint's cult in each case differs so radically that the ideological configurations—the representation of the saint, the monastery's relationship to society, the role of gender—must also differ.

Looking at the ideological implications of rhetorical formulations within a miracle collection provides us with one way of determining what cultural work the texts might be doing. A second way would situate the miracle collection relative to other textual and material products of the cult. Even if these products do not provide definitive proof, they are nonetheless highly suggestive of the role that written miracle texts played in the development of saints' cults.

Bernard of Angers, the inaugural author of the *Liber miraculorum sancte Fidis,* states explicitly the cultural work that his first book of miracles is capable of doing: In 1.34, "A Letter Intended for the Abbot and Monks, Which Is Considered the Conclusion of the First Book," Bernard announces that "a new edition of the miracles of Sainte Foy has been made, just as you asked." Though he does not elaborate on how the monks plan to use his *Liber,* he implies that it should be employed by the monastery to exalt the "miraculous deeds" of Foy. He then reveals how he has used the *Liber* to enhance his reputation among northern clerics. He tells the monks: "I showed this little book to my highly revered teacher, Reynold, master of the school of Tours, a man who is highly educated in the liberal arts." Rather surprisingly, Bernard reports that on this occasion the book was made to do the cultural work of healing: Reynold "considered my book to be of such great value that when he was afflicted with a serious illness while in my house he had it placed on his head just as if it were the text of the holy gospel and trusted that he would recover through Sainte Foy's power."

However, beyond the forwarding of Bernard's career, the broader cultural work performed in the north of Francia by Bernard's *Liber* was the dissemination of the cult itself. That the *Liber miraculorum* was somehow essential to the founding of new cult sites is suggested by the example of two brothers to whom Bernard loaned it—"My friends, Wantelme and Leowulf, canons of St-Quentin in the Vermandois, men distinguished as much by the reputation of their ancestral stock as by their own refined wisdom." In a reception that would gladden the heart of any author, these men "received it with such avid hearts that they almost tore it away from me violently, asserting that in a certain way it was rightfully theirs, because, due to the new reputation of Sainte Foy's powers, a new church dedicated to her was then being established in their city of Noyon. But because I did not have a copy in another place, they left empty-handed, insistently pleading with me to send one to them without delay." In this case, the new church was under way, but Bernard makes it obvious that the patrons find a copy of his *Liber* essential for the full authority of the foundation.

In a few other cases, however, it is clear that Bernard's book has, in fact, acted as the trigger for new foundations dedicated to Foy; Bernard tells us that "many respected people have heard of Sainte Foy for the first time through my writing, and through me her previously unknown miracles became known to many. Among them is my lord Hubert, bishop of the city of Angers, an unusually kind-hearted man who pursues a cultured way of life. In the cathedral he himself rebuilt from the ground up, he will declare the perpetual memory of Sainte Foy by dedicating an altar to her."

Bernard goes on to mention a number of other clergymen who have decided to found cult sites because they had heard of Foy from Bernard's book. These include Lord Gautier, "the very reverend bishop of Rennes," who "promised that a secondary altar will be built in honor of Sainte Foy in the basilica dedicated to Saint Thomas the apostle which that very notable man is building in that city." Also, Guy, "priest of the church of the holy mother in Angers . . . . has been consumed with such love for Sainte Foy that he arranged for a glorious oratory to be made to the holy martyr in his own church." With his usual mixture of self-promotion and humility, Bernard concludes by commenting, "I could name many more people who have become devotees of Sainte Foy, but I have thought that to include them in these pages would result in a repetitive and very boring text. Until recently, these people had hungered for banquets of such miraculous and renowned deeds. It is as if my promulgation of the miracles revived them with rich food. They thank God that I (although they greatly magnify the value of a sinner) took such great care and diligence and was eager to preserve with the service of my pen the great deeds of Sainte Foy, lest time pass and they be forgotten." Bernard thus claims that the cultural work of his miracle redactions is to celebrate the powers of Foy, the concrete outcome of which will be the foundation of new cult sites far from Conques.

The monk-continuators are even more explicit about the cultural work they expect the miracle collection to perform, that is, the spreading of Foy's fame and thus the dissemination of her cult. At the opening of book 4 the author makes a case for continuing to write down the deeds of the "unconquerable Foy." He says that he returns to the task of writing: "I feel compelled to lay claim to the time for writing that I once had and, for so long since, have not had." He interprets the miracles as signs of her power: "for even if she can't show herself to people as a corporeal being, still she manifests herself perpetually through the revealed signs of her miracles." He implies that it is the writing down of the miracles, the signs of her power, that produces the fame of the saint and the expansion of the cult: "There is no land from one pole to the other where her fame and the praise of her name are not known."

The same linkage is made by the monk-continuator of 3.1. As we have earlier pointed out, this first miracle in the post-Bernardian books documents the expansion of Foy's cult from Aquitaine to Normandy. The author grounds this new narrative in Bernard's suggestion that the cult was beginning to spread toward the north: "As is quite clearly evident in the preceding pages written by Bernard, Sainte Foy's power was traversing the farthest regions of the universe." In the Norman miracle then recounted, a noble woman, Goteline, was revived from death by Foy's power. As a substitute for traveling to the shrine at Conques, Goteline built a church in honor of Sainte Foy near her home, presumably the foundation at Conches. Within the *Liber miraculorum,* therefore, the principal reason for turning miracle stories into written narratives was to provide a concrete sign for use in the cultural work of promulgating Foy's cult.

As we described in our introduction to this book, the original collection of the miracles known as the *Liber miraculorum* and made at Conques (which Robertini calls alpha), became the prototype for other cult manuscripts which were essential to monastic foundations dedicated to Foy in other parts of Europe. Although most of these manuscripts contain substantial numbers of miracle narratives, they also include other texts regarded as essential to the performance of the cult. One kind of book or *libellus* contained not only a selection of miracle stories but also texts of Foy's *Passio* and *Translatio* as well as other texts to be used in celebrating the feast day of the saint. The only known example of the "Chanson de Sainte Foy," a Provençal epic version of Foy's martyrdom, is found in one of these manuscripts. Frédéric de Gournay suggests that this manuscript was made for a priory which the monks of Conques may have founded at Morlaas in Béarn, the southwest corner of France.[12] Its function of providing the monks at the new foundation with the materials they needed to celebrate and promote the cult of Sainte Foy presumably determined the subset of miracle narratives that it includes. Another copy of the materials needed for the practice of the saint's cult was evidently sent from Conques to the priory of Sainte-Foy in Sélestat, Alsace, from which the miracle narratives were adapted as instruments in the expansion of the cult into Germanic lands. Despite Bernard of Angers's presumption that he was insuring his own fame even as he commemorated Foy's, revisions of the miracle narratives in some later manuscripts (for example, Bodl. Lyell 64) actually remove all references to him. The cultural work of the narratives in monastic foundations or other religious institutions did not require his autobiographical glosses. Manuscripts containing selections of the miracles of Foy were also central to Foy foundations in England. The spread of Foy's cult to new sites was, as we have suggested, evidently enabled by the collection of miracles begun by Bernard of Angers and continued by the monks at Conques.

As the fame of Sainte Foy flourished in the eleventh century, in part because of the existence of written miracle stories, the chief shrine at Conques achieved its height of prosperity and power. Foy the miracle worker attracted pilgrims from the region and across Europe who made offerings that enriched the monastery. Although the *Liber miraculorum* relates stories in which the saint acquires precious metals and jewels, the monastery's cartulary records gifts of lands, priories, churches, and farms as well. The most lasting testimony to the success of the cult of Sainte Foy, and especially of its dissemination in the form of the *Liber miraculorum,* is the still-extant Romanesque church in Conques. Displaying features of a "Pilgrimage Road" basilica, the cruciform-plan church begun in the mid eleventh century has continuous aisles that allow pilgrims to circumnavigate the building, barrel vaults, and many carved capitals, among them one illustrating Sainte Foy's *Passio.* Begun at the choir end, to which the reliquary-statue was transferred by 1065, the church was under construction well into the twelfth century, when the beautifully preserved tympanum representing the Last Judgment was carved.[13] Included on the right-hand or Paradise side of the tympanum is a representation of Sainte Foy kneeling, hands clasped, as God's hand reaches toward her in blessing. The interaction signals God's positive response to Foy's intercession on behalf of those who request miracles from her. Above Foy hang shackles and chains, the offerings of freed prisoners, which function as signs of her efficacy. The context and history of the shackles and chains brought to the basilica are an important theme in the *Liber miraculorum.* As a visualization of the miracle book, the tympanum's representation of Foy the potent intercessor once more indicates the book's success in memorializing the miracle-working child martyr Sainte Foy.

At about this time Conques became an important stop on the pilgrimage road to Santiago de Compostela, which functioned to popularize her cult internationally. As we know from both the cartulary and surviving buildings, many new cult sites were founded around 1100, for example, Horsham Saint Faith in Norfolk, England; Santa Fede pres Cavagnolo in Italy's Piedmont; a number of churches in Navarre, Spain, and even a mosque in Barbastro, Aragon, part of which was reconsecrated after the Reconquista as a monastery dedicated to Foy.[14]

The history of the *Liber miraculorum* as a monastic production of Conques strongly suggests that this kind of text performed important cultural work during the period between the ninth and the twelfth centuries. Collections of miracles of local saints became the vehicles for linking regional cult centers to larger economic and political networks. By using their saint to enhance their prestige, the sponsoring institutions also enhanced their power and authority. After the twelfth century other kinds of texts and documents appear to have done this cultural work, and, while miracle stories did not cease to circulate and be recorded, they never again performed so crucial a cultural task.

NOTES

Preface

1. Rosenwein, Head, and Farmer, "Monks and Their Enemies," 769.
2. Lifshitz, *Norman Conquest,* 113.

Introduction

1. Head, "Hagiography," 433.
2. Knowles, *Great Historical Enterprises,* 9. For an excellent introduction to the scholarly study of hagiography see Dubois and Lemaître, *Sources et méthodes.*
3. Head, "Hagiography," 433.
4. "pridie nonas octobris: in Gallis civitate Agenno natale sancte fedis martyris." See Poulin, "Fides," col. 434. On martyrologies see Quentin, *Les martyrologies;* Dubois, *Les martyrologies.*
5. Cabaniss, "Florus."
6. Montpellier, Bibliothèque de l'Ecole de médicine, MS H 152, fols. 231v–237r, dated to the late ninth or early tenth century (BHL 2934). A somewhat different version of *Passio I* is preserved in Paris, BNF, lat. 5301 (BHL 2936a); the *Passio* is on fols. 328r–329v, a double leaf of the early tenth century inserted into the manuscript, which is dated to the end of the eleventh century and is from Saint-Martial of Limoges. For an edition based on the collation of these two texts see Bouillet and Sevières, *Sainte Foy,* 707–11.
7. On the *Passio* of Fides, Spes, and Karitas, and specifically its role as the source of Hrotswit's play on the subject, see Robertini, "Il 'Sapientia'" and Simonetta, "Le fonti."
8. Head, "Hagiography," 435.
9. Sheingorn, *Book of Sainte Foy,* 37.
10. Desjardins, *Cartulaire,* no. 4.
11. Geary describes the monastery's failed attempt to acquire the body of St. Vincent of Saragossa in that year (*Furta Sacra,* 61–62).
12. For a discussion of Foy's relics in the context of a pattern of relic transfers in the ninth through eleventh centuries see Geary, *Furta Sacra.* Specifically with regard to Foy's relics, Geary concludes:

"In the final evaluation, the facts of the case are these: by 883 Conques was recognized to be in possession of the remains of Saints Foy and Vincent, and so recognized by those who counted most—donors and patrons of the monastery. Just how this possession came about may well not have been decided for almost two centuries. It is immaterial that Agen may have continued to claim possession of the remains, or even that this claim may have been legitimate" (173–74).

13. On Angers as ecclesiastical and intellectual site see Fanning, *A Bishop and His World*.

14. For a fuller discussion of Bernard's literary strategies in the context of cult history see Ashley and Sheingorn, "Translations of Sainte Foy": "In this complex, multi-layered process of translation, therefore, Bernard is translating first from oral into literate culture, primarily (as he makes clear) for Fulbert and other literati back in northern France for whom his book was destined; second, he translates from the vernacular into Latin. Subsequently he translates his notes into complete narratives and those narratives into literary and rhetorical compositions" (34).

15. Bernard's two books are BHL 2942. This miracle collection exists in a number of editions and translations. We will be relying primarily on the edition of Luca Robertini (*Liber*). Our translations from the Latin were either made specifically for this book and stay close to a literal reading of the text or come from Sheingorn, *Book of Sainte Foy*. Here, we will use the term "Liber" to refer to the entire collection of miracles; we employ the term "book" as it was employed in the Middle Ages to refer to a group of individual chapters that made up a subsection of a *Liber*.

16. On this chronology see the summary in Sheingorn, *Book of Sainte Foy*, 24–25.

17. For a more detailed discussion of the manuscript history of the *Liber miraculorum sancte Fidis* see Robertini's chapter, "La Situazione Testuale del *Liber miraculorum sancte Fidis*" (*Liber*, 3–55).

18. Robertini, "Le *Liber*," 70.

19. "era stato concepito come strumento di propaganda per il culto di s. Fede e venne probabilmente inviato ad altri monasteri, desiderosi di ricevere documentazione sulla santa" (Robertini, *Liber*, 40).

20. For a recent edition and translation into modern French of the "Chanson" see Lafont.

21. Analyses of these rewritings and other kinds of hagiographic materials produced as the cult of Sainte Foy was disseminated to other sites will be central to our projected book on the cults of Sainte Foy.

22. "By that time [1557], the Protestant reaction to the cult of the saints had certainly contributed to give rise to a Catholic answer in the form of the Commission headed by Cardinal Baronius during the Council of Trent. This was to lead to the publication of the reformed Breviary in 1568, missing several apocryphal lives as well as some of doubtful authenticity" (Dunn-Lardeau, "From the *Légende*," 300). This revision of the canon of saints has continued; a number of

saints, including Catherine of Alexandria and George, were removed from the canon of the Roman Catholic Church in 1969.

23. *De probatis sanctorum historiis ex Al. Lipomani et mss. codicibus collectus.*

24. "Dans la transcription qu'ils en ont donnée, les Bollandistes, ignorant l'oeuvre du moine anonyme, que cependant ils soupçonnaient, et remarquant dans trois des récits des particularités et des détails qui leur semblaient étranges et inexplicables, les ont supprimés complètement. Quant aux autres, ils les ont groupés en dix chapitres répartis en trois livres" (Bouillet, *Liber,* xvi).

25. "Malheureusement certains scribes jugèrent à propos de faire un choix parmi les miracles; ils les tronquèrent, modifièrent l'ordre primitif, confondirent même ceux du moine anonyme avec ceux de Bernard, et donnèrent leur compilation comme l'oeuvre de ce dernier" (Bouillet, *Liber,* xiv). In sharp contrast, Julia Smith, who uses Gregory of Tours's rhetorical question, "Should we say the life or the lives of the saints?" to structure her review of early medieval hagiography, notes the theme in recent hagiographic research of the "particularity, indeed individuality, of every *vita* and every cult" ("Review Article," 75).

26. Dunn-Lardeau, "From the *Légende,*" 302. Dunn-Lardeau is here summarizing the Jesuit Pedro da Ribadeneira, the prologue to his *Flos Sanctorum,* a collection of lives of approved saints, published 1599–1601.

27. "Aucun chroniqueur ne nous fait connaître l'histoire des provinces du Midi de la France et leur état social durant le haut moyen-âge. Les nombreuses chartes qui nous ont été conservées de cette région, si importantes qu'elles soient, sont impuissantes cependant à combler cette lacune. Aussi, à ce point de vue spécial, les renseignements fournis par l'écolâtre d'Angers et par son continuateur sont-ils d'une haute valeur, et leur intérêt ne saurait être révoqué en doute. . . . Les moeurs souvent brutales des seigneurs, l'oppression des faibles et des petits par les grands et les puissants, mille détails de moeurs et de coutumes, mille renseignements sur les institutions et les usages de la vie privée et de la vie sociale, tout cela passe sous nos yeux à mesure que nous lisons le *Livre des Miracles* de sainte Foy" (Bouillet, *Liber,* xxix–xxx). Historians of the region continue to place a high value on the *Liber miraculorum sancte Fidis.* In his 1985 book, Jean Dunbabin wrote, "Bernard of Angers's two books of the *Miracles of St Foy,* along with those of his anonymous continuator, still shed light on an area of the far south on which there is little other information" (*France in the Making,* 128). The following passage gives a specific example of the way Dunbabin draws historical evidence from the miracle narratives: "Within the Rouergue itself, comital authority declined rapidly. The third and fourth books of the *Miracles of St Foy,* written in the second half of the century, never mention the count (though the Auvergnat social influence is easily detected). As a consequence, local political life became purely a matter of balancing out rival castellans' interests. For the monks of Conques, the only protection they could devise against the depredations inflicted on them by the neighboring castellan was to carry the standard of the Cross and the statue of St Foy into the centre of the town, calling publicly for God's vengeance. It worked— the castellan, all his sons, and his three daughters came rapidly to unpleasant ends;

even his castle was blown down. But for those without direct divine assistance, the absence of any superior authority was no doubt painful" (214–15).

28. Delehaye, *Legends,* 2. For a biography of Delehaye and a selected bibliography of his work see Heffernan, "Hippolyte Delehaye."

29. Bonnassie, "Descriptions of Fortresses," 132.

30. Zimmermann, *Les sociétés méridionales,* 4.

31. For a recent overview of hagiographic scholarship which comes to many of the same conclusions see Geary, "Saints, Scholars, and Society: The Elusive Goal," in *Living with the Dead,* 9–29.

32. Lifshitz, "Beyond Positivism," 95.

33. Robertini attributes the continued prominence of the *Liber miraculorum sancte Fidis* in historical writing to eminent French historian Georges Duby: "Il *Liber miraculorum sancte Fidis* ha acquisito una certa notorietà nell'ultimo ventennio, dopo che Georges Duby ha dedicato ad esso alcune pagine nel suo volume *L'An Mil,* pubblicandone anche qualche estratto in traduzione; la storiografia francese in particolare ha volorizzato il *Liber* per la ricca mèsse di informazioni sulla cultura materiale e sulla storia della mentalità nella Francia tra il primo e il secondo millennio. Il *Liber* si è rivelato inoltre fonte preziosa per i filologi romanzi e soprattutto per gli storici dell'arte" (*Liber,* vii). Historian Julia Smith points out, however, that in regions like Brittany and Wales saints' "cults flourished without written *miracula,*" and "secondary relics such as bells, croziers and bibles were at least as important as a saint's bodily relics" ("Review Article"; see especially her essay "Oral and Written").

34. Wilson, *Saints and Their Cults,* 6–7.

35. Ward, *Miracles and the Medieval Mind,* 215.

36. *Ibid.,* 42.

37. Kleinberg, *Prophets in Their Own Country,* 5, 6.

38. For the foundational study in this area see Delooz, *Sociologie et canonisation.*

39. Sigal, *L'homme et le miracle,* 275.

40. Goodich, *Vita perfecta,* 8. Goodich takes exception to the general practice, arguing that "in understanding a study of thirteenth century sainthood, one cannot therefore disregard the traditional, ahistorical themes of Christian piety, whereby each concrete example relied upon the stereotypical themes of saintly behavior laid down by Scripture, Gregory the Great, Athanasius, Sulpicius Severus or Jerome. While these prototypes were often folkloristic, Scriptural or even non-Christian, the saint's very conformity to antique models insured his acceptance by the community" (6).

41. Wilson, *Saints and Their Cults,* 16.

42. Patrick Geary, with reference to the French "historical anthropologists" who have studied popular religion (Jacques LeGoff and Jean-Claude Schmitt), notes their view that "the elements of the cultural system are shared, but each group—elites and masses, lay and clerical—articulates the system in its own way depending on its social, political, and intellectual circumstances" (*Living with the Dead,* 33).

43. Brown's classic article "The Rise and Function of the Holy Man in Late

Antiquity" (1971) demonstrates how religious developments of the fifth and sixth centuries have broad historical relevance, shedding light on the "values and functioning of the entire society" (*Society and the Holy,* 105).

44. Brown, *Cult of the Saints,* 42.

45. Patrick Geary identifies Brown's 1971 essay, "The Rise and Function," as "the work that gave the greatest impetus to the functionalist tradition of hagiographic research" (*Living with the Dead,* 13).

46. Wilson, *Saints and Their Cults,* 8.

47. Geary, *Furta Sacra,* xi.

48. Stock, *Implications of Literacy,* 66. Because his major topic is literacy and textuality in the eleventh century, Stock is able to pay close attention to Bernard's textual practices, one of our major topics as well. However, he treats neither books 3 and 4 of the *Liber miraculorum* nor the late miracle narratives, which were written by anonymous monk-continuators and do not support his thesis as neatly as Bernard's books do.

49. Farmer, "Down and Out and Female," 370.

50. Benedicta Ward too has discussed Sainte Foy's miracle stories as products of a "traditional shrine" (*Miracles and the Medieval Mind,* 33). Though she pays some attention to accounts as "propaganda," she does not otherwise analyze the textual constructions of miracles.

51. Abou-El-Haj, *Medieval Cult,* 12. As Bonnassie writes specifically with regard to the early medieval hagiography of the Midi: "Tout récit hagiographique est à l'évidence un texte publicitaire, qui vise à assurer la promotion d'un sanctuaire déterminé. Mais il n'est pas que cela: il ne se contente jamais de décrire le comportement des hommes (saints ou pécheurs) qu'il met en scène, mais il l'interprète. C'est tout un système de représentations de la société qu'il propose. Parfois même (ainsi dans le cas des Vies de saints écrits au XIe siècle à l'appui du mouvement de la Paix de Dieu), il se fait le vecteur d'une idéologie" (Bonnassie, "Avant-propos," 383).

52. On the contestations around the cult site of Sainte Foy in Sélestat (Alsace) see our "'*Discordia et lis.*'" For a related argument about the use of liturgical ritual in the medieval cult of Foy see our "Liturgy as Social Performance."

53. Schulenburg, "Saints' Lives," 285–86. See also her *Forgetful of Their Sex.*

54. Robertson, "Corporeality of Female Sanctity," 269.

55. Wogan-Browne, "Virgin's Tale," 165.

56. See Hollywood, "Suffering Transformed," for her critique of the current feminist narrative; see also her *Soul as Virgin Wife.*

57. For a political reading of Osbern Bokenham's Saint Faith very different from the eroticized martyr figures described above see Delany, *Impolitic Bodies.*

58. See Dronke, *Women Writers of the Middle Ages.*

59. Pizarro, A *Rhetoric of the Scene,* vii. A similar argument is made by Alexandra Hennesey Olsen that although hagiography is "one of the most important medieval literary genres," literary critics have failed to take it seriously ("'De Historiis Sanctorum,'" 407).

60. Signori, "The Miracle Collection and Its Ingredients," 279.

61. "Die Hagiographie trotz ihres Umfangs und ihrer Bedeutung sehr stief-mütterlich in den literarischen Handbüchern behandelt worden war . . . wird Hagiographie immer noch selten als literarische Kunst betrachtet und beurteilt" (Rydén, "Ueberlegungen," 47). We note that in 1974 Roger D. Ray ("Medieval Historiography") suggested that literary analysis of hagiography would be fruit-ful. Pointing out that "the study of historical genres is bound to be hard in ref-erence to an age that drew faint lines between history, hagiography, exegesis, preaching, and poetry" (35), Ray asks the modern historian to be "sensitive . . . to the medieval historian's basically rhetorical purposes and equipment" (56) and finds it "probable that methods heretofore reserved only for the explication of lit-erary narrative will carry over productively into the study of medieval historiog-raphy" (56).

62. Roberts, *Poetry and the Cult of the Martyrs,* 7.

63. *Ibid.,* 194.

64. Pizarro, *A Rhetoric of the Scene,* vii.

65. *Ibid.*

66. Speaking as a historian, Bonnassie identifies Robertini's primary focus as philological: "L'auteur est un latiniste et on sent bien à travers ses commentaires que ses préoccupations sont davantage d'ordre littéraire ou linguistique que d'or-dre proprement historique" (Bonnassie, Review, 476).

67. Jules-Rosette, "Semiotics and Cultural Diversity," 6.

68. Hodge and Kress, *Social Semiotics,* 1.

69. The dilemmas produced by this desideratum are fully articulated by Ga-brielle Spiegel in "History, Historicism, and the Social Logic of the Text in the Middle Ages." She concludes, "The most fruitful means of investigating this ma-terial and discursive mutuality, I would suggest, is to focus analysis on the moment of inscription, that is, on the ways in which the historical world is internalized in the text and its meaning fixed." Spiegel defines "inscription" as representing "the moment of choice, decision, and action that creates the social reality of the text, a reality existing both 'inside' and 'outside' the particular performance incorpo-rated in the work, through the latter's inclusions, exclusions, distortions, and stresses. . . . Historians must insist, I think, on the importance of history itself as an active constituent of the elements that themselves constitute the text" (84). The essay has been reprinted in a collection of Spiegel's essays, *The Past as Text.* Virtually all of the essays in the volume take up the question of how to do histori-cal analysis given the new understandings of textuality and ideology, and the result is a subtle dismantling of positivist definitions of "history." See especially chap-ter 3, "Towards a Theory of the Middle Ground" (44–56).

70. Patrick Geary's related but nonsemiotic formulation is that "to understand a hagiographic work, we must consider the hagiographic tradition within which it was produced; the other texts copied, adapted, read, or composed by the hagi-ographer; and the specific circumstances that brought him or her to focus this tra-dition on a particular work. The text stands as a threefold intersection of genre, total textual production, and historical circumstance" (*Living with the Dead,* 23).

While Geary focuses on the losses to "broader meaning" resulting from this approach, and projects a pessimistic tone about the future of hagiographic studies, we see social semiotics as a way of revealing the dynamic processes by which medieval people used their saints to make meaningful frameworks for their lives.

71. As Lester Little points out: "From the late eleventh century onwards, the aggressiveness of European warriors had to be directed against outsiders. There could be no sanctioning of Latin Christians' plundering of each other. Instead the Moslems in Spain, on the Mediterranean islands, on the coast of North Africa, and in the Holy Land were now fair game, as were also the Slavs on Germany's eastern borders. This category of victims eventually included Greek Christians, whose leading city, Constantinople, the Venetians and their warrior allies plundered in the opening years of the thirteenth century. But there were also 'outsiders' within Europe who could be subject to plunder: the Jews, who periodically suffered pogroms; and heretics, whose land, according to canon law, became the legitimate property of the Catholic warriors who conquered it" (*Religious Poverty*, 8).

72. Evidence of the historical shift toward a money economy is found in A.1, where a bereaved mother pleading for her son's resurrection promises the saint an annual offering of two gold coins, "just as if it were tribute that she owed under the law."

Chapter One

1. See Forsyth, *Throne of Wisdom*, for example. Most recently see *Gesta* issue on medieval body-part reliquaries.

2. In order to use miracle stories as historical sources the miraculous element must be rationalized. Thus Dunbabin employs the *Liber* miracle story in which Sainte Foy obtains a golden bracelet from Countess Arsinde in exchange for a promise to grant her a child to point out how important it was to the stability of the French nobility that they produce heirs (*France*, 105). And, as Robertini observes (*Liber*, 352), C. Erdmann (*Die Entstehung des Kreuzzugsdankens*, Stuttgart, 1935, pp. 69–70) sees in the colorful character Gimon, monk and prior of Conques in the mid tenth century, a prototype of the warrior-monk who anticipates the ideal knight. Bonnassie treats the miracles of Sainte Foy as a transparent source for historical data on such subjects as fortresses (*From Slavery to Feudalism*, 132–48) and eleventh-century violence. For example, he says, "This *Liber miraculorum*, many episodes in which concern Languedoc, provides a very full picture of all the various types of violence practiced at that period, and thus makes it possible to establish a veritable typology of exactions by nobles in the eleventh century period" (119).

3. " . . . est un véritable tableau, vivant et détaillé, de la vie dans le Rouergue et ses alentours aux environs de l'an mille" (Caitucoli, "Nobles et Chevaliers," 401).

4. Stock, *Implications of Literacy*, 64–71.

5. For an analogous investigation of a medieval religious text see Pizarro, *Writ-*

ing Ravenna. Pizarro looks at the *Liber pontificalis ecclesiae Ravennatis* as a literary creation reflecting the local and international interests of the Ravenna clergy.

6. Among the best known of the symbolic anthropologists and cultural critics who developed the terms "liminality," "reflexivity," "metasocial commentary," etc., in connection with the trickster paradigm are: Turner, "Myth and Symbol," "Betwixt and Between," and *The Ritual Process,* 94–118, 166–77; Babcock, "'A Tolerated Margin of Mess,'"147–48, and "Arrange Me into Disorder," 102–28; Geertz, "Deep Play," 443–53. Their insights have generated a rich literature, especially in anthropology and multicultural literatures, on trickster/sacred clown phenomena. See, for example, Babcock and Cox, "The Native American Trickster"; Wiget, "His Life in His Tail"; Handelman, "The Ritual Clown"; Handelman and Kapferer, "Symbolic Types"; Ricketts, "The North American Indian Trickster"; Ashley, "An Anthropological Approach"; Bouissac, *Circus and Culture;* Segal, *Dionysiac Poetics;* Ohnuki-Tierney, *The Monkey as Mirror;* Shulman, *The King and the Clown;* Ortiz, *The Tewa World;* Vizenor, "Trickster Discourse" and *Narrative Chance;* Ammons and White-Parks, *Tricksterism;* Cypess, *La Malinche;* Gates, *The Signifying Monkey;* Roberts, *From Trickster to Badman;* Pelton, *The Trickster in West Africa.*

7. Röckelein, "Miracle Collections," 268.

8. Head, "Hagiography," 434. Further, as Röckelein discusses, the difficulty of identifying any specific source is rendered virtually impossible by the widespread practices of borrowing and of combining from a wide range of sources ("Miracle Collections," 271–72).

9. In their hagiographic writing Bernard and his predecessors are using the humility *topos* in accordance with classical norms Curtius has described (*European Literature,* 407–13). Curtius attributes medieval uses of the humility *topos* to the "stylistic Mannerism of late Antiquity" (*European Literature,* 412). As Robertini observes, Bernard's letter also follows the structure of a classical epistle: *salutatio, exordium, narratio, petitio, conclusio* (*Liber,* 319). For a general survey of classical literary conventions of the preface see Janson, *Latin Prose Prefaces.* Not all miracle collections, however, were as literarily elaborated. For example, the first book of the *Miracles of Saint Benedict,* written in the ninth century by Adrevald of Fleury, was most probably known to Bernard of Angers, since it circulated widely and survives in over twenty manuscripts. Adrevald's collection has no prefatory epistle and does not exploit the rhetoric of authorial humility and other narrative topoi. For the Latin edition of the *Miracles of Saint Benedict* see Certain. For the best and fullest analysis see Head, *Hagiography and the Cult of Saints.*

10. Curtius traces the trope of "affected modesty" back to oratory, citing Cicero's *De inventione,* I, 16, 22. The orator's acknowledgment of his infirmities or his inadequate preparation "is intended to dispose the judges favorably. But it is very early transferred to other genres. . . . Such 'modesty formulas' achieve an immense diffusion, first in pagan and Christian late Antiquity and then in the Latin and vernacular literature of the Middle Ages. Now the author protests his inadequacy in general, now bemoans his uneducated and rude speech . . ." (*European*

Literature, 83). On "the familiar trope of *captatio benevolentiae* . . . a humble servant having been asked to complete a work which far exceeds his ability" (*Sacred Biography,* 134), Thomas Heffernan adds, "The use of the *captatio* persona, *facultas exigua,* although a stock motif in the classical exordium, was to become a part of the tradition of medieval sacred biography in the West through the influence of Sulpicius's dedicatory letter to his friend Desiderius with which he prefaced his *Vita Sancti Martini*" (138).

11. Head, "Hagiography," 434. The miracles of Saint Martin first recorded by Sulpicius and added to by Gregory of Tours played a foundational role in the establishment of the miracle collection as a genre; see Van Dam, *Saints and Their Miracles;* Rousselle, *Croire et guérir;* Stancliffe, *Saint Martin and His Hagiographer;* Loyen, "Les miracles de saint Martin."

12. Although he was to write the text that modeled hagiography for several centuries, Sulpicius dedicated his life of Martin to his friend Desiderius with the humble statement, "for I am the weakest of creatures and was loath to submit it to the world's judgment, for fear that an all too unpolished diction should prove displeasing to the reader (as indeed I think it will) and that I should be deemed the proper object of general reprobation for having had the effrontery to annex a subject that should have been reserved for writers of competence" (Sulpicius Severus, *Life of Saint Martin,* 3–4).

13. Odo of Cluny, *Life of Saint Gerald of Aurillac,* 295.

14. "You know that I am not learned in literature and being simple and unskilled would not dare describe such awe-inspiring miracles. Would that Severus or Paulinus were alive, or indeed that Fortunatus were present to describe these deeds! Since I am incompetent, I would incur shame if I tried to do this" (Gregory of Tours, "Preface of the First Book of 'The Miracles of Blessed Martin the Bishop,'" trans. McDermott, "Bishops," 133–34). For a slightly different translation see Gregory of Tours, *Miracles,* trans. Van Dam.

15. Gregory of Tours, "Glory of the Confessors," trans. Van Dam, 16.

16. MacKinney comments on "Fulbert's letters of effusive flattery to monastic friends," in which he adopted a "florid rhetorical style" (*Bishop Fulbert and Education,* 9). Bernard's prefatory letter is very much in Fulbert's effusive style of flattery and reveals his imitation of the norms of literate letter writing.

17. Constable, ed. *Letters of Peter,* 2:1–44, offers an excellent survey of medieval letter-writing tropes and conventions.

18. As Constable shows, in his letters Peter the Venerable also resisted the practice of brevity (*Letters of Peter,* 38, 41). François Dolbeau comments that "en matière stylistique, les hagiographes ne forment pas une catégorie speciale d'écrivains"—in other words, their compositional techniques followed medieval norms. Dolbeau points out that typically the hagiographer began with a redaction in a simple, unfigurative style and then used all the resources of stylistic elaboration to produce a revised text ("Les hagiographes au travail," 61). This is exactly the process of revision Bernard of Angers describes.

19. Herkommer, *Die Topoi,* analyzes the eyewitness *topos* in prefaces to Roman

histories; Sigal, "Le travail des hagiographes," surveys the *topos* of the eyewitness in the prologues to hagiographic works (151–53).

20. Isidore of Seville, *Etymologiarum,* 2, 8.

Rita Copeland has discussed the trope of "paene inusitata" in Notker the German of St. Gall, who wrote in the late tenth to early eleventh century. When Notker glosses Latin works in the vernacular, he says his undertaking is "almost unprecedented" and apologizes for the shock his reader may have from their unfamiliarity; see *Rhetoric, Hermeneutics,* 98–103. According to Martin Irvine, Isidore of Seville (c. 560–636) produced "the most widely used grammatical encyclopedia of the Middle Ages" (*Making of Textual Culture,* 209). Isidore was "able to apply the Augustinian model of *grammatica* as the discipline devoted to language and texts at every level from elementary literacy to exegesis to the needs of the textual community of the monastery and cathedral," and his *Etymologiae* "was a text held in common that, along with the Scriptures and Donatus, one can safely assume almost every library would have possessed" (210).

21. Remensnyder, "Un problème," 369–71.

22. Odo of Cluny, *Life of Saint Gerald of Aurillac,* 296.

23. *Ibid*.

24. Although we see few examples of symbolism in Bernard's text and view them as anomalous, Brian Stock says that "symbols abound" in the text (Stock, *Implications of Literacy,* 68). Stock is certainly correct in pointing to Bernard's allegorizing of Foy's costume in 1.1, but this is an isolated example.

25. Gregory of Tours, preface to *Life of the Fathers;* see Heffernan's translation: "Whence it is clear that it is preferable to speak of the life of the fathers than lives, because although there is a diversity of merit and virtue, in the world one life nourishes all bodies" (*Sacred Biography,* 7).

26. Pizarro, *Rhetoric,* 63.

27. Dominique Barthélemy has commented on the uses of the term *rusticus* in the writings of both Gregory of Tours and Bernard of Angers, saying that the term does not always mean a literal peasant but implies a lack of education or manners as opposed to cultural elite norms ("La paix de Dieu," 22). See also Peter Brown, *Society and the Holy,* 230–33; Brown points out that for Gregory of Tours *rusticitas,* meaning "boorishness" or "slipshodness," was the antithesis of *reverentia,* a key concept for "the focusing of belief onto precise, if invisible, objects, in such a way as to lay the participant under specific obligations," whereas "any gaffe in the punctilio demanded by the supernatural was *rusticitas*" (230, 232).

28. Collections of miracle stories were expected components of the saints' lives and the books of martyrs since at least the time of Augustine. In his *City of God,* book XXII, chapters 8–10, Augustine takes up the topic of miracles, their definition, and their function in the world. In Augustine we already have the typology of miracles that will characterize miracle collections for over a millenium. "Nous y trouvons déjà en germe tout ce qui donne à cette classe d'écrits sa physionomie et sa valeur un peu spéciale. A peu près tous les genres de faveurs temporelles y sont représentés: des aveugles, des sourds, des paralytiques, des malades de toute sorte sont guéris, des morts ressuscités, des biens recouvrés, des captifs délivrés,

tantôt le miracle est instantané, tantôt il est le fruit de la persévérance; souvent le saint lui-même se montre à son client" (Hippolyte Delehaye, "Les premiers 'libelli miraculorum,'" *Analecta Bollandiana* 29 [1910]: 434, as cited by Röckelein, "Miracle Collections," 267). On the conventions—such as healing and punishment miracles—established by Gregory of Tours see Oury, "Le Miracle dans Grégoire de Tours."

29. The connection between blindness and lechery was conventional. In this context, the punishment inflicted upon the first protagonist, Guibert—whose eyeballs were torn out after an accusation of adultery—is not unfitting by medieval norms; see Sheingorn, *Book of Sainte Foy,* 289, n. 17.

30. Odo of Cluny, *Life of Saint Gerald of Aurillac,* 305.

31. Curtius, "Jest in Hagiography," *European Literature,* 425–28. Auerbach, however, considers the combination of the grotesque, the humorous, and the miraculous in hagiography as an example of Christian *sermo humilis.* See *Literary Language and Its Public,* 96–101; 27–66.

32. Odo of Cluny, *Life of Saint Gerald of Aurillac,* 360.

33. Gregory of Tours, *Miracles,* 1.20.

34. McDermott, "Bishops," 165.

35. Poulin *(L'idéal de sainteté),* discussing the ideal of sanctity in Aquitaine in the eighth through the tenth centuries, argues strongly that the extant texts of saints' lives follow a set of hegemonic monastic norms in constructing their saints. Most saints from this period were either monks or other religious, and he argues that the exceptions like the layman Gerald of Aurillac still demonstrate the strength of the monastic virtues of chastity, humility, etc. The portrait of Sainte Foy in the Bernardian texts is in almost every way an anomaly for the early eleventh century.

36. Remensnyder, "Un problème," 376.

37. Wirth, *L'image médiévale,* 193. For Wirth, the development of a cult like Foy's implied the subversion of Carolingian rationalism by carnivalesque modes.

38. See also the arguments of Gurevich, "Peasants and Saints," in *Medieval Popular Culture,* 39–77. Much of his description of the nature of saints' cults until the eleventh century is relevant to the cult of Foy as represented in her miracle stories. Gurevich argues that "the teachings of the church were embedded in a rich context of folkloric tradition" (78). The resemblances between the folklore trickster and Celtic saints are analyzed by William Heist, "Hagiography, Chiefly Celtic."

39. Heinzelmann, "Une source," 247. Gregory of Tours's collection of posthumous miracles of St. Martin was important in setting the chronological pattern; as Heinzelmann shows, Gregory's collection is arranged according to the liturgical year, so that Gregory must have collected the miracles over a period of time. Perhaps Bernard of Angers's short visits to Conques precluded his ability to employ chronology and forced him to seek another arrangement.

40. Aimo began to write miracles of Saint Benedict in 1005, and Letaldus composed miracles of Saint Maximin of Micy after 982 (Head, "Hagiography," 74).

41. Sigal, *L'homme et le miracle,* 312. Outside of the corpus of miracle col-

lections that Sigal examines, Benedicta Ward finds joking miracles among the miracles of St. Thomas of Canterbury (*Miracles and the Medieval Mind,* 213), but Remensnyder ("Un problème," 375–76) sees Thomas's miracles as distinctly different from those of Foy.

42. The representation of Sainte Foy in these miracles adheres to the well-known folklore type of the trickster tricked.

43. "une opposition entre une conception plus populaire, plus folklorique, et une autre plus intellectuelle" (Sigal, *L'homme et le miracle,* 271).

44. Remensnyder, "Un problème," 378–79.

45. [Cicero], *Rhetorica ad Herennium,* 263.

46. Eugene Vance, "Chaucer's Pardoner," 730.

47. As Barbara Rosenwein observes, "Martin's 'perseverance in abstinence and in fasts, his capacity for vigils and prayers' had, by Sulpicius' time, become *topoi* in the accounts of early Christian ascetics. All of these were appropriate to the world-rejecting stance that Sulpicius gave his saint. Part of that stance was the rejection of the military life as incompatible with a religious vocation" (Rosenwein, *Rhinoceros,* 64).

48. On the folklore trickster as the mediator figure in binary mythical systems see structuralists Lévi-Strauss, *Structural Anthropology,* 223–27, and Edmund Leach, "Genesis as Myth." Lévi-Strauss says, "Thus, like Ash-Boy and Cinderella, the trickster is a mediator. Since his mediating function occupies a position halfway between two polar terms, he must retain something of that duality—namely an ambiguous and equivocal character. . . . Not only can we account for the ambiguous character of the trickster, but we can also understand another property of mythical figures the world over, namely, that the same god is endowed with contradictory attributes—for instance, he may be *good* and *bad* at the same time" (226, 227). Leach's formulation is that "in every myth system we will find a persistent sequence of binary discriminations as between human/superhuman, mortal/immortal, male/female, legitimate/illegitimate, good/bad, . . . followed by a 'mediation' of the paired categories thus distinguished. 'Mediation' (in this sense) is always achieved by introducing a third category which is 'abnormal' or 'anomalous' in terms of ordinary 'rational' categories. Thus myths are full of fabulous monsters, incarnate gods, virgin mothers. This middle ground is abnormal, nonnatural, holy. It is typically the focus of all taboo and ritual observance" (320).

49. Much has been written by ethnographers and cultural anthropologists about this paradox that the mythical breaker of taboos is also their enforcer and has a vital communal function. See Makarius, "Le mythe du 'Trickster.'" For the ritual figure (or sacred clown) who violates social norms but who is usually the policer of boundaries for others in the community see Hieb, "Meaning and Mismeaning"; Makarius, "Ritual Clowns"; also, Ashley, "An Anthropological Approach."

50. Monika Otter, *Inventiones,* has made a strong case for the existence of literary playfulness in Latin clerical writing of the twelfth century; "There is a good deal more flexibility, creative skepticism, and polyvocality than these critics [of vernacular literature] are willing to recognize. We shall see that many of the au-

thors about to be discussed—clerics all, though to various degrees semisecular in their professional lives and outlook—are perfectly capable of the textuality, the self-conscious voicing, the self-referencing, the playfulness, the 'parodic' quality that has been diagnosed so persuasively in their vernacular counterparts" (17–18). What Otter perceives in twelfth-century Latin clerical writing, we see in Bernard a century earlier, as we discuss more fully in the next chapter.

51. Robertini, *Liber,* 328, has identified Pliny's *Natural History* as the source from which Bernard crafted his anecdote about the lethal effects of goat's milk. On milk in general see Pliny, *Natural History,* book 28, section 33–36. On various cures for eye diseases, including goat's dung, goat's cheese, and goat's liver, see 28.47. On curing ulcers or wounds with a variety of substances, including goat's products, see 28.74. In 28.78 the brain of a she-goat is given drop by drop to babies before they are fed with milk to guard them against epilepsy. "The horn or hair of she-goats, when burnt, is said to keep serpents away, and the ash from the horn, whether taken in drink or applied, to be efficacious for their bites; as are also draughts of their milk with taminian grapes, or of their urine with squill vinegar; so too an application of goat cheese with marjoram, or of goat suet with wax" (28.42). Pliny goes on to give all kinds of other remedies with goat's dung for wounds. As Robertini notes, Bernard has combined several natural history "facts" from Pliny, but turned the cure into a producer of death. For a useful introduction to the scientific writing of the Elder Pliny see Duff, *Literary History,* 281–310. Duff points out that a primary interest of Pliny in his massive *Natural History* is the medications that can be procured from the animal world.

52. See Minnis, *Medieval Theory of Authorship,* for these developments in the twelfth century and beyond.

53. For a concise description of the reliquary-statue and further references see Boehm, *Medieval Head Reliquaries,* 207–12. On a rock crystal carving of the Crucifixion on the throne of the reliquary-statue see Kornbluth, *Engraved Gems.*

54. In one of the miracles of Saint Benedict written by Adrevald of Fleury between 865 and 877, Benedict similarly beats a man who threatened his authority, Raho, count of Orléans, who was plotting to kill the abbot of Saint-Benoît-sur-Loire. An old man wearing the habit of a monk appeared to Raho in a dream and spoke to him: "O count, how have I deserved that you want to kill my abbot?" When Raho denied the charge, the old man, whom Raho recognized as Benedict, "gave him a fierce look and struck his head with the crooked staff that he carried, saying 'Through your head I bear witness to the punishment that is going to be inflicted on you injuriously for this deed.'" Raho awoke in terror, related the dream, and died the next night (1.18; Certain, *Miracles,* 42–47). For a discussion of the significance of this episode for the abbey see Head, *Hagiography and the Cult of Saints,* 144.

55. In this reading of Bernard's "conversion" we differ from Brian Stock, who assigns Bernard of Angers to the same category as Guibert of Nogent, describing both as "critics of popular religion" who classify "a certain type of ritualism" as "primitive" (*Implications of Literacy,* 529).

56. Sigal, "Le travail des hagiographes," notes that there are few miracle col-

lections in which the author himself is the recipient or beneficiary of miracles" (157). In this, obviously, Bernard is exceptional, though see Van Dam on Gregory of Tours's repeated cures by St. Martin; according to his biographer, "Each time Gregory was ill, he ran to his own St. Martin and was quickly cured; this happened often" (*Leadership and Community*, 273). Van Dam suggests that in Gregory illness is linked to sin, so that a physical healing symbolized spiritual cleansing, but that link appears to be absent in the Bernardian miracles of the eleventh century.

57. Barre Toelken, interviewing tellers of Navaho coyote tales, elicited the response that "through the stories everything is made possible" ("'Pretty Languages' of Yellowman," 155). Trickster narratives make ideas available for thought; they can therefore function to critique the *status quo* as well as to model other possible arrangements. See also Ashley, "Interrogating Biblical Deception and Trickster Theories," 113–14).

Chapter Two

1. Critics have noted ways that the fourteenth-century English romance, *Sir Gawain and the Green Knight,* for example, is reflexive of the romance genre of the previous three centuries; see Gradon, *Form and Style,* 193; Bercovitch, "Romance and Anti-Romance"; Finlayson, "The Expectations of Romance."

2. For an excellent analysis of the "carefully worked out and consistently argued conception of the nature and role of the artistic image" in the *Libri Carolini* see Chazelle, "Matter, Spirit and Image in the *Libri Carolini.*"

3. For the classic description of the estates model see Duby, *The Three Orders.* Duby gives the year 1000 as the date when bishops adopted the "triangular figure" of the three estates. "Thirty or forty successive generations have imagined social perfection in the form of trifunctionality. This mental representation has withstood all the pressures of history. It is a structure" (5). However, Duby points out that the first explicit statement only appears in the third decade of the eleventh century in the work of Adalbero of Laon and Gerard of Cambrai (7). Although the division into these three orders is now the best known, other orderings were also used, as Constable shows in his discussion of "The Orders of Society" (*Three Studies,* 251–360).

4. For the history of this phenomenon see LeGoff, "Licit and Illicit Trades in the Medieval West" (*Time, Work and Culture,* 58–70).

5. See Aubrun, "Mythe et réalité."

6. See Little, "Pride Goes before Avarice."

7. The miracle of punishment for work on a feast day is a standard type in miracle collections; see, for example, the miracles of Saint Benedict. What is exceptional about the Bernardian version is its attribution to townspeople, who are negatively portrayed.

8. Curtius, *European Literature,* 428.

9. As C. Jan Swearingen points out, Cicero argued for the integration of rhetoric, philosophy, and literature: "Many in his era continued to see rhetoric as

a practical *techne* and to determine its merit solely by its persuasive success. Cicero does not deny to rhetoric its practical and technical elements, but he makes extensive reading in history, philosophy, religion, and literature prerequisite to the study of these elements. . . . The written materials which could provide this prerequisite curriculum did not exist in Latin in the first century B.C. One of Cicero's purposes, then, is to simultaneously argue for and exemplify the production of the liberal arts texts necessary for the training of the new, improved orator-citizen" (*Rhetoric and Irony*, 137). Swearingen adds that "Cicero's *artes liberales* and *eloquentia* represent an unprecedented and encyclopedic reconceptualization of Greek knowledge, literature, and education not simply through translation into Latin but also through cultural transformation" (139). It was this relocation of rhetoric "within a formal written literary milieu" that provided the basis for the literary liberal arts tradition the Middle Ages received and in which Bernard of Angers was schooled.

10. Behrends, "Introduction," in *Letters and Poems of Fulbert of Chartres*, xxx. For a broader picture of the teaching of Gerbert at Reims see Riché, "L'enseignement de Gerbert à Reims dans le contexte européen," in *Education et culture*, 51–69, and especially Lutz, *Schoolmasters of the Tenth Century*, 126–47. In his analysis of *The Cathedral School of Laon from 850 to 930: Its Manuscripts and Masters*, John Contreni summarizes the manuscript holdings (and therefore presumably the school's curricular emphases): "Greek studies and exegesis, history and geography, computation and chronology, medicine, law, and letter-writing represented special areas of interest in the library" (75).

11. MacKinney, "Bishop Fulbert," 286. See also MacKinney, *Bishop Fulbert and Education*. Since there is no evidence earlier than the twelfth century for Fulbert's period of study at Reims, Jeauneau (*L'age d'or*, 29) and Riché (*Gerbert d'Aurillac*, 76) doubt its truthfulness.

12. See, for example, Behrend's comments on the cathedral school at Chartres, which achieved preeminence under Fulbert (Behrends, ed., *Letters and Poems*, xv, xxviii–xxxvi; see also MacKinney, "Bishop Fulbert," 285–300; and MacKinney, *Bishop Fulbert and Education*).

13. In an excellent article on "The Hagiography of Hucbald of Saint-Amand," Julia Smith has demonstrated this Carolingian hagiographer's use of literary techniques that Bernard of Angers also employs: ". . . the hallmark of Hucbald's work was his easy familiarity with the authors on whom he depended, a familiarity so comfortable that he rarely drew his audience's attention to it. He generally chose not to flaunt his knowledge of patristic *auctors* by flagging his sources' identity, preferring instead to integrate into his work silent and unacknowledged quotations and paraphrases. This erudition was all the more effective for being concealed" (536). Smith has used Hucbald's "habit of adorning his saints' lives with a dense texture of biblical citations and with many unacknowledged quotations or paraphrases from a wide range of authors" to explore the holdings of the monastic library at Saint-Amand ("A Hagiographer at Work," 152).

14. See Robertini, *Liber*, 351.

15. Robertini (*op. cit.*, 359) indicates that this is taken word for word from Se-dulius's *Paschale carmen* III, 56. As Carl Springer comments, "For the Carolingians Sedulius enjoyed a reputation equal or even superior to Virgil," and his *Paschale carmen* evidently continued to be read in schools throughout the medieval period (*Gospel as Epic*, 132, 134).

16. For a study of the renewed popularity of Boethius in tenth-century Europe see Van de Vyver, "Les étapes du développement philosophique."

17. Robertini, *Liber*, 324–25, gives precise details of Bernard's repeated bor-rowings from Boethius in this scene.

18. Copeland, *Rhetoric, Hermeneutics*, 158.

19. *Ibid.*

20. Augustine, *On Christian Doctrine*, 37, 38. See also Augustine's suggestions throughout this treatise for interpretation of difficult passages. The burden of preparation is always on the reader, who must approach the text with the right will, prepared in languages, using good editions (78). Beyond that, the ambiguous signs of scriptural texts arise from the possibility that they can be read either liter-ally or figuratively (79). Augustine therefore offers detailed instructions on how to deal with this ambiguity. Biblical exegesis even before Augustine and throughout the Middle Ages used a "fourfold division of the [figurative] 'senses' of Scripture into literal, allegorical, anagogical and tropological," as G. R. Evans notes (*Lan-guage and Logic of the Bible*, 114). Interestingly, Bernard of Angers avoids using these figurative modes of interpretation in his miracle narratives, at least in com-parison with the monk-continuators.

21. Irvine, *Making of Textual Culture*, 257.

22. *Ibid.*, 259.

23. *Ibid.*, 260.

24. *Ibid.*, 270.

25. Copeland, *Rhetoric, Hermeneutics*, 158. On reading ambiguous signs and the principle of polyvalence see 156ff.

26. Cited by Evans, *Language and Logic of the Bible*, 106.

27. Jaeger, *Envy of Angels*, 110. Odo of Cluny describes St. Gerald as follows: "Gerald, therefore, was of medium height and well-proportioned. And while beauty encompassed all his members, his neck was of such shining white and so adorned to suit the eye, that you would think you had hardly seen another so beautiful. His beauty of mind further adorned the beauty of his body, so that the nature of his disposition shone forth in his appearance" (306–7).

28. Jaeger, *Envy of Angels*, 116.

29. *Ibid.*, 111–112.

30. *Ibid.*, 126.

31. *Ibid.*, 62.

32. Our argument, which draws on Jaeger's formulations, differs fundamentally from that of Gerald Bond in *The Loving Subject*. Bond tries to make a sharp dis-tinction between the "Christian curriculum" aligned with the ideologies of the traditional schools and an emerging secularism in literature and behavior. In Bond's view, monastic historians decry the new male courtesy (see 106–10).

33. Southern in *Medieval Humanism* asserts: "I believe the period from about 1100 to about 1320 to have been one of the great ages of humanism in the history of Europe," a statement he bases on "the reassertion of the claims of human dignity" (31). For Southern, the twelfth century represents a break in nearly every area of human life. He has, however, reconsidered (and substantially diminished) the place of Chartres in this twelfth-century Renaissance in "Chartrian Humanism: a Romantic Misconception," in *Scholastic Humanism* I: 58−101. On the twelfth-century Renaissance see also Constable, *Reformation of the Twelfth Century;* Chenu, *Nature, Man, and Society;* Evans, *Anselm and a New Generation;* and the older classic which first applied the term "Renaissance" to this period, Haskins, *Renaissance of the Twelfth Century.*

34. Stock acknowledges this point when he asks, "How characteristic is Bernard's obviously precocious mentality of broader aspects of eleventh- and twelfth-century religious change?" (*Implications of Literacy,* 71).

35. See Bynum, *Resurrection of the Body.*

36. Lifshitz, "Beyond Positivism and Genre," 104.

37. *Ibid.,* 105.

38. A broader application of the term "new men" to the period beginning in the fourteenth century is made by Duby (*Age of Cathedrals,* 195−220). With particular application to developments in artistic production and consumption, Duby identifies the "new man" who is an artist with a sense of professional freedom and secular values. See also Middleton, "Chaucer's 'New Men.'"

39. Southern, *Scholastic Humanism,* vol. I: *Foundations,* discusses the new alliance between the schools and centralizing governments in "The Men and Their Rewards" (163−97).

40. Jaeger, *The Origins of Courtliness.*

41. See Raybin, "Social Strain"; Hanning, "*Engin* in Twelfth Century Romance."

42. Bernard's critique of monasticism anticipates major themes of the reformation of the twelfth century (Constable, *The Reformation of the Twelfth Century*).

43. Gimon in his role as guardian of the sanctuary and scolder of the saint is reminiscent of a character named Christian who combines those traits in 1.26 of the miracles of Saint Benedict.

Chapter Three

1. Bonnassie and Gournay, "Sur la datation," discuss the dating of individual chapters. Robertini dates both books between 1030 and 1040 (*Liber,* 65).

2. Minnis, *Medieval Theory of Authorship,* 16.

3. *Ibid.,* 19. According to Minnis, by the eleventh century this "type C" prologue-paradigm emerges as the dominant rhetorical form.

4. "Le Midi s'est distingué par la quantité et la qualité de sa production. Dès l'époque mérovingienne, l'Aquitaine livre des oeuvres nombreuses et souvent riches d'informations. Les temps carolingiens ne sont pas en reste. Mais ce sont les Xᵉ et XIᵉ siècles qui voient la grande floraison de la littérature hagiographique.

Saint-Martial de Limoges, Sainte-Foy de Conques, Saint-Victor de Marseille en sont alors les foyers les plus prestigieux. Mais ils ne sont pas isolés: partout, dans tous les *scriptoria* monastiques ou canoniaux—à Périgueux, à Figeac, à Mauriac, à Mende, à Saint-Michel de Cuxa, par example—on a à coeur d'écrire la biographie du ou des saints locaux et de relater les prodiges qui se manifestent sur leurs tombeaux (Bonnassie, "Avant-Propos," 382). For descriptions of these materials and details of publication see Bonnassie, Sigal, and Iogna-Prat, "La Gallia du Sud. 930–1130."

5. "The work was an extended narrative of how a German nobleman named Henry had come to Micy and been cured of his lameness there through the intercession of St Maximinus. Since Henry remained for seven years as a servant in the abbey, the narrative was almost certainly recorded by a monk who knew him. It was written down in a somewhat careless hand in a crudely fashioned *libellus*. This little booklet was made from several scraps of poor-quality parchment, several of which had been scraped down after previous use as charters. The author recorded a story popular in his community on what was essentially scrap paper saved from the abbey's chancery, possibly with an eye to preserving the story for inclusion in a more formal collection of miracle stories. The booklet was fortuitously preserved, in incomplete form, as part of a collection of various hagiographic works from Micy bound together in the early modern period. It is impossible to determine how many similar booklets were kept in the archives of religious houses, which probably consisted of little more than a wooden cupboard or chest, waiting to serve as source material for later authors" (Head, *Hagiography and the Cult of Saints,* 78).

6. Sulpicius Severus, "Life of Saint Martin of Tours," 4.

7. A *libellus* is made up of a collection of texts about a single saint, as distinct from a legendary, which contains texts about more than one saint. Phillipart says that every pilgrimage center would have distributed small booklets containing texts about its saint (*Les légendiers latin,* 100). Such a book would also be called a *libellus.* We have no evidence of such booklets from Conques. It appears that the book compiled by the Conques monastery about their saint functioned to provide necessary liturgical materials for introducing Sainte Foy into the liturgy at other cult sites devoted to her.

8. According to Robertini, the word *Panaretos* is an epithet that authors such as Jerome, Cassiodorus, Isidore, and Bede normally reserve for biblical books (*Liber,* 383).

9. Fau, *Rouergue roman,* 26; Gournay, *Documents.*

10. Coleman, *Ancient and Medieval Memories,* 137–54, esp. 139–40; 151.

11. Hildebrandt, *External School,* 115. See also the map on p. 114, plotting the locations of members of the Reichenau prayer confraternity in about 826. It is important to note that the Reichenau prayer confraternity lasted until the twelfth century. On the Reichenau confraternity book see also Herrin, *Formation,* 480–87.

12. Hildebrandt, *External School,* 118.

13. As Knowles points out, the deliberate program of Alcuin in the Carolin-

gian period was to collect exemplars of classical works from Italy and urge monastic scriptoria to recopy them: "It was now that there began the quest and interchange of manuscripts, that multiplication of texts and that imitation of the Latin authors that continued for almost four centuries. . . . It was to the activity of the monks and bishops of this age that the transmission of the Latin classics was largely due" ("Preservation of the Classics," 142). On the contents and organization of Carolingian monastic libraries see also McKitterick, *Carolingians and the Written Word,* especially 165–210.

14. Fichtenau, *Living,* 292.

15. Birger Munk Olsen, "Production of the Classics," 8. On manuscripts of classical texts in this period see also Olsen, "La popularité," and Olsen, "Chronique," as well as Olsen, *L'étude.*

16. Mostert, "Tradition of Classical Texts," 26. Very little is known about the monastic library at Conques; no medieval catalogue survives and few manuscripts, most of them late medieval, can be assigned to such a library; for descriptions of surviving manuscripts from Conques see Lemaître, "Note sur les manuscrits."

17. Gournay, "Relire," 399.

18. Kendall, "Voice in the Stone," figure 4, p. 170.

19. *Ibid.,* 173.

20. Robertini, *Liber,* 333, n. 2, notes that the name Arseus is found neither in the cartulary of the monastery nor in other documents from the region.

21. Desjardins, *Cartulaire.*

22. See Rosenwein, *To Be the Neighbor of Saint Peter,* which deals with the gifts of land, specifically land that was repeatedly in circulation, as a way of forming bonds of community between lay donors and the monastery. See also McKitterick, *Carolingians and the Written Word,* especially chapter 3: "A Literate Community: The Evidence of the Charters" (77–134). It is also important to note that the monastery was growing both in its holdings and in the number of monks. From his detailed analysis of the cartulary, Gournay concludes that during the abbacy of Odalric (1031–65), which is when Conques's period of great acquisition begins, there were 212 monks of Conques, a number that includes those assigned to priories (*Etude du cartulaire,* 1 : 28).

23. Jean-Yves Tilliette, "Les modèles de sainteté," comments on the erudition, in particular training in the *trivium,* required to write hagiographic poetry: "écrire un poème, souvent long, en hexamètres ou en distiques élégiaques à cette époque requiert de la part de son auteur un très bon entrainement intellectuel, une connaissance solide et maîtrisée des arts du *trivium*" (383). Verse hagiographers were especially influenced by the Christian poets of late Antiquity, he notes (384).

24. "Il est remarquable de constater que le Moine Anonyme de Conques était au moins aussi cultivé que lui. Voilà qui suffit à balayer toutes les assertions que continue parfois à véhiculer l'historiographie actuelle sur la prétendue 'ignorance crasse' du clergé méridional avant la réforme grégorienne" (Bonnassie, Review of *Liber miraculorum,* 477).

25. This corporate voice of the monk-continuators is closer than Bernard's in-

dividualistic voice to norms of miracle collections; see, for example, the narrative voice in the miracles of Saint Benedict.

26. Bonnassie and Gournay, "Sur la datation," 464–70; Robertini, *Liber,* 65–66.

27. After giving their reasons for Odolric's authorship, Bonnassie and Gournay admit, "L'hypothèse est fragile car le secret a été bien ficelé" ("Sur la datation," 472).

28. Bonnassie and Gournay, "Sur la datation," 473: "Si ce n'est pas lui, ce ne peut être qu'un moine de Conques aux contacts nombreux, aux horizons très vastes et d'une culture hors du commun."

29. Michel Foucault, "What Is an Author?" See also the discussion by Donald Pease, "Author." Pease comments that "produced by the practices whose reproduction it guarantees, the name of the author turns otherwise unrelated discursive practices into a coherent cultural realm over which it maintains jurisdiction" (113).

30. In 3.1 Foy is called "medicabile"; in 3.11 the word "medicantibus" refers to Foy's actions.

31. For a discussion of this ritual as an example of liturgical cursing see Little, *Benedictine Maledictions.*

32. The Foy of this monk-continuator is a martyr whose life mimics the master narrative of Christ's Passion. Bernard's master narrative is closer to Victor Turner's idea of social drama, where the powers of the saint are appropriated by groups in conflict to enhance their positions (see "Social Dramas").

33. On the great changes in the cult of Mary in the later eleventh and twelfth centuries see Johnson, "Marian Devotion."

34. According to Poulin, it is a hagiographic *topos* that resurrection of the dead is reserved for the greatest of saints (*L'idéal de sainteté,* 112).

35. "Alma," used to characterize Foy, is a Roman epithet for nurturing goddesses.

36. Nancy Siraisi suggests, "In reality, the most serious competitor to the healing power of the saints in the early Middle Ages was probably less the surviving tradition of ancient secular medicine than the non-Christian religious or magical folk practices and beliefs widespread in a partially or superficially Christianized society" (*Medieval and Early Renaissance Medicine,* 11). In the introductory poem of 4.23 (4.28) the monk-author positions Foy above both of these traditions.

37. On this point see Arbesmann, "Concept of 'Christus Medicus'"; Fichtner, "Christus als Arzt"; and Honecker, "Christus medicus."

38. "According to this theory, when the Devil beguiled men into sin he won the right to take them in death. In order to redeem mankind, the deity disguised himself in human flesh, and the disguise tricked the Devil into attempting to kill one who was not mortal. This abuse of the Devil's legitimate power cancels the Devil's claim to men's souls after the coming of Christ" (Ashley, "The Guiler Beguiled," 128). The narrative of atonement which casts Christ as trickster was developed and elaborated by virtually every major theologian after Irenaeus (second

century) in the Greek and Latin traditions. Augustine and Gregory the Great were particularly fond of the images of Christ's flesh as bait on a hook or in a mousetrap to entice the Devil, and Christ's harrowing of hell—leading the patriarchs from Death towards the light of heaven—was an important image for Christ the divine trickster.

39. The narrative of the hernia miracle parodies the figure of the blacksmith, who was associated with the low, the sinister, and even the demonic in the medieval imagination. But Foy's blacksmith is a kind of joke on this usual medieval image, for he is reluctant in the extreme, afraid of collaborating in the warrior's self-annihilation, aware of legal penalties he might have to pay to the victim's next of kin, and generally a man of conscience who refuses to play the lethal games of Foy the trickster. As her chosen agent, however, he is a reminder that in world folklores the blacksmith is a figure of liminal powers. On "the blacksmith prince" of West Africa, see Balendier, "Blacksmith"; see also McNutt, "The African Ironsmith as Marginal Mediator."

40. As medical historian Ynez Violé O'Neill notes, "There are two ancient authorities on the subject of hernias, Aulus Cornelius Celsus and Paul of Aegina" (Personal communication, December 14, 1992). In his *De medicina,* written in Latin in the first century C.E., Celsus describes procedures for the treatment of hernia, and specifically for inguinal hernia, that condition in which the peritoneum ruptures and allows the intestines to descend into the scrotum. For any patient other than a child, surgery was required. John Raaf describes Celsus's recommended procedure: "An incision was to be made in the groin and the testis carefully dissected out. This however, should not be performed in a strong man but only 'when the patient is of a tender age and the mischief is moderate.' It is thought that Celsus then recommended ligation of the sac and possibly its removal. After dissecting away as much of the structures as the operator considered necessary he was to cut away the skin edges and let the wound heal in by granulation. This produced scar tissue and a firm cicatrix at the external ring. If the hernia was large the actual cautery was used; probably for the purpose of producing more scar tissue" (Raaf, "Hernia Healers," 379). During this procedure Celsus recommends that the patient's body should be in a specific position for which he uses the word "*resupinato.*" Celsus writes, "At, cum infra incidi oportet, resupinato homine. . . ." ("When it is necessary that an incision be made down below, after the patient has been tilted back or laid flat on his back . . ." ["*Resupinato*" can be read either way.]) (*De medicina,* VII, 19, as quoted in Belloni, "Historical Notes," 372). Paul of Aegina, writing in the seventh century, recommends essentially the same procedure, and a post-medieval Latin translation of his Greek uses the same phrase: "*homine resupinato*" (*De re medica,* VI, 65, cited in Belloni, "Historical Notes," 372).

Similar techniques are described in the earliest surgical treatise written in Latin in the medieval West: that of Ruggero Frugardi of Salerno, also called Roger of Parma, who wrote in the 1170s, and in later commentaries on it. Their treatment of scrotal hernia is as follows:

"If the intestines descend into the scrotum, first restore them to their proper place. If this cannot be done easily, clyster or purge, then apply mollifacients and replace the intestines as we have said. Have an assistant place a finger on the rupture while the physician cuts into the thin skin above the testicle at this point. Having extracted the testicle [from the peritoneum], scrape the inguinal canal even to the top with an instrument. If there is wind in the canal decompress it internally. Suture [the top of the inguinal canal] well with thread, and bind with thread leaving it detached at each end so that it hangs an inch outside the suture. Placing the patient on a plank, burn the inguinal canal with cauteries thrice, up to the thread" (MacKinney, *Medical Illustrations,* 79, quoting from what he calls "the similarly detailed accounts of Rogerius [*Chirurgia,* III, 33] and Rolandus [*Chirurgia,* III, 32]").

Folio 24v in a late thirteenth-century manuscript of the *Chirurgia Rolandina,* Rolando of Parma's commentary on Ruggero Frugardi's surgical treatise, shows this operation in progress. The caption reads "First the patient is made to lie down on a board with head and shoulders depressed so that the entire intestine descends towards the chest" ("In primis patiens collocetur in bance caput et humeros habens depressos, ut tota intestina descentant ad pectus" [Belloni, "Historical Notes," 372 and figure 1]). For a facsimile edition of Rolando's treatise see *Chirurgia.*

The position of the body described here is of great interest to medical history. The medical historian Luigi Belloni firmly states, "Roland's text and illustration represent the earliest documentary and quite incontestable evidence of the use of the inverted position in human surgery" ("Historical Notes," 373). Physicians today know it by the term "the Trendelenburg position," named for Friedrich Trendelenburg (1844–95), professor of surgery in the Universities of Rostock, Bonn, and Leipzig. Trendelenburg devised a special operating table for securing patients in the desired position (illustrated in Belloni, "Historical Notes," figure 10).

41. Medical historians have found no definitive evidence that the inverted position for hernia operations, presumably coming from the classical authorities Celsus and Paul of Aegina, was used before the thirteenth century. But the joking use of the inverted position here suggests that the monk-author of this miracle was familiar with one of these authors. The availability of these texts is still a vexed issue. Paul of Aegina wrote in Greek in the seventh century. His work was translated into Arabic in the ninth century. Abulcasis (died after 1009) incorporated Paul's description of hernia treatment into his work. Belloni says that Abulcasis "hinted at the use of the inclined inverted position in operating for hernia" (Belloni, "Historical Notes," 372). However, Abulcasis was translated into Latin by Gerard of Cremona only in the last quarter of the twelfth century and in Latin translation his description of the position uses entirely different language: "Tum jacet in cervicem suam inter manus tuas et elevet crura sua" (*De chirurgia,* II, 65, cited in Belloni, 372). The monks of Conques could have known Paul only in Greek or Arabic.

Celsus wrote in Latin in the first century; three copies of Celsus were made in northern Italian monasteries in the ninth and tenth centuries (Siraisi, *Medieval and Early Renaissance Medicine*, 213, citing L. D. Reynolds, *Texts and Transmissions: A Survey of the Latin Classics,* Oxford, 1983). Some historians of medicine have assumed that, as Nancy Siraisi puts it, "Celsus' work . . . was too long and complicated to be of practical use to early medieval western *medici*" (161). Others have assumed that Celsus was completely unknown in the Christian West and ignored in the Christian East because he was a pagan ("Le tome VI de *Encyclopédie* de Celse, consacré à la Médicine, réserve ses 7ᵉ et 8ᵉ livres à la chirurgie. Il ne fut retrouvé que tardivement par le Pape Nicolas V [1397–1455]. Ce fut, après qu'il ait été perdu pendant près de 1400 ans, le premier livre de médecine imprimé [1478]. La meilleure édition latine est celle d'Angelo Del Lungo [Florence 1904]. Ignoré des médicins contemporains grecs qui appréciaient peu l'oeuvre d'un profane, le traité de Celse fut, en fait, à peine connu au Moyen-Age et n'exerça une influence réelle qu'à partir de la Renaissance" [Huard and Grmek, *Mille ans de chirurgie en Occident,* 8–9]).

However, Foy's treatment of hernia suggests that knowledge of these ancient authorities, and most likely of Celsus, had circulated in southern France by the mid eleventh century.

42. Foy's cure offers a striking contrast to a cure for hernia in the miracles of Saint Thomas Becket, illustrated in the stained glass at Canterbury Cathedral. The miracle took place between 1171 and 1173. James, son of Roger, Earl of Clare, developed an inguinal hernia while still an infant "owing to over-violent crying" (from the account by Benedict of Canterbury, who completed a book of Saint Thomas Becket's miracles before 1175. See Abbott, *St. Thomas of Canterbury*). His mother took James to Thomas's shrine at Canterbury and was advised there to "wash the boy's diseased parts with the healing Water" (that is, water imbued with the martyr's blood). "By merely washing she gained complete health for him whom she washed. No other kind of cure was employed" (from the description of this miracle by William of Canterbury, who issued his book of Saint Thomas's miracles before 1189. See Abbott, *St. Thomas,* 2.202).

This miracle is illustrated in window S.VII of Trinity Chapel, executed between 1213 and 1220. The illustration shows the totally magical character of this miracle attributed to Thomas Becket—as the mother applies the healing liquid the boy stands erect, the worst possible position for treating an inguinal hernia. We therefore must concur with the author of the miracle story, William of Canterbury, that "faith alone reduced the intestines into their place." The warrior in our narrative also needed faith, but in the form of Foy, the trickster-physician, who effected his cure through a parody of a procedure known to medical science.

43. For a compilation of materials on the *prosimetrum* form see Pabst, *Prosimetrum;* see also Charles Wittke's review cautioning that Pabst's "characterization of the different phases of hagiographic prosimetra (788–92) may depend too much on the accidental preservation of the texts."

Some authors use the term "Menippean satire" interchangeably with *prosime-*

trum but, as Peter Dronke points out, "the uses of the mixed form, in many periods, extend far beyond the Menippean" (*Verse with Prose,* 1). The form was especially popular among the *grandes rhétoriqueurs* at the fifteenth-century Burgundian court; see "Versiprosa" in Kittay and Godzich, *Emergence of Prose,* 46–76.

44. Dronke (*Verse with Prose,* 2) finds the earliest use of the term in a treatise by Hugh of Bologna, *Rationes dictandi,* ca. 1119. "Hugh . . . defines the *prosimetrum* as a branch of poetic composition. For him the poetic aspect is integral to the form and determines its nature, even if 'we call it a *prosimetrum* when a part is expressed in verse and a part in prose.'"

45. It is not clear that this example should even be considered *prosimetrum* since Bernard doesn't mix verse and prose, but switches to verse entirely.

46. Pabst, *Prosimetrum,* 670. Pabst attributes these effects to the author's powers of composition; as Robertini shows, they are heavily adapted from Venantius Fortunatus (*Liber,* 396).

47. Michael Roberts has analyzed the techniques of this "jeweled style" of poetry (which flourished in late Antiquity) that the Foy miracle incorporates (*The Jeweled Style*).

Chapter Four

1. See Krötzl, *Pilger, Mirakel und Alltag.*

2. Robertini, *Liber,* 368.

3. *Ibid.,* 369, discusses Raymond's supposed departure from Luna "vocabulo ab antiquis celebratam": "Il riferimento a Luni è di probabile origine letteraria. . . . Il riferimento a Luni ha qui probabilmente soltanto carattere generico per indicare la costa ligure: l'impianto fortemente letterario su cui è strutturato il miracolo induce a credere che Bernardo abbia voluto inserire, come in molti altri casi, un'allusione erudita alle sue letture, per altro esplicitamente ammessa (*ab antiquis celebratam*)."

4. Olivia Remie Constable, "Muslim Spain and Mediterranean Slavery," 266.

5. See Williams, "*Generationes Abrahae,*" for a discussion of Hagar and Muslim women and their association with sexuality; as John Boswell points out, this polemic grows during the First Crusade, and by the thirteenth century "wanton and violent sexuality were prominent and regular attributes of Muslim society in most Western literature" (*Christianity, Social Tolerance, and Homosexuality,* 281). See also Mark Jordan's characterization of Hrotswitha's "Passion of Saint Pelagius" as a "project of moral codification" (*The Invention of Sodomy,* 21).

6. Moore, *Formation of a Persecuting Society,* 91–94. It is important to acknowledge, however, that for Moore, "the accusation of homosexuality became an acceptable and accepted basis for persecution" only in the thirteenth century (94).

7. Pabst, *Prosimetrum,* 671.

8. Bouillet, *Liber,* xvi.

9. Stevens, *Sidonius Apollinaris,* 176–77. See also the characterization by Erich Auerbach in *Literary Language and Its Public:* "The great model for epideictic description was Sidonius . . . the gaudy peacock, as Alan of Lille called him" (196;

also 197–98 and 255 ff.). Auerbach comments that there is something "spooky" about Sidonius's playfulness: "His art resembles a difficult game which consists in capturing the truth and even the concrete reality of things in a mesh of rhetorical figures; . . . his style was highly esteemed and much imitated in the schools of the Middle Ages. But it is a game for the initiate; only a small clique could appreciate without effort his incessant parallel figures, his unduly rich and select vocabulary, and his tricky sentence structure" (258).

10. Weyman, "Apollinaris Sidonius," was the first modern scholar to discover the extensive use of Sidonius in the V–L group.

11. Robertini, *Liber,* 67. For an edition of Sidonius see Sidonius, *Poems and Letters.*

12. Stevens, *Sidonius Apollinaris,* 32.

13. *Ibid.,* 87.

14. The italicized words are taken from Sidonius. See Robertini, *Liber,* who identifies each Sidonian borrowing.

15. The monks' eyewitness to the miracle is expressed in more Sidonian word-play: "acclamatur ab omnibus, conclamatur a nobis" (compare Sidonius, *Poems and Letters, Epist.* I, 7, 10: "acclamatur ab accusatoribus, conclamatur a iudicibus").

16. Other puns on Foy in V–L include: L.3: "Fidem enim habuit" (For they had faith); L.4: "salva fidei reverentia, dixerim, virgo Fidis" (with all due reverence for faith, I would say, the virgin Faith); L.5: "fides firmarat" (faith fortified); L.6: "Aderit statim sancte Fidei meritum, que dabit cunctos cernere future fidei signum" (At once Saint Faith's power was present, she who was about to give them all a sign of faith in the life to come).

17. Sidonius, *Epist.* I, 2, 9: "two men known for their biting wit." Robertini, *Liber,* 422, says the words "mimici sales" come from Sidonius and in this context mean "actors"; W. B. Anderson in Sidonius, *Poems and Letters,* translates them as "the banter of low comedians."

18. "ut de eorum discutiendis nominibus non sit adeo posteritas elaboratura," taken from "ut de nominibus ipsorum quandoque reminiscendis sit posteritas laboratura: namque improborum probra aeque ut praeconia bonorum immortalia manent" (Sidonius, *Poems and Letters, Epist.,* V, 8, 3).

Translator W. B. Anderson comments on the line from Sidonius that is part of a letter complimenting a friend on his satiric verse: "The meaning, if I am right, is 'The names of the wicked today will not be so utterly forgotten in future ages that your satire about them will fall flat.'"

19. "apud quos iugiter status seriarum peregrinatur actionum" (Sidonius, *Poems and Letters, Epist.* I, 5, 10).

20. *Ibid.,* I, 7, 7.

Chapter Five

1. Tension between the two originated with the founding of a monastery at Figeac in 838 to be called the "New Conques." Whether there was continuing

friction from that time forward is a subject of scholarly disagreement. A papal intervention of 1084 is evidence of open conflict in the later eleventh century, which was surely a live issue at the time the late miracle narratives were written. On the founding of Figeac and its relationship with Conques see Remensnyder, *Remembering Kings Past,* 271–76.

2. For a brief overview of this history see the introduction to Sheingorn, *Book of Sainte Foy,* 6–21. For a thorough treatment up to 1250 see Bousquet, *Le Rouergue,* 273–363.

3. For an introduction to these theoretical approaches to texts see Hawkes, *Structuralism and Semiotics,* and Eagleton, *Criticism and Ideology,* especially 64–101.

4. This aim was not unique to the Foy cult. Wendy Davies has made a strong argument that "property rights and property claims were a preoccupation of the earliest Welsh hagiographic writing—as of much Celtic hagiography" ("Property rights and property claims," 515). Davies speculates that the emphasis in Welsh hagiography on defending property rights may be connected to the "unstable political structure of Wales in the tenth and eleventh centuries" (527).

5. The absence of rival male ecclesiastical institutions is obviously a function of the semiotic paradigm in force in the *Liber,* since many such institutions existed in the region. However, the absence of nuns in *Liber* narratives may be closer to historical reality, since evidently there were very few female monasteries in the Midi before 1100. See Venarde, *Women's Monasticism,* 46.

6. Moore, *Formation of a Persecuting Society,* 68, citing Gratian's *Decretals.* Moore says that "heresy exists only insofar as authority chooses to declare its existence" (68), and he argues that it was only in the eleventh century that the reforming Church chose to label certain behaviors as heretical because it was attempting to impose uniformity of belief and practice. See also G. R. Evans's discussion of antiheretical formulations as "a missionary theology" connected to the consolidation of Catholic orthodox positions (*Old Arts and New Theology,* 137–66). Brian Stock discusses the vexed historiography of early eleventh-century heresy in *Implications of Literacy,* 92–151, and concludes there was a "making of heresies" by "placing of relatively isolated events in a literary format of shared assumptions among authors and readers" (146). See also R. I. Moore's claim that "the literacy of the eleventh century was the restricted literacy of all traditional societies, and had its usual corollaries—the mystification of the book, the social and political aggrandisement of those who had access to it, the consequent extension and reinforcement of social hierarchy, the identification of orthodoxy with privilege and illiteracy with unfreedom, and the elaboration of a concept of heresy to police the frontier between them" ("Literacy and the Making of Heresy," 20).

7. Bouillet, *Liber,* 213, reads "canum attegiam forensem," which is translated in Sheingorn, *Book of Sainte Foy,* as "doghouse." However, Robertini, *Liber,* 258, amends to "camini attegiam forensem," which would translate literally as "a public tent with an open furnace," and presumably refers to a rough structure over a smelting furnace.

8. For a discussion of early eleventh-century uses of the term "heresy" see

Pierre Bonnassie and Richard Landes, "Une nouvelle hérésie est neé dans le monde," in M. Zimmermann, ed., *Les sociétés méridionales autour de l'an mil,* 435–59.

9. Pizarro, *Rhetoric of the Scene,* 8. His theory is that "features of the new narrative manner . . . were taken over from traditional oral storytelling." Pizarro notes a "convergence of high and popular culture" which "leaves its unmistakable stamp upon the new style" (15).

10. *Ibid.,* 9.

11. Patrick Geary, for example, has noted that in the writings of eleventh-century historians women are represented on the whole negatively in contrast to their role in historical texts of the East: "Memorial texts of France, especially chronicles and histories roughly contemporary with imperial ones—that is, the late tenth and eleventh centuries—present a radically different image of women from that in the empire period. One looks in vain for a positive image of a woman in Rodulfus Glaber and Ademar of Chabannes. . . . The images of the role of women in the two societies as reflected in eleventh-century historiography thus cannot be explained by a difference in their social condition, actual access to property, or public involvement. Rather the varying images of tenth-century women created by authors of the eleventh century results neither entirely from events, inheritance law, or mortality tables but come also from differing ideologies closely tied to different power relationships within the two regions and the perceived roles of women within the traditions of liturgical *memoria*" (Geary, *Phantoms of Remembrance,* 67–68). Though we refer to the pervasive denigration of women in clerical culture, we recognize that misogyny has a history and increased markedly after the "exceptionally well documented restructuring of the gender system" in the early twelfth century so convincingly analyzed by Jo Ann McNamara ("The *Herrenfrage*"). For a sophisticated analysis of the semiotic role played by a female patron saint in a male monastery after the gender shift, see Otter, "Temptation of St. Æthelthryth."

12. One striking exception to Bernard's overall lack of misogyny is also exceptional in many other ways, including its rather positive construction of a warrior. In 2.2, after Raymond's wife is given reason to believe that he has died in a shipwreck, she "feigned grief for a while, but did not turn it into a matter of heavy weeping or long sighs as is the custom of good women. Instead, she quickly made herself an elegant spectacle for men and threw herself with unbridled passion into faithless and untrustworthy love in its many and varied forms." Out of her "blind lust" the woman not only endangers the inheritance of her daughters, but also plots her husband's murder when he returns. It seems significant that neither monks nor the Conques monastery is even mentioned in this tale of adventure, which stands completely outside Bernard's central gender system. However, we would read this construction not as undercutting our generalization, but as an antitype to both the good wife and the Conques locale.

13. "This *Liber miraculorum,* many episodes in which concern Languedoc, provides a very full picture of all the various types of violence practiced at that pe-

riod, and thus makes it possible to establish a veritable typology of exactions by nobles in the eleventh century" (Bonnassie, "From the Rhône to Galicia," 119). Recently there has been a trend in historiography to emphasize the importance of this movement as well as to connect it, in some cases, to the apocalypticism of the year 1000. See, for example, Head and Landes, *Peace of God;* Landes, *Relics, Apocalypse.* Most recently Dominique Barthélemy has dissented, arguing that early eleventh-century texts have been misconstrued by other scholars; the "real historical background" of the "*peaces* of God" was "neither a social crisis nor an eschatological one" ("La paix de Dieu," 3). Barthélemy sees the crisis of the year 1000 as a construction of nineteenth-century historiography. Marcus Bull also plays down the impact of the Peace of God, though from the perspective of the First Crusade, with which it has been linked (*Knightly Piety,* 21–69).

14. "After the year 1000, the size of the nobility again expanded as a new group of families, the castellans, began to consolidate their power and marry the daughters of older noble families, as had the viscounts before them. By the eleventh century, the old nobility, enlarged by the inclusion of the former viscounts, had begun to lose part of its wealth due to generations of partible inheritance and of generous gifts to local monasteries. At this time a new social group, the castellans, accumulated and consolidated sufficient power to join the noble ranks. The castles that had sprung up across Europe in the tenth and eleventh centuries in the wake of the invasions became central points around which power could be built" (Bouchard, "Origins of the French Nobility," 521).

15. Farmer, "Persuasive Voices," 521. The existence of the "pious matron" as supporter of emerging Christian institutions is a recurrent motif in histories of the early Middle Ages. Even as they were creating misogynistic discourses the early Church fathers often benefited from communities of pious women who supported their proselytizing efforts. A little later the churchmen supported noblewomen who wished to escape onerous marriages; as Dyan Elliott has pointed out, "The women in question were highly connected, often better Christians than their husbands, and better potential patrons of the Church. Moreover, the institution of marriage was by no means as stable as it was to become, nor had the Church yet surfaced as its chief protector" ("Dress as Mediator," 285). See also Schulenburg, "Sexism;" Nelson, "Les femmes." Georges Duby has also noted the importance of noble wives as symbolically powerful figures between 1050 and the end of the twelfth century, a role the lady plays in letters of clerical direction ("Women and Power").

16. Elisabeth Magnou-Nortier, who has studied the presence of women in tenth- and eleventh-century documents from Languedoc, concludes: "Les femmes de l'aristocratie méridionale, les seules qui aient laissé une trace, paraissent ressembler à des pièces d'un jeu d'échec qui les familles ont souvent maniées avec habileté" ("Ombres féminines," 56). It would not be in the nature of such documents, however, to record the kinds of mediating actions described in the *Liber miraculorum.*

17. Geary, *Phantoms of Remembrance,* makes a similar semiotic point (though

without using our terminology) about the negative portrayal of women in some French liturgical *memoria* of the eleventh and twelfth century: ". . . the so-called French model was not so much French as monastic. Who should be responsible for the *memoria* of the family? The answer given in the West was offered not coincidentally by reformed monks such as Odilo and Rodulfus Glaber. Not women, but men—or better reformed monks, angels in Cluniac ideology—can best guard both the liturgical commemoration of the dead and the narrative, formal memory of the past, a memory in which women are present only in a passive manner. In the following century the contrast between Cluny's efficacy and the unreliability of even well-intentioned women in the care of the dead was underlined in Peter the Venerable's *De miraculis*" (68). Geary concludes that "women were the primary rivals of the reformed monastic tradition in the domain of memory" (73).

18. "Lord Ebalus" is Ebles I of Comborn, then lord of Turenne; see Bull, *Knightly Piety,* 215, for a discussion of the viscounts of Turenne.

19. As Bull (*Knightly Piety,* 51) notes, "There is good circumstantial evidence that the Aquitanian Peace petered out in the mid- and late 1030s."

20. Vogel, in his survey of penitentials, identifies two types of penance used in the period from the eighth through the eleventh century: public penance for serious public misbehavior and penitential penalties for sins committed out of the public eye. Beginning in the twelfth century and codified in the thirteenth century and after, a three-part penitential system developed, including solemn public penance, sacramental private penance, and the penitential pilgrimage (*Le pécheur et la pénitence,* 36). Payen has described the importance of theories of contrition for the twelfth- and thirteenth-century development of penitential systems; this transformation in understanding of the penitential process coincided not just with the Gregorian reform but also with new forms of affective piety ("La pénitence," esp. 402).

21. Brundage analyzes the work of the "major German canonist of the early tenth century, Regino of Prüm, who compiled his *Two Books Concerning Synodal Cases and Ecclesiastical Discipline* about 906, as his major example of the teaching of the Church before the era of reform. Regino's penitential was centrally concerned with "ritual purity and the need to cleanse oneself from sexual defilement as a condition for participation in the sacred mysteries of the Church" (*Law, Sex, and Christian Society,* 172, 174). Brundage bases his analysis of sexual purity in the penitentials on the theories of Mary Douglas in *Purity and Danger.*

22. The description of communal rejoicing within the church in this narrative resembles that of Augustine (*City of God,* XXII, 8) when a young man afflicted with trembling of his limbs was cured at the shrine of St. Stephen: "Who could then refrain from giving praise to God? The whole church was filled in every corner with shouts of thanksgiving. . . . The church was packed, and it rang with the shouts of joy: 'Thanks be to God! God be praised!' The cries came from all sides; not a mouth was silent" (1046). Compare to the Foy miracle 4.3: "Everyone was filled with indescribable joy by this; the air rang mightily with their exuberant

shouts; with their voices rivaling one another they made the whole basilica reverberate with declarations of praise."

23. Caroline Bynum surveys the late twentieth-century fascination with body as construct and what she calls the "cacophony of [medieval] discourses" about the body, sexuality, and gender. She argues however that in contrast to the twentieth century the Middle Ages was much more concerned with "the body that dies" than the sexual body ("Why All the Fuss?" 7, 8).

24. It is also significant that, as Jody Enders points out, classical rhetorical theories, such as those of Pseudo-Cicero and Quintilian, taught that ugliness, deformation, violence, and comic effects were believed to increase the usefulness of images as memory devices ("Rhetoric, coercion, and the memory of violence").

25. See Victor Turner on "Social Dramas." See also Ashley and Sheingorn, "An Unsentimental View of Ritual," 74–77. We note that—although Turner's model of social drama assumes that the dissident factions or individuals will eventually be reintegrated—the society represented in the *Liber* "more frequently produces resolution by expelling the incongruent element, thus ritually reestablishing group boundaries" (74).

26. A.1 tells a similar story of the inevitable losses associated with worldly responsibilities. Here there is only one child: "He brought up his son with the greatest care, for Raymond was his sole heir and he expected that this boy would be the precious consolation of his life, a universal feeling among humankind." The narrator is aware of the emotional investment involved in raising a child to adulthood: "And what could be more painful for them, now that he had been with them for so long and stood on the brink of a successful adult life, than to lose him to harsh Death?" Despite the sympathetic tone in the monk-narrator's voice, the moral is clear: life in the world entails pain.

27. Sigal, "Le travail des hagiographes," offers two purposes for hagiographic composition: the liturgical one of celebrating the feast day of the saint and an economic one of attracting pilgrims to the shrine (150). The *Liber miraculorum* we have analyzed served both purposes, although our rhetorical and ideological analyses suggest the importance of the second purpose in shaping the text by emphases and exclusions.

28. Katrien Heene, in "*Audire, legere, vulgo,*" points to a shift away from pastoral uses of hagiography in the Carolingian period. "The fact that hagiographical texts, which seem to have been an important pastoral medium in the Merovingian Age, almost totally ceased to be used as such after the beginning of the ninth century, could, however, be at least partly due to the fact that reformed Latin became the language of communication of a restricted group, while it was then incomprehensible for the man in the street" (155).

Conclusion

1. The posthumous miracles of Saint Benedict are included, as are the Miracles of Sainte Foy, in the statistical analyses of Sigal (*L'homme et le miracle*).

2. Head, *Hagiography and the Cult of Saints,* situates the miracles of St. Benedict written at Fleury within the corpus of the hagiographic writing from the Orléanais. For overviews of these miracle stories see Leclercq, "Violence et dévotion"; Rollason, "The Miracles of St Benedict"; Ward, "The Miracles of Saint Benedict"; and Ward, *Miracles and the Medieval Mind.*

3. Monks of Fleury continued to compose miracles of St. Benedict in the twelfth century, but we have not included these later authors in our comparisons with the miracles of Sainte Foy. The editor of the Benedict miracles, Eugène de Certain, supplied sequential book numbers to the collections written by the various Fleury monks, and scholarly convention follows that numbering. Thus, Adrevald wrote book 1, Aimo is the author of books 2 and 3, and Andrew composed books 4 through 7. On the authors and the relationships among their compositions see Vidier, *L'historiographie.*

4. This is confirmed by charter evidence: "The monks of Fleury had another special friend of great power: their king. The history of this relationship can be traced in the relatively few charters which survive for Fleury during this period. In 818 Louis the Pious bestowed a set of exemptions including judicial *immunitas,* the right of the community to elect its own abbot, and certain fiscal exemptions. The king promised his *defensio* of these rights in return for the prayers of the monks for the benefit of his soul and of his kingdom. In various versions these privileges were renewed by Carolingian rulers and by Hugh Capet. The monks were friends of Hugh Capet not only because he was the successor to the Carolingians but also because they had a long-standing relationship with the Robertian family. Royal privileges, of course, could only exempt the monks of Fleury from temporary lordship and claims made against it in secular courts. Nevertheless, when respected and enforced, such exemptions could provide a 'royal monastery' such as Fleury with an impressive weapon to be wielded against their neighboring secular and ecclesiastical magnates. Moreover, it should be remembered that the Capetian king wielded more direct power over the Orléanais during this period than he did over the contemporary Mâconnais or over Touraine during the later eleventh and twelfth centuries" (Rosenwein, Head, and Farmer, "Monks and Their Enemies," 779–80).

5. Due to the initial weakness of the Capetians and their failure to defend the rights of the monastery, Abbot Abbo felt it necessary to produce a biography of King Edmund of East Anglia to model pious royal behavior: "Although Hugh Capet had indeed renewed the traditional Carolingian privileges of the abbey of Fleury, Abbo [abbot at the time] recognized that such a guarantee of royal defence would no longer suffice in and of itself. It was necessary to redefine what royal support of monastic rights entailed and in the process to reformulate the very definitions of the offices of king, bishop, and abbot" (Head, *Hagiography and the Cult of Saints,* 241).

6. The differences among monastic institutions, even those from the same period and practicing the same form of monasticism, remain great, as Rosenwein, Head, and Farmer demonstrate ("Monks and Their Enemies"). In their compari-

son of Cluny, Fleury, and Marmoutier these authors show that "regional political variations decisively affected" the ways that each institution handled conflict (766).

7. On the Peace League of Bourges see Head, "The Judgment of God."

8. As David Rollason notes, "Much attention is lavished on the history of Fleury. . . . But the writers' horizon extended beyond Fleury and its properties to take in the history of Western Francia. Adrevald draws, for example, a picture of the later Merovingians and the accession of the Carolingians; and his successors devote chapters to the transference of power to the Capetians, the heresy which arose in Orléans and was condemned in 1022, the troubles of Henry I with his mother Constance and so on. The reader frequently has the impression of dealing with a chronicle rather than with a miracle-collection, an impression reinforced by the inclusion of information about eclipses, floods and famines which are standard elements in full-blown chronicles" ("The Miracles of St Benedict," 76–77).

9. Head, *Hagiography and the Cult of Saints,* 139.

10. Rollason, "The Miracles of St Benedict," 87.

11. Head, *Hagiography and the Cult of Saints,* 5.

12. Gournay, "Relire." The practice of a monastery's sending a collection of miracles about its patron saint to one of its priories is documented for this same period at Fleury, from which a collection of the miracles of Saint Benedict was sent to the priory of Perrecy (Head, *Hagiography and the Cult of Saints,* 127).

13. For a description of the former abbey church of Sainte Foy and other extant monastic buildings see Shaver-Crandell and Gerson, *Pilgrim's Guide,* 179–81, with relevant bibliography. In addition, see Fau, *Rouergue roman,* 3rd ed., 104–247, which includes many illustrations.

14. See Bousquet, *Le Rouergue au premier Moyen Age,* 298–345. His comparative list of the possessions of Conques, based largely on twelfth- and thirteenth-century papal bulls and other official documents, is found on 347–63.

BIBLIOGRAPHY

Primary Sources

Acta Sanctorum, Octobris, III (1770); 3rd edition, 1866.

Augustine. *Concerning the City of God against the Pagans.* Ed. David Knowles. Trans. Henry Bettenson. Harmondsworth: Penguin, 1972.

———. *On Christian Doctrine.* Trans. D. W. Robertson, Jr. Library of the Liberal Arts. Indianapolis: Bobbs-Merrill, 1958.

Bouillet, Auguste, ed. *Liber miraculorum sancte Fidis.* Paris: Alphonse Picard et fils, 1897.

Cazelles, Brigitte, ed. and trans. *The Lady as Saint: A Collection of French Hagiographic Romances of the Thirteenth Century.* Philadelphia: University of Pennsylvania Press, 1991.

Certain, Eugène de, ed. *Les miracles de Saint Benoit écrits par Adrevald, Aimon, André, Raoul Tortaire et Hugues de Sainte Marie, moines de Fleury.* Paris, 1858.

Chirurgia de Maestro Rolando da Parma detto dei Capezzuti, La. Riproduzione del codice latino no. 1382 della R. Biblioteca Casanatense, Roma. Vulgarizzamento e note del Dott. Giovanni Carbonelli. Rome: Instituto Naz. Medico-Farmicologico, 1927.

[Cicero]. *Ad C. Herennium de ratione dicendi (Rhetorica ad Herennium).* Trans. Harry Caplan. Loeb Classical Library. Cambridge: Harvard University Press, 1954.

Desjardins, Gustave, ed., *Cartulaire de l'abbaye de Conques-en-Rouergue.* Documents Historiques Publiés par l'École des Chartes. Paris: Alphonse Picard, 1879.

Gregory of Tours, *The Miracles of the Bishop St. Martin.* Trans. Raymond Van Dam. In Raymond Van Dam. *Saints and Their Miracles in Late Antique Gaul.* Princeton: Princeton University Press, 1993. 199–303.

———. *Glory of the Confessors.* Trans. and intro. Raymond Van Dam. Liverpool: Liverpool University Press, 1988.

Isidore of Seville. *Etymologiarum sive originum libri XX.* Ed. W. M. Lindsay. 2 vols. Oxford: Clarendon Press, 1911; rpt. 1962.

Lafont, Robert, ed. and trans. *La chanson de Sainte Foi*. Geneva: Droz, 1998.

Liber miraculorum sancte Fidis (facsimile edition). Sélestat, 1995.

McDermott, William C. "Bishops: The World of Gregory of Tours." In *Monks, Bishops and Pagans: Christian Culture in Gaul and Italy, 500–700*. Ed. and intro. Edward Peters. Philadelphia: University of Pennsylvania Press, 1975. 117–218.

Quintilian. *Institutio oratoria*. Ed. and trans. H. E. Butler. 4 vols. Loeb Classical Library. 1920; rpt. Cambridge, Mass.: Harvard University Press, 1980.

Odo of Cluny. *The Life of Saint Gerald of Aurillac*. Trans. Gerard Sitwell, O.S.B. In *Soldiers of Christ: Saints and Saints' Lives from Late Antiquity and the Early Middle Ages*. Ed. Thomas F. X. Noble and Thomas Head. University Park, Penn.: Pennsylvania State University Press, 1995. 293–362.

Pliny. *Natural History*. Trans. W. H. S. Jones. Loeb Classical Library. Vol. 8 (books XXVIII–XXXII). Cambridge, Mass.: Harvard University Press, 1963.

Robertini, Luca, ed., *Liber miraculorum sancte Fidis: Edizione critica et commento*. Spoleto: Centro italiano di studi sull'alto medioevo, 1994.

Sheingorn, Pamela, trans. and intro. *The Book of Sainte Foy*. Philadelphia: University of Pennsylvania Press, 1995.

Sidonius. *Poems and Letters*. Trans. W. B. Anderson. 2 vols. Cambridge, Mass.: Harvard University Press, 1936, 1965.

Sulpicius Severus. "The Life of Saint Martin of Tours." Trans. F. R. Hoare. In *Soldiers of Christ: Saints and Saints' Lives from Late Antiquity and the Early Middle Ages*. Ed. Thomas F. X. Noble and Thomas Head. University Park, Penn.: Pennsylvania State University Press, 1995. 1–29.

Secondary Sources

Abbott, Edwin. *St. Thomas of Canterbury: His Death and Miracles*. 2 vols. London, 1898; rpt. in one vol. New York: AMS Press, n.d.

Abou-El-Haj, Barbara. *The Medieval Cult of Saints: Formations and Transformations*. New York: Cambridge University Press, 1994.

Ammons, Elizabeth, and Annette White-Parks, eds. *Tricksterism in Turn-of-the-Century American Literature: A Multicultural Perspective*. Hanover, N.H.: University Press of New England, 1994.

Arbesmann, Rudolph. "The Concept of 'Christus Medicus' in St. Augustine." *Traditio* 10 (1954): 1–28.

Ashley, Kathleen M. "An Anthropological Approach to the Cycle Drama: The Shepherds as Sacred Clowns." *Fifteenth-Century Studies* 13 (1988): 127–38.

———. "Interrogating Biblical Deception and Trickster Theories: Narratives of Patriarchy or Possibility?" *Semeia: An Experimental Journal for Biblical Criticism* 42 (1988): 103–16.

———. "The Guiler Beguiled: Christ and Satan as Theological Tricksters in Medieval Religious Literature." *Criticism* 24 (1982): 126–37.

Ashley, Kathleen, and Pamela Sheingorn. "Liturgy as Social Performance." In

Teaching the Medieval Liturgy. Ed. Thomas Heffernan and E. Ann Matter. Kalamazoo: Medieval Institute Publications, forthcoming.

————. "'*Discordia et lis*': Negotiating Power, Property, and Performance in Medieval Selestat." *The Journal of Medieval and Early Modern Studies* 26, no. 3 (Fall 1996): 419–46.

————. "Translations of Sainte Foy: Bodies, Texts, Places." In *The Medieval Translator,* vol. 5. Ed. Roger Ellis. Turnhout, Belg.: Brepols, 1996, 29–49.

————. "An Unsentimental View of Ritual in the Middle Ages or, Sainte Foy was no Snow White." *Journal of Ritual Studies* 6 (1992): 63–85.

Aubrun, Michel. "Mythe et réalité: aux origines de l'avaritie auvergnate. VIIIᵉ–XIᵉ siècle." *Revue d'Auvergne* 97 (1983): 65–67.

Auerbach, Erich. *Literary Language and Its Public in Late Latin Antiquity and in the Middle Ages.* Trans. Ralph Manheim. Bollingen Series LXXIV. New York: Pantheon Books, 1965.

Babcock, Barbara. "Arrange Me into Disorder: Fragments and Reflections on Ritual Clowning." In *Rite, Drama, Festival, Spectacle: Rehearsals toward a Theory of Cultural Performance.* Ed. John J. MacAloon. Philadelphia: ISHI, 1984. 102–128.

————. "'A Tolerated Margin of Mess': The Trickster and His Tales Reconsidered." *Journal of the Folklore Institute* 11 (1975): 147–86.

Babcock, Barbara, and Jay Cox. "The Native American Trickster." In *Handbook of Native American Literature.* Ed. Andrew Wiget. New York: Garland, 1996. 99–105.

Balendier, Georges. "Blacksmith." In *Dictionary of Black African Civilization.* Ed. Georges Balendier and Jacques Maquet. New York: Leon Amiel, 1974. 62–63.

Barthélemy, Dominique. "La paix de Dieu dans son contexte (989–1041)." *Cahiers de civilisation médiévale* 40 (1997): 3–35.

Behrends, Frederick, ed. and trans. "Introduction." *Letters and Poems of Fulbert of Chartres.* Oxford: Clarendon Press, 1976.

Belloni, Luigi. "Historical Notes on the Inclined Inverted or So-called Trendelenburg Position." *Journal of the History of Medicine and Allied Sciences* 4 (1949): 371–81.

Bercovitch, Sacvan. "Romance and Anti-Romance in *Sir Gawain and the Green Knight.*" *Philological Quarterly* 44 (1965): 30–37.

Bochm, Barbara Drake. *Medieval Head Reliquaries of the Massif Central.* Ph.D. diss., New York University, 1990.

Bond, Gerald. *The Loving Subject: Desire, Eloquence, and Power in Romanesque France.* Philadelphia: University of Pennsylvania Press, 1995.

Bonnassie, Pierre. "Avant-Propos." *Annales du Midi* 107 (1995): 381–83.

————. Review of *Liber miraculorum sancte Fidis,* edizione critica e commento a cura di Luca Robertini, Spoleto, Centro Italiano di Studi sull'Alto Medioevo, 1994. *Annales du Midi* 107 (1995): 476–77.

————. "Descriptions of Fortresses in the Book of Miracles of Sainte-Foy of

Conques." In *From Slavery to Feudalism in South-Western Europe.* Trans. Jean
Birrell. Cambridge: Cambridge University Press, 1991. 132–48.

————. "From the Rhône to Galicia: Origins and Modalities of the Feudal Order." In *From Slavery to Feudalism in South-Western Europe.* Trans. Jean Birrell.
Cambridge: Cambridge University Press, 1991: 104–31.

Bonnassie, Pierre, and Frédéric de Gournay. "Sur la datation du *Livre des miracles
de sainte Foy de Conques." Annales du Midi* 107 (1995): 457–73.

Bonnassie, Pierre, Pierre-André Sigal, and Dominique Iogna-Prat. "La Gallia du
Sud, 930–1130." *Hagiographica* 1 (1994): 289–344.

Boswell, John. *Christianity, Social Tolerance, and Homosexuality.* Chicago and London: University of Chicago Press, 1980.

Bouchard, Constance B. "The Origins of the French Nobility: A Reassessment."
American Historical Review 86 (1981): 501–32.

Bouillet, Auguste, and L. Servières. *Sainte Foy, vierge et martyre.* Rodez, France:
E. Carrère, 1900.

Bouissac, Paul. *Circus and Culture: A Semiotic Approach.* Bloomington: Indiana
University Press, 1976.

Bousquet, Jacques. *Le Rouergue au premier Moyen Age (vers 800–vers 1250).* Vol. I:
Les pouvoirs, leurs rapports, et leurs domaines. Archives Historiques du Rouergue
XXIV. Rodez: Société des Lettres, Sciences et Arts de l'Aveyron, 1992.

Brown, Peter. *Society and the Holy in Late Antiquity.* Berkeley and Los Angeles:
University of California Press, 1982.

————. *The Cult of the Saints: Its Rise and Function in Latin Christianity.* Chicago:
University of Chicago Press, 1981.

Brundage, James A. *Law, Sex, and Christian Society in Medieval Europe.* Chicago
and London: University of Chicago Press, 1987.

Bull, Marcus. *Knightly Piety and the Lay Response to the First Crusade: The Limousin
and Gascony, c. 970–c.1130.* Oxford: Clarendon Press, 1993.

Bynum, Caroline Walker. *The Resurrection of the Body in Western Christianity, 200–
1336.* New York: Columbia University Press, 1995.

————. "Why All the Fuss about the Body? A Medievalist's Perspective?" *Critical
Inquiry* 22 (Autumn 1995): 1–33.

————. *Holy Feast and Holy Fast: The Religious Significance of Food to Medieval
Women.* Berkeley: University of California Press, 1982.

Cabaniss, Allen. "Florus of Lyons." *Classica et mediaevalia* 19 (1958): 212–32; rpt.
in his *Judith Augusta, a Daughter-in-law of Charlemagne, and Other Essays.* New
York: Vantage Press, 1974. 153–73.

Caitucoli, Christiane. "Nobles et Chevaliers dans le *Livre des miracles de Sainte
Foy." Annales du Midi* 107 (1995): 401–16.

Chazelle, Celia. "Matter, Spirit, and Image in the *Libri Carolini." Recherches Augustiniennes* 21 (1986): 163–84.

Chenu, M.-D. *Nature, Man, and Society in the Twelfth Century: New Theological Perspectives.* Selected, ed. and trans. Jerome Taylor and Lester K. Little. Chicago:
University of Chicago Press, 1968.

Coleman, Janet. *Ancient and Medieval Memories: Studies in the Reconstruction of the Past.* Cambridge: Cambridge University Press, 1992.

Constable, Giles. *The Reformation of the Twelfth Century.* Cambridge: Cambridge University Press, 1996.

———. *Three Studies in Medieval Religious and Social Thought: The Interpretation of Mary and Martha; The Ideal of the Imitation of Christ; The Orders of Society.* Cambridge: Cambridge University Press, 1995.

———, ed. *The Letters of Peter the Venerable.* Vol. II. Cambridge: Harvard University Press, 1967.

Constable, Olivia Remie. "Muslim Spain and Mediterranean Slavery: the medieval slave trade as an aspect of Muslim-Christian relations." In *Christendom and Its Discontents: Exclusion, Persecution, and Rebellion, 1000–1500.* Ed. Scott L. Waugh and Peter D. Diehl. Cambridge: Cambridge University Press, 1996: 264–84.

Contreni, John J. *The Cathedral School of Laon from 850 to 930: Its Manuscripts and Masters.* Munich: Arbeo-Gesellschaft, 1978.

Copeland, Rita. *Rhetoric, Hermeneutics, and Translation in the Middle Ages: Academic Traditions and Vernacular Texts.* Cambridge: Cambridge University Press, 1991.

Cowdrey, H. E. J. *The Cluniacs and the Gregorian Reform.* Oxford: Clarendon Press, 1970.

Curtius, Ernst Robert. *European Literature and the Latin Middle Ages.* New York: Harper & Row, 1963.

Cypess, Sandra Messinger. *La Malinche in Mexican Culture.* Austin: University of Texas Press, 1991.

Davies, Wendy. "Property rights and property claims in Welsh 'Vitae' of the eleventh century." In *Hagiographie, cultures et société IVe–XIIe siècles.* Actes du Colloque organisé à Nanterre et à Paris (2–5 mai 1979). Paris: Etudes Augustiniennes, 1981. 515–33.

Delany, Sheila. *Impolitic Bodies: Poetry, Saints and Society in Fifteenth-Century England.* Oxford: Oxford University Press, 1997.

Delehaye, Hippolyte. *The Legends of the Saints.* Trans. Donald Attwater. New York: Fordham University Press, 1962; orig. pub. as *Les Légendes hagiographiques,* 1905.

Delooz, Pierre. *Sociologie et canonisation.* Liège and The Hague: Faculté de droit de l'Université de Liège, 1969.

Dolbeau, François. "Les hagiographes au travail: collecte et traitement des documents écrits (ixe–xiie siècles)." In *Manuscrits hagiographiques et travail des hagiographes.* Ed. Martin Heinzelmann. Sigmaringen, Germany: Jan Thorbecke Verlag, 1992. 49–76.

Douglas, Mary. *Purity and Danger: An Analysis of the Concepts of Pollution and Taboo.* New York: Frederick A. Praeger, 1966.

Dronke, Peter. *Verse with Prose from Petronius to Dante: The Art and Scope of the Mixed Form.* Cambridge, Mass.: Harvard University Press, 1994.

———. *Women Writers of the Middle Ages: A Critical Study of Texts from Perpetua (d. 203) to Marguerite Porete (d. 1310)*. Cambridge: Cambridge University Press, 1984.

Dubois, Jacques. *Les martyrologies du Moyen Age latin*. Typologie des sources du Moyen Age occidental, 26. Turnhout, Belg.: Brepols, 1978.

Dubois, Jacques, and Jean-Loup Lemaître. *Sources et méthodes de l'hagiographie médiévale*. Paris: Les Editions du Cerf, 1993.

Duby, Georges. "Women and Power." In *Cultures of Power: Lordship, Status, and Process in Twelfth-Century Europe*. Ed. Thomas N. Bisson. Philadelphia: University of Pennsylvania Press, 1995.

———. *The Age of the Cathedrals: Art and Society 980–1420*. Trans. Eleanor Levieux and Barbara Thompson. Chicago: University of Chicago Press, 1981.

———. *The Three Orders: Feudal Society Imagined*. Trans. Arthur Goldhammer. Chicago: University of Chicago Press, 1980. *Les trois ordres ou l'imaginaire du féodalisme*. Paris: Editions Gallimard, 1978.

Duff, J. Wight. *A Literary History of Rome in the Silver Age: From Tiberius to Hadrian*. Ed. A. M. Duff. New York: Barnes and Noble, 1960.

Dunbabin, Jean. *France in the Making, 842–1180*. Oxford: Oxford University Press, 1985.

Dunn-Lardeau, Brenda, "From the *Legende dorée* (thirteenth century) to the *Fleurs des vies de saints* (seventeenth century): A New Image of the Saint and Sainthood?" *History of European Ideas* 20, nos. 1–3: 299–304.

Eagleton, Terry. *Criticism and Ideology*. London: Verso, 1978.

Elliott, Alison Goddard. *Roads to Paradise. Reading the Lives of Early Saints*. Hanover, N.H.: University Press of New England, 1987.

Elliott, Dyan. "Dress as Mediator between Inner and Outer Self: The Pious Matron of the High and Later Middle Ages." *Mediaeval Studies* 53 (1991): 279–308.

Enders, Jody. "Rhetoric, coercion, and the memory of violence." In *Criticism and Dissent in the Middle Ages*. Ed. Rita Copeland. Cambridge: Cambridge University Press, 1996. 24–55.

Evans, G. R. *The Language and Logic of the Bible in the Earlier Middle Ages*. Cambridge: Cambridge University Press, 1984.

———. *Anselm and a New Generation*. Oxford: Clarendon Press, 1980.

———. *Old Arts and New Theology: The Beginnings of Theology as an Academic Discipline*. Oxford: Clarendon Press, 1980.

Fanning, Steven. *A Bishop and His World before the Gregorian Reform: Hubert of Angers, 1006–1047*. Transactions of the American Philosophical Society 78, Part I. Philadelphia: American Philosophical Society, 1988.

Farmer, Sharon. "Down and Out and Female in Thirteenth-Century Paris." *American Historical Review* 103 (1998): 345–72.

———. *Communities of Saint Martin: Legend and Ritual in Medieval Tours*. Ithaca, N.Y.: Cornell University Press, 1991.

———. "Persuasive Voices: Clerical Images of Medieval Wives." *Speculum* 61 (1986): 517–43.

Fau, Jean-Claude. *Rouergue roman.* 3rd ed. La nuit des temps 17. Saint-Léger-Vauban: Zodiaque, 1990.

Fichtenau, Heinrich. *Living in the Tenth Century: Mentalities and Social Orders.* Trans. Patrick J. Geary. Chicago: University of Chicago Press, 1991.

Fichtner, Gerhard. "Christus als Arzt: Ursprünge und Wirkungen eines Motivs." *Frühmittelalterliche Studien* (Münster) 16 (1982): 1–18.

Finlayson, John. "The Expectations of Romance in *Sir Gawain and the Green Knight.*" *Genre* 12 (1979): 1–24.

Finucane, Ronald C. *Miracles and Pilgrims: Popular Beliefs in Medieval England.* 1977; rpt. New York: St. Martin's Press, 1995.

Forsyth, Ilene. *The Throne of Wisdom: Wood Sculptures of the Madonna in Romanesque France.* Princeton, N.J.: Princeton University Press, 1972.

Foucault, Michel. "What Is an Author?" In *Language, Counter-Memory, Practice: Selected Essays and Interviews.* Ithaca, N.Y.: Cornell University Press: 1977. 113–38.

Gates, Henry Louis. *The Signifying Monkey: A Theory of African American Literary Criticism.* New York: Oxford University Press, 1988.

Geary, Patrick J. *Living with the Dead in the Middle Ages.* Ithaca, N.Y., and London: Cornell University Press, 1994.

———. *Phantoms of Remembrance: Memory and Oblivion at the End of the First Millennium.* Princeton, N.J.: Princeton University Press, 1994.

———. *Furta Sacra: Thefts of Relics in the Central Middle Ages.* Princeton, N.J.: Princeton University Press, 1978; revised ed. 1990.

Geertz, Clifford. "Deep Play: Notes on the Balinese Cockfight." In *The Interpretation of Cultures.* New York: Basic Books, 1973: 412–53.

Gesta 36, no. 1 (1997). Issue devoted to essays on medieval body-part reliquaries.

Goodich, Michael. *Vita perfecta: The Ideal of Sainthood in the Thirteenth Century.* Stuttgart: Anton Hiersemann, 1982.

Gournay, Frédéric de. "Relire la *Chanson de sainte Foy.*" *Annales du Midi* 107 (1995): 385–99.

———. *Les documents écrits de l'abbaye de Conques (IXᵉ–XIIIᵉ s.).* Université de Toulouse-Le Mirail. U.F.R. d'histoire. D.E.A. (Mémoire). Sous le direction de Pierre Bonnassie, Sept. 1992.

———. *Etude du Cartulaire de l'abbaye de Conques (actes postérieurs à 1030).* Université de Toulouse-Le Mirail. U.F.R. d'histoire. Mémoire de maîtrise. Sous la direction de Pierre Bonnassie, October 1988. 2 vols.

Gradon, Pamela. *Form and Style in Early English Literature.* London: Methuen, 1971.

Gurevich, Aron. "Peasants and Saints." In *Medieval Popular Culture.* Cambridge: Cambridge University Press, 1988.

Handelman. Don. "The Ritual Clown: Attributes and Affinities." *Anthropos* 76 (1981): 321–70.

Handelman, Don, and Bruce Kapferer. "Symbolic Types, Mediation and the

Transformation of Ritual Context: Sinhalese Demons and Tewa Clowns." *Semiotica* 30 (1980): 41–71.

Hanning, Robert. "*Engin* in Twelfth Century Romance: An Examination of the Roman d'Eneas and Hue de Rotelande's Ipomedon." *Yale French Studies* No. 51 (1974): 82–101.

Haskins, Charles H. *The Renaissance of the Twelfth Century.* Cambridge: Harvard University Press, 1927.

Hawkes, Terence. *Structuralism and Semiotics.* Berkeley: University of California Press, 1977.

Head, Thomas. "Hagiography." In *Medieval France: An Encyclopedia.* Ed. William Kibler and Grover Zinn. New York: Garland, 1995. 433–37.

———. "Saints, Cult of." In *Medieval France: An Encyclopedia.* Ed. William Kibler and Grover Zinn. New York: Garland, 1995. 851–55.

———. *Hagiography and the Cult of Saints: The Diocese of Orléans, 800–1200.* Cambridge: Cambridge University Press, 1990.

———. "The Judgment of God: Andrew of Fleury's Account of the Peace League of Bourges." In Head and Landes, *The Peace of God,* 219–238.

Head, Thomas, and Richard Landes, eds. *The Peace of God. Social Violence and Religious Response in France around the Year 1000.* Ithaca, N.Y., and London: Cornell University Press, 1992.

Heene, Katrien. "*Audire, legere, vulgo:* An Attempt to Define Public Use and Comprehensibility of Carolingian Hagiography." In *Latin and the Romance Languages in the Early Middle Ages.* Ed. Roger Wright. London: Routledge, 1991. 146–63.

Heffernan, Thomas J. "Hippolyte Delehaye (1859–1941)." In *Medieval Scholarship: Biographical Studies on the Formation of a Discipline.* Vol. 2: *Literature and Philosophy.* Ed. Helen Damico. New York: Garland, 1998. 215–27.

———. *Sacred Biography: Saints and Their Biographers in the Middle Ages.* New York and Oxford: Oxford University Press, 1988.

Heinzelmann, Martin. "Une source de base de la littérature hagiographique latine: le recueil de miracles." In *Hagiographie, cultures et société IVᵉ–XIIᵉ siècles.* Actes du Colloque organisé à Nanterre et à Paris (2–5 mai 1979). Paris: Etudes Augustiniennes, 1981. 235–59.

Heist, William W. "Hagiography, Chiefly, Celtic, and Recent Developments in Folklore." In *Hagiographie, cultures et société IVᵉ–XIIᵉ siècles.* Actes du Colloque organisé à Nanterre et à Paris (2–5 mai 1979). Paris: Etudes Augustiniennes, 1981. 121–41.

Herkommer, Elmar. *Die Topoi in den Prooemien der römischen Geschichtswerke.* Tübingen, 1968.

Herrin, Judith. *The Formation of Christendom.* Princeton, N.J.: Princeton University Press, 1987.

Hieb, Louis A. "Meaning and Mismeaning: Toward an Understanding of the Ritual Clown." In *New Perspectives on the Pueblos.* Ed. Alfonso Ortiz. Albuquerque: University of New Mexico, 1972: 163–95.

Hildebrandt, M. M. *The External School in Carolingian Society.* Leiden: Brill, 1992.

Hodge, Robert, and Gunther Kress. *Social Semiotics.* Ithaca, N.Y.: Cornell University Press, 1988.

Hollywood, Amy. *The Soul as Virgin Wife: Mechthild of Magdeburg, Marguerite Porete, and Meister Eckhart.* Notre Dame, Ind., and London: University of Notre Dame Press, 1995.

————. "Suffering Transformed: Marguerite Porete, Meister Eckhart, and the Problem of Women's Spirituality." In *Meister Eckhart and the Beguine Mystics: Hadewijch of Brabant, Mechthild of Magdeburg, and Marguerite Porete.* Ed. Bernard McGinn. New York: Continuum, 1994. 87–113.

Honecker, Martin. "Christus medicus." In *Der kranke Mensch in Mittelalter und Renaissance.* Ed. Peter Wunderli. Studia humaniora, vol. 5. Düsseldorf: Droste, 1986. 27–43.

Huard, Pierre, and Mirko Drazen Grmek. *Mille ans de chirurgie en Occident: V^e–XVe siècles.* Paris: Les Editions Roger Dacosta, 1966.

Irvine, Martin. *The Making of Textual Culture: 'Grammatica' and Literary Theory 350–1110.* Cambridge: Cambridge University Press, 1994.

Jaeger, C. Stephen. *The Envy of Angels: Cathedral Schools and Social Ideals in Medieval Europe, 950–1200.* Philadelphia: University of Pennsylvania Press, 1994.

————. *The Origins of Courtliness: Civilizing Trends and the Formation of Courtly Ideals, 939–1210.* Philadelphia: University of Pennsylvania Press, 1985.

Janson, Tore. *Latin Prose Prefaces: Studies in Literary Conventions.* Stockholm: Almquist and Wiksell, 1964.

Jeauneau, Edouard. *L'âge d'or des écoles de Chartres.* Chartres: Editions Houvet, 1995.

Johnson, Elizabeth A. "Marian Devotion in the Western Church." In *Christian Spirituality: High Middle Ages and Reformation.* Ed. Jill Raitt. New York: Crossroads, 1987. 392–414.

Jordan, Mark D. *The Invention of Sodomy in Christian Theology.* Chicago: University of Chicago Press, 1997.

Jules-Rosette, Bennetta. "Semiotics and Cultural Diversity: Entering the 1990's." *Semiotica* 7 (1990): 5–26.

Kendall, Calvin B. "The Voice in the Stone: The Verse Inscriptions of Ste.-Foy of Conques and the Date of the Tympanum." In *Hermeneutics and Medieval Culture.* Ed. Patrick J. Gallacher and Helen Damico. Albany: State University of New York Press, 1989. 163–82.

Kieckhefer, Richard. *Unquiet Souls: Fourteenth-Century Saints and Their Religious Milieu.* Chicago: University of Chicago Press, 1984.

Kittay, Jeffrey, and Wlad Godzich. *The Emergence of Prose: An Essay in Prosaics.* Minneapolis: University of Minnesota Press, 1987.

Kleinberg, Aviad M. *Prophets in Their Own Country: Living Saints and the Making of Sainthood in the Later Middle Ages.* Chicago: University of Chicago Press, 1992.

Knowles, David. *Great Historical Enterprises: Problems in Monastic History.* London: Thomas Nelson, 1963.

Knowles, M. D. "The Preservation of the Classics." In *The English Library before 1700: Studies in Its History*. Ed. Francis Wormald and C. E. Wright. London: Athlone Press, 1958. 136–47.

Kornbluth, Genevra. *Engraved Gems of the Carolingian Empire*. University Park, Penn.: Pennsylvania State University Press, 1995.

Krötzl, Christian. *Pilger, Mirakel und Alltag: Formen des Verhaltens im skandinavischen Mittelter*. Helsinki: Suomen Historiallinen Seura, 1994.

Labande, Edmond-René. "L'historiographie de la France de l'ouest aux Xᵉ et XIᵉ siècles." *Settimane* 17 (1970): 751–91.

Landes, Richard. *Relics, Apocalypse and the Deceits of History: Ademar of Chabannes, 989–1034*. Cambridge, Mass.: Harvard University Press, 1995.

Leach, Edmund. "Genesis as Myth." In *European Literary Theory and Practice*. Ed. Vernon W. Gras. New York: Dell, 1973. 317–330.

Leclercq, Jean. "Violence et dévotion à Saint-Benoît-sur-Loire au moyen âge." In *Etudes ligériennes d'histoire et d'archéologie médiévales. (Mémoires et exposés présentés à la Semaine d'études médiévales de Saint-Benoît-sur-Loire du 3 au 10 juillet 1969)*. Ed. René Louis. Auxerre: Société des fouilles archéologiques et des monuments historiques de l'Yonne, 1975. 247–56.

LeGoff, Jacques. *Time, Work and Culture in the Middle Ages*. Trans. Arthur Goldhammer. Chicago: University of Chicago Press, 1980.

Lemaître, Jean-Loup. "Notes sur les manuscrits conservés de l'abbaye de Conques." *Scriptorium* 41 (1987): 264–71.

Lévi-Strauss, Claude. *Structural Anthropology*. Trans. Claire Jacobson and Brooke Grundfest Schoepf. New York: Doubleday, 1967.

Lifshitz, Felice. *The Norman Conquest of Pious Neustria*. Toronto: Pontifical Institute of Mediaeval Studies, 1995.

———. "Beyond Positivism and Genre: 'Hagiographical' Texts as Historical Narrative." *Viator* 25 (1994): 95–113.

Little, Lester K. *Benedictine Maledictions: Liturgical Cursing in Romanesque France*. Ithaca, N.Y., and London: Cornell University Press, 1993.

———. *Religious Poverty and the Profit Economy in Medieval Europe*. Ithaca, N.Y.: Cornell University Press, 1978.

———. "Pride Goes before Avarice: Social Change and the Vices in Latin Christendom." *American Historical Review* 76 (1971): 16–49.

Loyen, André. "Les miracles de saint Martin et le débuts de l'hagiographie en Occident." *Bulletin de littérature ecclésiastique* 123 (1972): 147–57.

Lutz, Cora E. *Schoolmasters of the Tenth Century*. Hamden, Conn.: Archon, 1977.

MacKinney, Loren C. *Medical Illustrations in Medieval Manuscripts*. Publications of the Wellcome Historical Medical Library, n.s., 5. London, 1965.

———. *Bishop Fulbert and Education at the School of Chartres*. Texts and Studies in the History of Medieval Education 6. Notre Dame, Ind.: The Medieval Institute, University of Notre Dame, 1957.

———. "Bishop Fulbert: Teacher, Administrator, Humanist." *Isis* 14 (1930): 285–300.

Makarius, Laura. "Ritual Clowns and Symbolical Behaviour." *Diogenes* 69 (1970): 44–73.

———. "Le mythe du 'Trickster.'" *Revue de l'histoire des religions* 175 (1969): 17–46.

McDermott, William C. "Bishops: The World of Gregory of Tours." In *Monks, Bishops and Pagans: Christian Culture in Gaul and Italy, 500–700.* Ed. Edward Peters. Philadelphia: University of Pennsylvania Press, 1949; rpt, 1975: 117–218.

McKitterick, Rosamond. *The Carolingians and the Written Word.* Cambridge: Cambridge University Press, 1989.

McNamara, Jo Ann. "The *Herrenfrage:* The Restructuring of the Gender System, 1050–1150." In *Medieval Masculinities: Regarding Men in the Middle Ages.* Ed. Clare A. Lees. Minneapolis: University of Minnesota Press, 1994. 3–29.

McNamara, Jo Ann, and John E. Halborg, with E. Gordon Whatley. Ed. and trans. *Sainted Women of the Dark Ages.* Durham, N.C.: Duke University Press, 1992.

McNutt, Paula M. "The African Ironsmith as Marginal Mediator: A Symbolic Analysis." *Journal of Ritual Studies* 5 (Summer 1991): 75–98.

Magnou-Nortier, Elisabeth. "Ombres féminines dans l'histoire de Languedoc, aux Xe et XIe s." *Cahiers de civilisation médiévale* 34 (1991): 51–56.

Middleton, Anne. "Chancer's 'New Men' and the Good of Literature in the Canterbury Tales." In *Literature and Society: Selected Papers from the English Institute, 1978.* Ed. Edward Said. Baltimore, Md.: Johns Hopkins University Press, 1980. 15–56.

Minnis, A. J. *Medieval Theory of Authorship: Scholastic Literary Attitudes in the Later Middle Ages.* 2nd ed. Philadelphia: University of Pennsylvania Press, 1988.

Moore, R. I. "Literacy and the Making of Heresy, c. 1000–c. 1150." In *Heresy and Literacy, 1000–1530.* Ed. Peter Biller and Anne Hudson. Cambridge: Cambridge University Press, 1994: 19–37.

———. *The Formation of a Persecuting Society* . Oxford: Blackwell, 1987, 1990.

Mostert, Marco. "The Tradition of Classical Texts in the Manuscripts of Fleury." In *Medieval Manuscripts of the Latin Classics: Production and Use.* Proceedings of the Seminar in the History of the Book to 1500, Leiden, 1993. Ed. Claudine A. Chavannes-Mazel and Margaret M. Smith. Los Altos Hills: Anderson-Lovelace, The Red Gull Press, 1996. 19–40

Nelson, Janet L. "Les femmes et l'évangelisation au IXe siècle." *Revue du nord* 68 (1986): 471–85.

Ohnuki-Tierney, Emiko. *The Monkey as Mirror: Symbolic Transformations in Japanese History and Ritual.* Princeton, N.J.: Princeton University Press, 1987.

Olsen, Alexandra Hennessey. "'De Historiis Sanctorum': A Generic Study of Hagiography." *Genre* 13 (1980): 407–29.

Olsen, Birger Munk. "The Production of the Classics in the Eleventh and Twelfth Centuries." In *Medieval Manuscripts of the Latin Classics: Production and Use.* Proceedings of The Seminar in the History of the Book to 1500, Leiden,

1993. Ed. Claudine A. Chavannes-Mazel and Margaret M. Smith. Los Altos Hills: Anderson-Lovelace, The Red Gull Press, 1996. 1–17.

———. "Chronique des manuscrits classiques latins (IX ᵉ–XII ᵉ siècles)." *Revue d'histoire des textes* 21 (1991): 37–76.

———. "La popularité des textes classiques entre le IX ᵉ et le XII ᵉ siècle." *Revue d'histoire des textes* 14–15 (1984–85): 169–81.

———. *L'étude des auteurs classiques latins aux XI ᵉ et XII ᵉ siècles.* 3 vols. Paris: Documents, études et répertoires publiés par l'Institut de Recherche et d'Histoire des Textes, 1982–89.

Ortiz, Alfonso, ed. *The Tewa World: Space, Time, Being and Becoming in a Pueblo Society.* Chicago: University of Chicago Press, 1969.

Otter, Monika. "The Temptation of St. Æthelthryth," *Exemplaria* 9, no. 1 (1998): 139–63.

———. *Inventiones: Fiction and Referentiality in Twelfth-Century English Historical Writing.* Chapel Hill and London: University of North Carolina Press, 1996.

Oury, Guy-Marie. "Le Miracle dans Grégoire de Tours." In *Histoire des miracles: Actes de la sixième rencontre d'Histoire Religieuse tenue à Fontevraud les 8 et 9 October 1982.* Angers: Presses de l'Université, 1983. 11–28.

Pabst, Bernhard. *Prosimetrum: Tradition und Wandel einer Literaturform zwischen Spätantike und Spätmittelalter.* 2 vols. Ordo: Studien zur Literatur und Gesellschaft des Mittelalters und der frühen Neuzeit. Vol. 4, part 1. Cologne, Weimar, Vienna: Böhlau, 1994.

Payen, Jean Charles. "La pénitence dans le contexte culturel des XII ᵉ et XIII ᵉ siècles des doctrines contritionnistes aux pénitentiels vernaculaires." *Revue des sciences philosophiques et théologiques* 61 (1977): 399–428.

Peacock, James L. "Symbolic Reversal and Social History: Transvestites and Clowns of Java." In *The Reversible World: Symbolic Inversion in Art and Society.* Ed. Barbara Babcock. Ithaca, N.Y.: Cornell University Press, 1978. 209–24.

Pease, Donald. "Author." In *Critical Terms for Literary Study.* Ed. Frank Lentricchia and Thomas McLaughlin. Chicago: University of Chicago Press, 1990. 105–17.

Pelton, Robert D. *The Trickster in West Africa.* Berkeley: University of California Press, 1980.

Petroff, Elizabeth A., ed. *Medieval Women's Visionary Literature.* New York: Oxford University Press, 1986.

Phillipart, Guy. *Les légendiers latins et autres manuscrits hagiographiques.* Turnhout, Belg.: Brepols, 1977.

Pizarro, Joaquín Martínez. *Writing Ravenna: A Narrative Performance in the Ninth Century.* Philadelphia: University of Pennsylvania Press, 1995.

———. *A Rhetoric of the Scene: Dramatic Narrative in the Early Middle Ages.* Toronto: University of Toronto Press, 1989.

Platelle, H. "Le problème du scandale: Les nouvelles modes masculines aux XI ᵉ et XII ᵉ siècles." *Revue belge de philologie et d'histoire* 53 (1975): 1071–96.

Poulin, J-C. "Fides." In *Lexikon des Mittelalters* 4. Munich / Zurich: Artemis Verlag, 1987. Cols. 434–35.

Poulin, Joseph-Claude. *L'idéal de sainteté dans l'Aquitaine carolingienne d'apres les sources hagiographiques (750–950)*. Quebec City: Presses de l'Université Laval, 1975.

Quentin, Henri. *Les martyrologies historiques du Moyen Age. Etude sur la formation du Martyrologe romain*. Paris, 1908.

Raaf, John E. "Hernia Healers." *Annals of Medical History* 4 n.s. (1932): 377–89.

Ray, Roger D. "Medieval Historiography through the Twelfth Century." *Viator* 5 (1974): 33–59.

Raybin, David. "Social Strain and the Genesis of Literary Genre in Twelfth Century France." *Works and Days* 3 (1984): 45–63.

Remensnyder, Amy G. "Legendary Treasure at Conques: Reliquaries and Imaginative Memory." *Speculum* 71 (1996): 884–906.

———. *Remembering Kings Past: Monastic Foundation Legends in Medieval Southern France*. Ithaca, N.Y.: Cornell University Press, 1995.

———. "Un problème de cultures ou de culture?: La statue-reliquaire et les *joca* de sainte Foy de Conques dans le *Liber miraculorum* de Bernard d'Angers." *Cahiers de la civilisation médiévale* 33 (1990): 351–79.

Reynolds, L. D., and N. G. Wilson. *Scribes and Scholars: A Guide to the Transmission of Greek and Latin Literature*. 2nd ed. Oxford: Clarendon Press, 1974.

Riché, Pierre. *Education et culture dans l'Occident médiéval*. Aldershot: Variorum, 1993.

———. *Gerbert d'Aurillac, le pape de l'An Mil*. Paris: Fayard, 1987.

Ricketts, Mac Linscott. "The North American Indian Trickster." *History of Religions* 5 (1965): 327–50.

Robertini, Luca. "Le *Liber miraculorum sancte Fidis* dans la tradition manuscrite entre Conques et Sélestat." *Annuaire des Amis de la Bibliothèque Humaniste de Sélestat* 44 (1994): 67–76.

———. "Il 'Sapientia' di Rosvita e le fonti agiografiche." *Studi Medievali* 30, no. 2, ser. 3 (1989): 647–59.

Roberts, John W. *From Trickster to Badman: The Black Folk Hero in Slavery and Freedom*. Philadelphia: University of Pennsylvania Press, 1989.

Roberts, Michael. *Poetry and the Cult of the Martyrs: The Liber Peristephanon of Prudentius*. Ann Arbor: University of Michigan Press, 1993.

———. *The Jeweled Style: Poetry and Poetics in Late Antiquity*. Ithaca, N.Y.: Cornell University Press, 1989.

Robertson, Elizabeth. "The Corporeality of Female Sanctity in *The Life of Saint Margaret*." In *Images of Sainthood in Medieval Europe*. Ed. Renate Blumenfeld-Kosinski and Timea Szell. Ithaca, N.Y.: Cornell University Press, 1991. 268–87.

Röckelein, Hedwig. "Miracle Collections of Carolingian Saxony: Literary Tradition versus Original Creation." *Hagiographica* 3 (1996): 267–75.

Rollason, D. W. "The Miracles of Saint Benedict: A Window on Early Medieval France." In *Studies in Medieval History Presented to R. H. C. Davis*. Ed. Henry Mayr-Harting and R. I. Moore. London: Hambledon, 1985. 73–90.

Rosenwein, Barbara. *To Be the Neighbor of Saint Peter: The Social Meaning of Cluny's Property, 909–1049*. Ithaca, N.Y.: Cornell University Press, 1989.

————. *Rhinoceros Bound: Cluny in the Tenth Century*. Philadelphia: University of Pennsylvania Press, 1982.

Rosenwein, Barbara H., Thomas Head, and Sharon Farmer. "Monks and Their Enemies: A Comparative Approach." *Speculum* 66 (1991): 764–96.

Rousselle, Aline. *Croire et guérir. La foi en Gaule dans l'Antiquité tardive*. Paris: Fayard, 1990.

Rydén, Lennart. "Ueberlegungen zum literarischen Wert oder Unwert hagiographischer Texte." *Eranos* 91 (1993): 47–60.

Schulenburg, Jane Tibbets. *Forgetful of Their Sex: Female Sanctity and Society ca. 500–1100*. Chicago: University of Chicago Press, 1998.

————. "Saints' Lives as a Source for the History of Women, 500–1100." In *Medieval Women and the Sources of History*. Ed. Joel T. Rosenthal. Athens: University of Georgia Press, 1990. 285–320.

————. "Sexism in the Celestial Gynaeceum from 500 to 1200." *Journal of Medieval History* 4 (1978): 117–33.

Segal, Charles. *Dionysiac Poetics and Euripides' Bacchae*. Princeton, N.J.: Princeton University Press, 1982.

Shaver-Crandall, Annie, and Paula Gerson, with Alison Stones. *The Pilgrim's Guide to Santiago de Compostela: A Gazetteer*. London: Harvey Miller, 1995.

Shulman, David Dean. *The King and the Clown in South Indian Myth and Poetry*. Princeton, N.J.: Princeton University Press, 1985.

Sigal, Pierre-André. "Les récits de miracles." In *Comprendre le XIIIᵉ siècle*. Eds. Pierre Guichard and Danièle Alexandre-Bidon. Lyon: Presses Universitaires de Lyon, 1995. 133–144.

————. "Le travail des hagiographes aux XIᵉ et XIIᵉ siècles: Sources d'information et méthodes de rédaction." *Francia* 15 (1987): 149–82.

————. *L'homme et le miracle dans la France médiévale (XI–XII siècle)*. Paris: Les Editions du Cerf, 1985.

Signori, Gabriela. "The Miracle Collection and Its Ingredients: A Methodological and Critical Approach to Marian Shrine Wonders (10th to 13th Century)." *Hagiographica* 3 (1996): 277–303.

Simonetti, Adele. "Le fonti agiografiche di due drammi di Rosvita." *Studi Medievali* 30 (1989): 661–95.

Siraisi, Nancy. *Medieval and Early Renaissance Medicine*. Chicago and London: University of Chicago Press, 1990.

Smith, Julia M. H. "A Hagiographer at Work: Hucbald and the Library of Saint-Amand." *Revue bénédictine* 106 (1996): 151–71.

————. "The Hagiography of Hucbald of Saint-Amand." *Studi Medievali* 35, ser. 3 (1994): 517–42.

————. "Review Article: Early Medieval Hagiography in the Late Twentieth Century." *Early Medieval Europe* 1, no. 1 (1992): 69–76.

————. "Oral and Written: Saints, Miracles, and Relics in Brittany, c. 850–1250." *Speculum* 65 (1990): 309–43.

Southern, Richard W. *Scholastic Humanism and the Unification of Europe*. Vol. I: *Foundations*. Oxford: Blackwell, 1995.

————. *Medieval Humanism*. New York: Harper and Row, 1970.

Spiegel, Gabrielle. *The Past as Text: The Theory and Practice of Medieval Historiography*. Baltimore, Md.: Johns Hopkins University Press, 1997.

————. "History, Historicism, and the Social Logic of the Text in the Middle Ages." *Speculum* 65 (1990): 59–86.

Springer, Carl P. E. *The Gospel as Epic in Late Antiquity: The Paschale carmen of Sedulius*. Leiden: Brill, 1988.

Stancliffe, Clare. *Saint Martin and His Hagiographer: History and Miracle in Sulpicius Severus*. Oxford: Clarendon Press, 1983.

Stevens, C. E. *Sidonius Apollinaris and His Age*. Oxford: Clarendon Press, 1933.

Stock, Brian. *The Implications of Literacy: Written Language and Models of Interpretation in the Eleventh and Twelfth Centuries*. Princeton, N.J.: Princeton University Press, 1983.

Swearingen, C. Jan. *Rhetoric and Irony: Western Literacy and Western Lies*. New York: Oxford University Press, 1991.

Taralon, Dominique. *"Le reliquaire de Pepin" du Trésor de Conques*. Mémoire pour l'obtention de la maitrise d'histoire de l'art. Université de Paris-Sorbonne, Paris IV—Art & Archeologie. Année Universitaire 1988/1989.

Thiébaux, Marcelle, ed. and trans. *The Writings of Medieval Women*. 2nd ed. New York: Garland, 1994.

Tilliette, Jean-Yves. "Les modèles de sainteté du IXe au XIe siècle, d'après le témoignage des récits hagiographiques en vers métriques." *Settimane* 36 (1988): 381–406.

Toelken, Barre. "The 'Pretty Languages' of Yellowman: Genre, Mode, and Texture in Navaho Coyote Narratives." In *Folklore Genres*. Ed. Dan Ben-Amos. Austin: University of Texas, 1976. 145–70.

Turner, Victor W. "Social Dramas and Stories about Them." In *On Narrative*. Ed. W. J. T. Mitchell. Chicago: University of Chicago Press, 1981: 137–64.

————. *The Ritual Process: Structure and Anti-Structure*. Ithaca, N.Y.: Cornell University Press, 1969.

————. "Myth and Symbol." *International Encyclopedia of Social Sciences*. New York: Macmillan, 1968. 576–82.

————. "Betwixt and Between: The Liminal Period in *Rites de Passage*." In *The Forest of Symbols: Aspects of Ndembu Ritual*. Ed. Victor W. Turner. Ithaca, N.Y.: Cornell University Press, 1967.

Van Dam, Raymond. *Leadership and Community in Late Antique Gaul*. Berkeley: University of California Press, 1985.

————. *Saints and Their Miracles in Late Antique Gaul*. Princeton, N.J.: Princeton University Press, 1993.

Van de Vyver, A. "Les étapes du développement philosophique du haut moyen-age." *Revue belge de philosophie et d'histoire* 8 (1929): 425–52.

Vance, Eugene. "Chaucer's Pardoner: Relics, Discourse, and Frames of Propriety." *New Literary History* 20 (1989): 723–45.

Vauchez, André. *The Laity in the Middle Ages: Religious Beliefs and Devotional Prac-*

tices. Ed. Daniel E. Bornstein. Trans. Margery J. Schneider. Notre Dame, Ind.: University of Notre Dame Press, 1993.

———. *La sainteté en Occident aux derniers siècles du Moyen Age d'après les procès de canonisation et les documents hagiographiques*. Bibliothèque des Ecoles françaises d'Athènes et de Rome 241. Rome: 1981.

Venarde, Bruce L. *Women's Monasticism and Medieval Society: Nunneries in France and England, 890–1215*. Ithaca, N.Y., and London: Cornell University Press, 1997.

Vidier, Alexandre. *L'historiographie à Saint-Benoît-sur-Loire et les Miracles de Saint Benoît*. Paris, 1965.

Vizenor, Gerald. "Trickster Discourse." *American Indian Quarterly* 14 (1990): 277–88.

———, ed. *Narrative Chance: Postmodern Discourse on Native American Literatures*. Albuquerque: University of New Mexico Press, 1989.

Vogel, Cyrille, ed. and trans. *Le pécheur et la pénitence au moyen âge*. Paris: Les Editions du Cerf, 1969.

Wands, Frances Terpak. *The Romanesque Architecture and Sculpture of Saint Caprais in Agen*. 2 vols. Ph.D. diss., Yale University, 1982.

Ward, Benedicta. *Miracles and the Medieval Mind: Theory, Record, and Event, 1000–1215*. Philadelphia: University of Pennsylvania Press, 1982.

———. "The Miracles of Saint Benedict," In *Benedictus: Studies in Honor of St Benedict of Nursia*. Ed. E. Rozanne Elder. Kalamazoo: Cistercian Publications, 1981. 1–14.

Weinstein, Donald, and Rudolph M. Bell. *Saints and Society: The Two Worlds of Western Christendom, 1000–1700*. Chicago: University of Chicago Press, 1982.

Wemple, Suzanne Fonay. "Sanctity and Power: The Dual Pursuit of Early Medieval Women." In *Becoming Visible: Women in European History*. Ed. Renate Bridenthal, Claudia Koonz, and Susan Stuard. 2nd ed. Boston: Houghton Mifflin, 1987. 130–51.

Weyman, Carl. "Apollinaris Sidionius und die 'Miracula Sanctae Fidis.'" *Historisches Jahrbuch* 20 (1899): 55–71.

Wiget, Andrew. "His Life in His Tail: The Native American Trickster and the Literature of Possibility." *Redefining American Literary History*. Ed. A. LaVonne Brown Ruoff and Jerry W. Ward, Jr. New York: MLA, 1990. 83–96.

Williams, John. "*Generationes Abrahae*: Reconquest Iconography in Leon." *Gesta* 16 (1977): 3–14.

Wilson, Stephen, ed. *Saints and Their Cults: Studies in Religious Sociology, Folklore and History*. Cambridge: Cambridge University Press, 1983.

Wirth, Jean. *L'image médiévale: Naissance et développements (VIᵉ–XVᵉ siècle)*. Paris: Méridiens Klincksieck, 1989.

Wittke, Charles. Review of Pabst, *Prosimetrum* in *Journal of Medieval Latin* 6 (1996): 226–32.

Wogan-Browne, Jocelyn. "The Virgin's Tale." In *Feminist Readings in Middle English Literature: The Wife of Bath and All Her Sect*. Ed. Ruth Evans and Lesley Johnson. London and New York: Routledge, 1994. 165–94.

Wogan-Browne, Jocelyn, and Glyn S. Burgess, trans. and intro. *Virgin Lives and Holy Deaths: Two Exemplary Biographies for Anglo-Norman Women*. London: J. M. Dent, 1996.

Zimmermann, Michel, ed. *Les sociétés méridionales autour de l'an mil: répertoire des sources et documents commentés*. Paris: CNRS, 1992.

index

abbots, 119
Abou-El-Haj, Barbara, *Medieval Cult of Saints,* 14–15
abuse-of-power theory of atonement, 92–93
Acta sanctorum (Bollandists), 9, 108
actors, role in miracle narrative, 113–14
Adelman of Liège, 55
Adrevald (author of Benedict miracles), 137–38, 154 n. 9, 159 n. 54
affirmation, ritual, 77, 80–81
Agen, 4–5
Aimo (author of Benedict miracles), 33, 137, 139
Alcuin, 164–65 n. 13
allegory, Bernard of Angers's avoidance of, 27
ambiguity, in Augustinian rhetoric, 52–53
Andrew (author of Benedict miracles), 137–39
anthropology, and study of hagiography, 13–15
antifeminism, clerical, 121
aphorism, use of, 109
artisans, urban, 48
Ashley, Kathleen, quoted, 148 n. 14
audience, for Bernard of Angers's writing, 50–51
Auerbach, Erich, quoted, 170–71 n. 9
Augustine, St., 52–53
  City of God, 156–57 n. 28, 175–76 n. 22
  De doctrina christiana, 52, 162 n. 20
Aurillac, 41
authenticity
  Bernard of Angers's interest in, 77
  evidence of, 31, 56–59, 80, 111–12
  through illiteracy, 51–52
author, naming of, 68–69

authorial conversion *topos,* 26–27, 40–42, 44, 59
authors, of *Liber miraculorum sancte Fidis. See* Bernard of Angers; miracle narratives, late; monk-continuator(s)
autobiography, Bernard of Angers and, 39–45, 77–79

Becket, St. Thomas, miracles of, 169 n. 42
behavior, Bernard of Angers's concern for, 128
Belloni, Luigi, quoted, 167–68 n. 40, 168–69 n. 41
Benedict, St. *See also* Benedict miracles
  as historical agent, 138–39
  iconography of, 140
Benedict miracles, 137–41, 154 n. 9, 159 n. 54, 177 n. 3
Bernard of Angers (author of books 1 and 2 of *Liber miraculorum sancte Fidis),* ix, 5–6, 8, 14. *See also* Conques monastery; *Liber miraculorum sancte Fidis;* miracle narratives, late; monk-continuator(s)
  autobiographical approach of, 39–45, 77–79
  as character in *Liber miraculorum sancte Fidis,* 43–44, 77–79
  and Conques monastery, 6, 28–29, 41–44, 47, 53, 59–64, 67–70, 80
  conversion from skepticism, 26–27, 40–44, 59
  on cultural work of *Liber miraculorum sancte Fidis,* 141–42
  education of, 41–42, 49–55, 95–96
  as eyewitness, 26, 40, 43, 57
  gender system of, 121–24
  as hagiographer, 6, 23–32
  intellectual approach of, 56–59

naming, of author, 68–69
narrative typology, and hagiographical
  texts, 17
narrative voice
  of Bernard of Angers, 19–20, 26–27,
    39–45, 56–59, 72, 77–79, 96–98, 132
  Conques monastery as, 19, 84, 110
  in late miracle narratives, 102
  of V-L group, 110–13
Natural History (Pliny the Elder), 39,
  159 n. 51
network, monastic, 70–71
"new man," 163 n. 38
  Bernard of Angers as, 55–59
noblewomen, as monastic allies, 122–24,
  140, 174 n. 15
Normandy, cult of Sainte Foy in, 74–75
Notker the German, 156 n. 20
novelty *topos,* 26
nuns, 172 n. 5

Odolric, Abbot, 84
Odo of Cluny
  life of St. Gerald of Aurillac, 24, 54
  quoted, 24–26, 162 n. 27
Olsen, Alexandra Hennesey, 151 n. 59
Olsen, Birger Munk, quoted, 71
O'Neill, Ynez Violé, quoted, 167–68 n. 40
Otter, Monika, quoted, 158–59 n. 50

Pabst, Bernhard, 107
  quoted, 98
Panaretos, use of term, 164 n. 8
Panaretos (Book of Foy's Powers), 68–69
paradox, Bernard of Angers's use of, 37–
  38, 51
Passio, of Sainte Foy, 3, 68, 143
  later versions, 7
  monk-continuator and, 69–70
  Passio I, 4–5, 147 n. 6
  Passio II, 7
patronage, in Benedict miracles, 137
Paul of Aegina, 167–68 n. 40, 168–69 n.
  41
Peace of God movement, 121, 123, 138,
  173–74 n. 13
peasants, as Other, 39. *See also* popular
  culture
Pease, Donald, quoted, 166 n. 29
penitential system, 127, 129, 175 n. 20

persecuting society, 106–7
Peter, Abbot, Bernard of Angers and, 54,
  68, 78
petitions and petitioning, 109, 113–15
physician, Sainte Foy as, 91–94
pilgrimage, 76
  to Conques, 81–83, 102–3, 112, 144–45
pilgrimage cults, 33
Pizarro, Joaquín Martinez, 173 n. 9
  quoted, 16–18, 27, 120
Plato, *Timaeus,* 50
Pliny the Elder, *Natural History,* 39,
  159 n. 51
pluralism, historical, 11–12
Poetry and the Cult of the Martyrs (Roberts), 17
political events, in Benedict miracles,
  138–39
popular culture, 29, 34, 39, 50–52
popular religion, 29, 42–43, 150 n. 42
poverty, ideal of, 63
power struggles, Fleury monastery and,
  139
power system, in *Liber miraculorum sancte
  Fidis,* 126–29
prayer, use of verse for, 98–99, 107–9,
  114–15
priests, in *Liber miraculorum sancte Fidis,* 117
prisoners, freeing of, 42, 46, 81
  in late miracle narratives, 113–14
prologue, "modern," of eleventh century,
  65–66
propaganda, cult, 7
prosimetrum, 97–99, 169–70 n. 43, 170 n. 44
  in late miracle narratives, 107–9
Prosimetrum (Pabst), 98
Protestant Reformation, and cult of saints,
  8–9, 148–49 n. 22

Ray, Roger D., quoted, 152 n. 61
Reims, cathedral school of, 49
relics, of Sainte Foy, 5, 147–48 n. 12. *See
  also* reliquary, body-shaped
  theft of, 13–14
reliquary, body-shaped, 28, 40–42, 47,
  128, 130, 133–34
  of St. Gerald of Aurillac, 41, 47
Remensnyder, Amy, 14, 26, 32–34
renaissance, twelfth-century, 54–55,
  163 n. 33